Praise for *Essence* bestselling author
Betty DeRamus

FREEDOM BY ANY MEANS

"DeRamus does a wonderful job painting the resolve of the actors and the drama of their situations. . . . [Her] documentation is meticulous. . . . Chromatic stories of passion and quick wits on the road out of slavery."

—*Kirkus Reviews*

FORBIDDEN FRUIT

"A soulful, sassy love song to our people."

—*Essence*

"Uplifting and sometimes heartbreaking. . . . DeRamus and her subjects do the valuable service of reminding readers what it means to be courageous enough to love."

—*Publishers Weekly*

"This impressive debut collection awes us with its stories of slave-era couples."

—*Kirkus Reviews*

"Add[s] a new perspective to the history of American slavery."

—*Booklist*

These titles are also available as eBooks.

Also by Betty DeRamus

Forbidden Fruit: Love Stories from the Underground Railroad

FREEDOM BY ANY MEANS

True Stories of Cunning and Courage on the Underground Railroad

———————

BETTY DeRAMUS

ATRIA PAPERBACK

NEW YORK LONDON SYDNEY TORONTO

ATRIA PAPERBACK
A Division of Simon & Schuster, Inc.
1230 Avenue of the Americas
New York, NY 10020

First Atria Paperback edition February 2010

ATRIA PAPERBACK and colophon are trademarks of Simon & Schuster, Inc.

For information about special discounts for bulk purchases,
please contact Simon & Schuster Special Sales at
1-866-506-1949 or business@simonandschuster.com.

The Simon & Schuster Speakers Bureau can bring authors to your live event.
For more information or to book an event contact the Simon & Schuster Speakers Bureau
at 1-866-248-3049 or visit our website at www.simonspeakers.com.

Designed by Level C

Manufactured in the United States of America

10   9   8   7   6   5   4   3   2   1

The Library of Congress has cataloged the hardcover edition as follows:

DeRamus, Betty.
    Freedom by any means : con games, voodoo schemes, true love, and lawsuits on the
Underground Railroad / by Betty DeRamus.—1st Atria Books hardcover ed.
        p.   cm.

    1. Underground Railroad—Anecdotes.   2. Fugitive slaves—United States—Biography—
Anecdotes.   3. African Americans—Biography—Anecdotes.   4. United States—Race
relations—Anecdotes.   I. Title.

    E450.D473   2009
    973.7'115—dc22
                                                                        2008047810

ISBN 978-1-4165-5110-2
ISBN 978-1-4391-2675-2 (pbk)
ISBN 978-1-4391-5648-3 (ebook)

To Ellen Holly, my great-great-grandmother, and all other enslaved Americans who turned oxtails into soup and made chicken feet the highlight of holiday dinners.

They could turn seashells into whistles. They could make dolls from grass.

When their souls needed saving, they prayed at midnight in ditches and fields, cabins and canyons.

When they yearned for fun, they stomped and clapped the rhythm of dances and made music by blowing on combs.

Yet there were some sorrows they couldn't banish.

Haunted by grief for lost spouses and children, they longed for love they could keep.

CONTENTS

BOOK II
TRICKS AND TRAPS ON THE
ROAD TO FREEDOM

BOOK III
THAT COLD BLACK MAGIC

FOREWORD

Much of what we think we know about African American history is only partly true.

According to the usual story, slaves gained their freedom by running away, being freed in their owners' wills, buying their way out of bondage or having someone else buy them. But how do we account for people like John Bowley, who bluffed his family's way to freedom, or Althea Lynch, a runaway slave whose cooking sprang her from jail? And what about all those enslaved blacks who managed to gain freedom by winning lawsuits in which state-appointed attorneys defended them?

Most people believe fugitive slaves ran only to northern states, or to Canada after it abolished slavery. But what about James Williams, a California Gold Rush miner and runaway, who journeyed to Mexico? What about the fugitives who wound up in Haiti, Nicaragua and the Caribbean? And what about places like Cass County, Michigan, once the site of black settlements where black freedmen and fugitives could vote, own land and enjoy other privileges not available in the rest of the country, North or South?

We've all heard that slave marriages had no legal standing, and that was certainly true. But what, then, are we to make of Nelson Gant, a free black man married to the enslaved Anna Maria? Their "marriage" not only withstood legal challenges but kept Nelson out of jail. Then there was Thomas Day, a free black man for whom the North Carolina legislature created a special loophole so that he could sidestep the law barring his free wife from entering the state?

Relationships between white men and black women are almost always portrayed as brutal or exploitive, yet a white South Carolinian named John L. Brown even forces us to rethink that image. After all, he risked being hanged to be with his beloved.

Runaways are most often portrayed as young single men who walked away from their families and never looked back. Many characters in this book defy that stereotype, too. They ran away with their families. They returned for their kin. And they rescued children whom they hadn't seen in years.

Lurid tales about voodoo spells and love charms dominate many biographies of black California entrepreneur Mary Ellen Pleasant. But the alleged voodoo queen played a key role in liberating slaves in a state that was supposedly free. She also was a brilliant investor who owned eight homes and other property but was savvy enough to pretend to be her white business partner's servant.

And speaking of magic, there often was more than a casual connection between enslaved people's religious beliefs and slave uprisings. We all know the story of Nat Turner, leader of a Virginia slave rebellion that spread terror and death for miles. But many conjurers and root workers became leaders on slave plantations, healing the sick, interpreting mysteries and expressing the longings and resentments of a stolen and sold-off people.

In the early and usually secret plantation churches, ancient beliefs from West and Central Africa would gradually mingle with Christianity, but the resulting faith would have a different spirit. It would be passionate. It would be intense. And sometimes it would be dangerous. Peter the Doctor, a free African, rubbed an alleged magic powder on the clothing of the nearly thirty slaves who participated in the 1712 New York City Slave Rebellion. As a result, the slaves who participated considered themselves an unstoppable force.

Clearly, the saga of runaway slaves who successfully escaped isn't just one story. It is the story of inventor Elijah McCoy's abolitionist parents, who hid runaways in cigar-carrying wagons in Ypsilanti, Michigan. And it is millions of other stories, including tales of the former slaves and freedmen who wound up owning department stores, coal mines and even towns.

I hope that this book will help bring forgotten heroes and heroines to life.

BOOK I

———◆———

PRISONERS OF LOVE

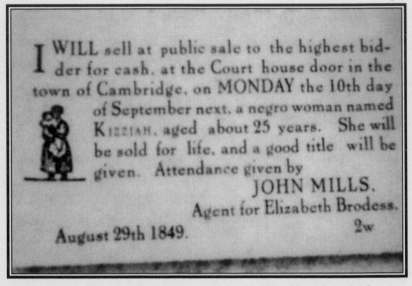

I WILL sell at public sale to the highest bidder for cash, at the Court house door in the town of Cambridge, on MONDAY the 10th day of September next, a negro woman named KIZZIAH, aged about 25 years. She will be sold for life, and a good title will be given. Attendance given by
JOHN MILLS,
Agent for Elizabeth Brodess.
August 29th 1849.   2w

Fig. 1. Ad from Cambridge Democrat *announcing the 1849 sale of Kessiah Bowley, an event that actually took place in December 1850. (Photo courtesy of William Jarmon)*

ONE

$\longrightarrow \bullet \bullet \bullet \longleftarrow$

THE BIG BLUFF

No one yelled for the sheriff when a free black man named John Bowley showed up at a Maryland slave auction in December 1850. To the small crowd at the Dorchester County courthouse, Bowley was just another black man saying good-bye to the enslaved family he was about to lose. But the thirty-four-year-old husband and father hadn't come to the courthouse to smell his children's fear or kiss their tears. He hadn't come to watch his wife shrivel up either—all her green hopes gone—as a slave trader hauled her away. He wasn't that kind of man. He was a man who could build a ship from prime white oak and tar, pegs and passion, and then make it dance with him across the sea. The kind of man who could sail through storms and laugh at the wind. He brought no cash to the sale of his wife and children on the steps of the old brick courthouse in Cambridge, Maryland, but he brought something equally powerful.

He brought a plan.

His scheme would have made a riverboat gambler grin, drag his chair to the nearest poker table and prepare to bluff. His scheme was brash, tricky, risky and in the eyes of most rational people—impossible. Yet it was Bowley's last hope. Unless it worked, his wife and children would be sold on the courthouse steps. Unless it worked, his family would become the property of men who wore good suits, oozed charm, smelled like they'd been born sipping whiskey and gambled on just about everything, including the fate of their slaves.

Cambridge was the seat of Dorchester County on Maryland's Eastern Shore, a place where quiet villages nestled along rivers with names that conjured up images of once-numerous Indian tribes—the Nanticoke, the Wicomico, the Pocomoke and, in the case of Cambridge, the two-mile-wide Choptank River. The Choptank churned with crabs so plentiful you could scoop them up from the sea grass at low tide. Bay trout, Spanish mackerel, shad, bluefish, herring, rockfish, white perch and oysters bathed in its waters, too. In the opinion of at least one observer, Cambridge was "the most picturesque town in Maryland in the eighteenth century." It was the home of bald eagles calling to each other, Colonial Revival, Queen Anne and Georgian buildings, black squirrels, red foxes and great blue herons hunting lunch. But Cambridge and the rest of sprawling, river-rich Dorchester County also was the home of many men and women as desperate as John Bowley.

HENNY

One of Cambridge's most memorable events had been the 1831 hanging of an enslaved woman named Henny. The recently whipped slave threw lye into her mistress's face, fatally stabbed her and stuffed her body into a closet. The two women had argued after Henny's mistress refused to give her sausage for breakfast. Two blacks, one free and one enslaved, also had been tried in Cambridge for trying to trigger a rebellion. The free black man was sentenced to seven years of hard labor in prison while the enslaved man was condemned to hang. Meanwhile, Hugh Hazlett, an Irishman working near Cambridge, would be convicted in 1858 of helping slaves escape and sentenced to forty-five years in the penitentiary. He was pardoned in 1864, but his original sentence surely made an impression. Even thinking about freedom could be dangerous. Reverend Samuel Green, a former slave in Dorchester

County, was sentenced to ten years in prison for owning a copy of the antislavery novel *Uncle Tom's Cabin,* the best-selling novel of the nineteenth century. He also had a map of Canada, schedule routes to the North, a railroad timetable and a letter from his son, a runaway slave in Canada, asking him to urge other slaves to flee to the far North. Green served five years of his sentence.

But in December 1850, John Bowley only had one thought, one goal, one wish and one prayer: saving his family. A small crowd of slave buyers gathered a little before lunchtime for the slave auction in front of the old courthouse on High Street at Spring. The sale had been advertised in newspapers before and then canceled: an August 1849 ad described John Bowley's wife, Kessiah, as "Kizziah, aged about twenty-five years. She will be sold for life, and a good title will be given." The county jail sat near the courthouse on Spring Street, housing slaves who had been sold or were about to be sold. Yet out-of-town visitors often clustered at Bradshaw's Hotel on the corner of High and Church streets diagonal to the courthouse.

Slave dealers or their agents came to Cambridge from other states and cities to buy slaves. They would sell them in the Deep South at twice the price they'd paid in Dorchester County where, by the 1850s, large-scale plantations were rare. At Bradshaw's Hotel, the men Frederick Douglass called "Georgia traders" could stand on the veranda and haggle with private sellers, wait for sales to begin, watch the auctions or, perhaps, drink. Methodist Episcopal Bishop John Fletcher Hurst, who lived in Cambridge as a boy, also remembered the "Georgia-man or slave trader, who sat in a splint-bottomed chair in the verandah of Bradshaw's hotel and sunned himself and waited for propositions from slave owners. We boys feared him as a hobgoblin." It is safe to assume that potential slave buyers inspected Bowley's wife and children, peering at their teeth, poking their stomachs, kneading their muscles for signs of broken bones and trading comments on what they saw and felt. According to Douglass, slave traders won and lost slaves "upon the turn of a single card" and while "in a state of brutal drunkenness." So some might have swapped bourbon-scented jokes about what a good breeder Kessiah Bowley would make.

John Bowley was a skilled, free ship's carpenter and most likely lived in a boarding house only a block from the courthouse. Yet he'd been unable to raise the money to buy his family's freedom. In fact, according to a notice he and his two brothers, Major and Richard, posted in a local newspaper in the winter of 1850, the Bowley brothers were waist-deep in debt and struggling to pay off their creditors. In a February 6 notice, they promised to "pay every cent" they owed by August 1, 1850, but it's not known if they managed to do that. It's also not clear what was draining the money of this family of skilled free seamen and tradesmen. At least one local historian believes John Bowley might have been "renting" Kessiah and her children from their owner, one way of keeping the family close together. All the same, cash-short John Bowley brought some not-so-obvious assets to his family's sale. They included a web of resourceful relatives and friends and the self-assurance he'd gained as a member of Maryland's free black community, a group that was then 12.8 percent of the total state population.

And his plot, his plan, would have made the Reverend Samuel Green, Hugh Hazlett and other freedom fighters proud. He meant to carry off his enslaved family in the stark light of midday rather than under a blanket of darkness. He intended to whisk Kessiah, James Alfred and Araminta away from courthouse officials and slave buyers and sellers without being questioned, stopped, restrained, jailed, whipped or re-enslaved.

John Bowley had no known history of helping to free slaves. Nor was he the kind of person that the first commissioners elected in Dorchester County in 1669 had worried about—he was no forger, no extortionist, no drunk, no practitioner of "witchcraft" and "enchantments," no trespasser and no price-gouger. He had been freed while a young boy by Levin Stewart, member of a powerful and wealthy clan, but that freedom didn't take effect until he was thirty-one years old. In the meantime, he and his brothers were trained as ship carpenters. That made them members of the county's black elite. According to the 1850 census, of all 673 free black men in Dorchester County, 78 percent were laborers, 11 percent were farmers, 2 percent were ship's carpenters, 5 percent were sailors, 1 percent worked as blacksmiths and 1 percent were general carpenters.

When the bidding for his family began, Bowley stood in the small crowd, waiting for the right moment to raise his voice and hopes. It is believed that he had managed to stall the sale of his family for about a year while he unsuccessfully tried to raise the money to buy them, but the time for stalling had passed. The value of a slave was determined by age, size, health, sex, disposition, whether the slave would be sold out of state and skills such as shoemaking, blacksmithing or carpentering. As a healthy young female with two children, Kessiah could have sold for as much as $500 to $600, the equivalent of nearly $10,000 in today's dollars. Bowley made a bid that satisfied John Brodess, who was acting on behalf of his mother, Eliza Brodess, who owned Kessiah Bowley. Someone then removed the enslaved woman from the courthouse steps and set her aside while the auctioneer left to eat his noonday meal. That's when John Bowley had to play the starring role in the drama that he and Kessiah's aunt, Harriet Tubman, had plotted while exchanging letters. Bowley, according to later testimony from family members, left the crowd at the courthouse and fled with his wife and children to the nearby home of a white woman. The question is: How in the world did he do it?

THE GETAWAY

"The breakaway occurred on the day his mother (Kessiah) was to be sold at auction to another slave-owner," wrote journalist Earl Conrad, repeating what he'd been told by Kessiah and John's son, Harkless Bowley, who was born after their escape. "During the course of the sale, conducted at the courthouse, the auctioneer went to dinner. Meanwhile (Kessiah) was hidden in a house only a five minutes walk from the courthouse."

It is tempting to dismiss this story as a bowl of oral history seasoned with spicy speculation and then stretched into a whole meal.

Harkless Bowley, after all, wasn't alive at the time his parents escaped and was relying on stories he'd heard from Tubman, his great-aunt.

Maryland historical researcher John Creighton still remembers what happened after he told the Bowley escape story to his eighth-grade American history class in the spring of 1972: A black student confronted him after class and insisted that the family's escape from a white crowd in front of the courthouse just did not seem possible.

In those days, doubts dogged Creighton, too. "For over a century before 1850, enslaved people presumably had been sold there under similar circumstances," he said. "Many precautions, probably including handcuffs, must have been taken by the enslaved person's owner and the auctioneer."

Yet, the Dorchester County courthouse contains testimony from a white farmer named Polish Mills that backs up Harkless Bowley's description of his parents' escape. Polish Mills was the brother of John Mills, coadministrator of the personal estate of Edward Brodess, Kessiah Bowley's late owner. Edward Brodess's widow filed a complaint before the court in 1855, claiming that John Mills had sold some of her slaves but failed to give her any money. After John Mills's death, his brother, Polish, answered these charges. He repeated the story of Kessiah's mysterious escape.

"She was brought out to be sold in front of the Court House door in Cambridge," he testified, ". . . but it was found after the sale that she was purchased by her husband, a negro man, who when called in failed to comply—and they were then proceeding to sell her over, when it was discovered she had run away."

Did John Bowley simply put his arms around his wife and children and slowly walk away from the rear of the courthouse, giving observers the impression that he had paid for them already? Or did one of his accomplices lead them away? Did Bowley manage to convince whoever was guarding his family that he was taking them to the auctioneer to make his payment? Is it possible that they were left unguarded or in the care of someone who was sympathetic to the Bowley family? Or did he have accomplices in even higher places?

"The auctioneer must have been in on it or the clerk of the court," speculates Harriet Tubman biographer Kate Clifford Larson. "It seems inconceivable that [Bowley] would have been allowed to take possession of [Kessiah]. She would have been put somewhere secure. We think that perhaps the auctioneer may have been in on the deal— bribed perhaps, [or he was] a friend of Bowley's."

Whatever happened, John Bowley likely had help from several white and black residents of Cambridge, where he and his thirty-five-year-old brother, Richard, lived in the same boarding house and were well-respected craftsmen. When the conveniently absent auctioneer finally returned from his meal and called for the payment for Kessiah and her children, no one stepped forward. The auctioneer then began the bidding for the Bowley family again. Kessiah was "sold twice in one day," according to Harkless Bowley, the second time "sight unseen." By the time the auctioneer figured out that the family was missing, the Bowleys were hidden in the home of a white woman living in Cambridge, whose identity remains a mystery but whose house had to be nearby.

She probably was not a member of the Society of Friends or Quakers, a religious group often associated with antislavery movements. Members of that group did help Harriet Tubman move other slaves safely out of Dorchester County to Delaware. However, most Quakers in the Eastern Shore lived on farms distant from Cambridge. Most likely, the woman who hid the Bowleys was a closet abolitionist, someone whose antislavery sympathies weren't known and whose house no one would think of searching.

AUNT HARRIET

John Bowley had created his family rescue plan with the long-distance help of Harriet Tubman, a woman often identified as his wife's sister but who really was her aunt and was in Baltimore at the time. Slaves and free blacks had many ways of communicating. They gathered among bushes and in swamps for religious rituals. They swapped in-

Fig. 2. Harriet Tubman, the legendary slave rescuer honored in this highway sign, helped John Bowley pull off the bluff that freed his family. (Photo courtesy of William Jarmon)

formation while tending small private vegetable plots. They spread gossip about small and large events along an invisible wire that sometimes traveled for miles. Black educator and former slave Booker T. Washington described how a black man from his plantation who was sent to the post office for mail would linger there and gather gossip from the crowd. Washington called it the "grapevine telegram." In Bowley's case, his grapevine might have been enslaved or free black men who worked as deckhands, cooks or firemen or at other jobs on ships or loaded and unloaded cargo. It was they who spread news, personal messages, escape routes and gossip about people no longer in the area.

After hearing about Kessiah's upcoming sale, Tubman had moved from Philadelphia to Baltimore. John Bowley and Tubman had traded coded messages along the Underground Railroad, an antislavery network that moved information as efficiently as it moved fleeing slaves. Unable to read or write, Harriet would have dictated her letters to Bowley. Standing no more than five feet tall, Tubman was a woman with such a large vision of her role in the freedom movement that she believed God spoke to her directly and would not allow her to fail. She had been born in Dorchester County, not far from Cambridge, and three of her sisters had been sold away by their original owners. Today, Cambridge and the world remember Harriet Tubman with museums, posters, boats, historical markers, parks, tours, children's books, movies and a recent spate of adult books as well. In her day, though, she was a myth, a ghost, a slave rescuer whose existence many white Dorchester residents didn't suspect and whose name they didn't know for years.

"All of her trips . . . were carefully planned and brilliantly executed," noted Robert W. Taylor, financial secretary of Tuskegee Institute, in a 1901 letter to a newspaper editor. "She told me that when she found her mother unwilling to leave behind her feather bed tick, and her father his broad axe and other tools, she bundled up feather bed, broad axe, mother, father—all and landed them in Canada."

But if Tubman was Bowley's trump card in his bid to free his family, it was he who had had to shuffle, cut and play those cards. Though free Maryland blacks lived in a world so restricted that they couldn't captain ships, belong to secret societies or avoid paying property taxes supporting schools their children couldn't attend, a few became blacksmiths and carpenters or infiltrated other trades—thereby gaining a broader knowledge of transportation routes and the wider world. John Bowley was such a man. While he and his brothers were apprenticed to Joseph Stewart, brother of their original owner, they'd learned a variety of shipbuilding skills. By 1848 they were all free and by 1850, they were all ship's carpenters. They then hired themselves out as ship's carpenters, benefiting from a tangle of relationships that stretched from Cambridge to Baltimore and beyond.

In most accounts of the Bowley escape, John and his wife and children fled Cambridge on the same night they sneaked away from the slave buyers and sellers in front of the courthouse. It is equally possible that they hid out for a few days, waiting for the outrage over their escape to lose some of its heat. Though harbors were watched at night, the family finally made their way to the Choptank River, where a small sailboat had been left for them. It was most likely a canoe made from several logs lashed together and topped by a sail. If northwest winds were sweeping down from Baltimore, their boat might have had a rough time sailing, but a seaman like John Bowley would have known what to do. He would have veered in and out of various creeks and narrows, following a zigzag course that brought him close to the wind and then away from it. It was a ninety-mile journey sailing from the Choptank River into the Chesapeake Bay and into Baltimore's Patapsco River, and the Bowleys were targets for capture every mile of the way. Slaves were valuable commodities, and county slaveholders paid top prices to catch those who ran. A $150 reward was common for a runaway from the Eastern Shore, but during the 1850s, prices shot up. Fifteen hundred dollars was offered for a man named Joe Bailey, $300 for his brother Bill, and $800 for Peter Pennington in November 1856.

John Bowley's journey took at least a full day of sailing and possibly several days. Once their ship entered the water, he could have held to his course, manipulating the rudder and center board and raising and lowering its sail. Harriet Tubman biographer Kate Larson believed the family "more than likely would have stopped a couple times along the way." They most likely would have hidden in small, predominately black waterfront settlements such as Bellevue in Talbot County.

When the family finally reached Baltimore, one of Bowley's brothers, possibly Major Bowley, met them there. The city's thriving harbor provided many jobs that attracted free blacks and gave slaveholders a chance to hire out their slaves. In 1850, Baltimore had 140,666 whites, 25,442 free blacks and 2,946 slaves. John and Kessiah and their two children wound up in Fells Point, a famous downtown waterfront community that was within easy reach of the Patapsco River. Frederick Douglass had spent nine years of his childhood in this neighborhood where thousands would gather at shipyards to celebrate a ship's launching. It was a neighborhood that smelled like paint and tar, roasted peanuts and perch; it also was a neighborhood that resounded with the sounds of ship's craftsmen, who hammered, sawed and shouted. It teemed with merchants, shipbuilders and many free and enslaved black caulkers, stevedores, ship builders, carpenters and seamen. Several enslaved and free men from Dorchester County lived and worked in that neighborhood, including Tubman's two brothers-in-law, Tom and Evans Tubman. Harriet Tubman was there, too, having journeyed to Baltimore from Philadelphia to meet the Bowleys. She hid John and Kessiah and their children among friends and relatives, most of whom lived along Slemmers Alley, which ran for only four blocks and was the home of a cross-section of the city's free blacks.

Yet the southern city of Baltimore had its own trail of snares and traps. A law forbade blacks from leaving Baltimore by rail or water without being "weighed, measured and then given a bond signed by people well known locally." As always, Tubman had to use her knowledge and craftiness to work her way around such hazards. In fact, she and other Underground Railroad conductors had to treat any trip into slave territory as a military campaign, a raid upon an enemy that could result in the harassment, wounding, kidnapping, jailing, return to enslavement or even the hanging of everyone involved. The majority of slave escapes probably failed, in part because slave catchers had so many weapons at their disposal, including the law and its officials, hired slave catchers and freelance bounty hunters.

After the Bowleys rested for a few days, Tubman probably obtained fake passes for the whole group from black female vendors in Baltimore's marketplace. They then moved on to Philadelphia, the first large city north of the traditional slave states. At that moment, the

Bowley family joined the ranks of the nearly three hundred slaves who successfully escaped from the border state of Maryland in 1850. In Philadelphia, the Bowleys would have found a city with a strong anti-slavery movement and activists such as Robert Purvis, who had inherited a fortune from his white South Carolina father, a cotton broker. Purvis's home sheltered fugitives in a concealed room, and he and his wife used no slave-produced goods.

All the same, slave catchers operated in Pennsylvania, just as they did in other free states. In fact, in the days when Maryland's notorious Patty Cannon was still alive, she and members of her gang would hang out in Philadelphia bars and buy drink after drink for black customers. Once these freedmen became too drunk to put up a fight, the Cannon gang would kidnap them. "These unfortunate people . . . were kept locked up in the tavern's attic or on an island . . . until they could be loaded aboard schooners and sent away," according to one chronicler of those times.

The Bowleys remained in Philadelphia for nearly a year, working and saving their money. Tubman also worked as a domestic and cook. Late in 1851, though, John and Kessiah and their daughter Araminta moved to Canada, no doubt for the same reason other American fugitives fled to the far North after Congress passed the strict Fugitive Slave Act of 1850. With slave catchers increasingly snatching runaways from the northern United States, the family no longer felt safe either from slave catchers or from the kidnappers of free black people. Many moved to Canada, widely viewed as the Promised Land despite having been a slave society until 1834. Canada had its own set of obstacles, often including racial prejudice and segregated schools. Yet in the 1850s, it provided legal protections and freedom from violence for thousands of American fugitives and a chance for the Bowleys to create lives together.

IN CHATHAM

They settled in Chatham, Ontario, in what was then known as Canada West, a port city some eleven miles north of Lake Erie and sitting on the Thames River. By 1855, it would have an all-black fire brigade, and by 1861, it would have the largest black population and highest proportion of blacks of any city or town in Canada West. Mary Ann Shadd, founder of an antislavery newspaper called the *Provincial Freeman,* moved from Toronto to Chatham in 1855. Emma Lawrence ran a boarding house there on the corner of William and Church streets. Martin Delany moved to Chatham in 1856 and began a medical practice. During the Civil War, he would return to the United States, help raise the 54th Massachusetts Colored Infantry Regiment and become a major in command of the 102nd U.S. Colored Troops. During the black community's heyday in Chatham, several blacks also owned blocks—large buildings containing businesses. James Charity owned the Charity block on King and Adelaide streets, which housed the offices of the *Provincial Freeman* and Dr. Samuel C. Watson. Stanton Hunton owned the Hunton block on William Street near King. Nathaniel Murray built the Murray block on King Street East near William.

Chatham's black citizens worked as laborers, field hands on the rich agricultural and fruit-growing lands, artisans, teachers, and ministers as well. Thomas Doston cut hair. John W. Taylor cut hair and also styled it. John Bowley may have tried farming, blacksmithing or other manual labor or worked on the waterfront. In the 1861 Chatham census, he was said to be forty-five years old and Kessiah thirty-seven, while other members of their household ranged in ages from one to seventeen, five of them described as Canadian born. Between the summer of 1855 and spring of 1856, Ben Ross, who had changed his name to James Stewart, and his wife, Catherine, originally named Jane Kane, also lived with John and Kessiah. Ben Ross was Harriet Tubman's brother and Kessiah's uncle.

JAMES ALFRED BOWLEY

Though John and Kessiah brought their baby, Araminta, with them, they left their son, James Alfred, in Philadelphia with Tubman to continue his education. In an 1868 letter to a woman writing a book about Harriet Tubman, James Alfred remembered "the trouble that you [Tubman] have underwent for me in my childhood days when you were compelled to work in service for one dollar a week in Philadelphia, the city of brotherly love and then give me [one] half of it for my care."

The family's constant push to educate James Alfred would pay off after the Civil War when he moved to Georgetown, South Carolina. There, he edited a newspaper, taught for the Freedmen's Bureau and was elected to the state legislature. An 1867 newspaper article described him as "a laborer in the educational work." While James Alfred prospered in South Carolina, another son of John and Kessiah's—Harkless Bowley—became a teacher in Dorchester County, Maryland, during the 1880s. He then moved to Washington, D.C. He had benefited from living for a time with Tubman in Auburn, New York, where she would live for fifty years—not knowing that she would become the most celebrated black woman in America and have a street named for her in Ghana, West Africa, or that her rescue of Harkless's parents would wind up in brochures promoting tourism in Maryland.

What happened to John and Kessiah Bowley following the Civil War was almost as dramatic, though, as their near-miraculous escape from a slave sale in front of the Dorchester County courthouse. It began when they decided to return to the United States. It's not known exactly what made them go back, but they might have returned for economic reasons. By the late 1860s and early 1870s, for instance, "black businesses and professionals began to be squeezed out of the market causing a resurgence of the black migration" from Chatham, according to historical researcher Gwen Robinson. The end of American slavery also inspired some black Americans living in Canada to start wanting to believe in America's unfulfilled yet lofty promises. The desire to find and reunite with relatives spurred some migrations, too, and so, no doubt, did Canada's relatively chilly climate. Yet not even the abolition of slavery in the United States could end John Bowley's career as a slave rescuer.

Sometime between 1865 and 1867, he and his family lived with Tubman for a year or two, in Auburn, New York, the city that nurtured the legal talents of Lincoln's secretary of state, William H. Seward—the man who was shot but not killed on the same day as Lincoln's assassination. In 1867 or early 1868, the Bowleys returned to Dorchester County, Maryland, to live with Kessiah's father, Harkless Jolley, until they could buy their own land. That's when John Bowley, who had defied weather and slave traders to steer his family to safety, took on yet another rescue mission. Maryland had written a new constitution in November 1864, banning slavery; however, many slaveholders indentured or pressed the children of their former adult slaves into a short-term form of enslavement that kept parents as well as children tied to former masters. The child apprentice system was supposed to guarantee the necessities of life and training in a trade to black youngsters and orphans but often wound up providing neither. Many people regarded the system as slavery in new clothes.

JOHN STEWART

Once Bowley returned to Maryland, John Stewart—one of Harriet Tubman's brothers, who had changed his name from Robert Ross—asked Bowley to find his sons. Stewart had escaped to Canada to avoid being sold but had been unable to free his wife and children. He had not seen his sons, John Henry or Moses Ross, in more than a decade. John Bowley twice sailed across the Choptank River to rescue his two nephews, who held apprenticeships near Trappe, Maryland. Both youngsters were then sent to the crowded Tubman household in Auburn, New York.

Why did John Bowley keep risking his freedom and even life to rescue his kin? The answer might be more complicated than simply love for members of his family. As slaves and former slaves, Bowley and others like him would have understood that they could rely on no one but themselves for their continued survival. They also would have cherished the one thing no one could take from them—their ties to and memories of close relatives, distant relatives, sold-away relatives, lost relatives, dead relatives and people they had adopted informally on slavery-era plantations and farms.

This might have been why Harriet Tubman brought with her a whole group of family and friends, including two brothers and their families, when she settled near Auburn. This also could have been the reason Alfred Wood, a Civil War civilian scout and spy, brought home a fourteen-year-old boy who'd become separated from his regiment. The boy was wandering through Vicksburg, Mississippi, in the summer of 1864—a place then filled with people dazed by the roar of war and the smell of scorched lives. Once Wood decided to take the youngster home, it didn't really matter that, in 1864, home for Al and his wife, Margaret, both runaway slaves from Mississippi, was a Union Army camp.

John and Kessiah spent the rest of their lives in Dorchester County, Maryland, where their people had lived and died. They made their home among folks who went to camp meetings where they embraced visions and wrapped themselves in golden hopes for days.

The Cambridge, Maryland, that John and Kessiah Bowley and their children knew doesn't really exist today. The area's oyster and vegetable packing and canning industries are long gone. The old Dorchester County courthouse on High Street and many of its records burned in a fire in 1852 and the current courthouse replaced it in 1854. The mid-nineteenth-century businesses that once stretched along High Street are history now, too: The street no longer has a silversmith, a coachmaker, a printer, a peddler or a hotel. In the rural parts of the county, the white oaks so valued by ship's carpenters like Bowley— virgin trees that stood one hundred feet or more high—have all but vanished, too, though, here and there, younger oaks are rising up. Sharpshooter Annie Oakley is dead, though some visitors still recall how she made the town famous in the early twentieth century by shooting at waterfowl from the ledge of her home's second-story windows. In the 1960s, Cambridge became famous for clashes between civil rights activists marching for change and people who wanted to freeze things right where they were. Soon, there will be no one left there who actually heard black power activist H. Rap Brown declare in a 1967 speech, "It's time for Cambridge to explode, baby."

Some things—some memories, some habits, some relationships with the natural world—endure, though.

People still stand on the banks of the Choptank, fishing for white perch and striped bass, croackers [*sic*] and spot [*sic*] and trout. (Is it true that croackers make a sound that is just like their name?) Clusters of fat and forbidding flies still bite unlucky visitors just as they bit white and black laborers working in the fields in eighteenth- and nineteenth-century Dorchester County. Countless creeks and rivers still crisscross the county, though mechanical straw balers and combines have replaced most field laborers. Now and then, a wild turkey crosses a road or a back country church emerges from the shadow of a tree. A highway sign detailing the exploits of Harriet Tubman is an unexpected reminder of the haunting power of history. White-tailed deer are here, too, an animal that one admirer described in 1909 as "the least migratory, the least polygamous, the least roving, as well as the swiftest, keenest, shyest, wisest, most prolific . . . of our deer." But in much of rural Dorchester County, the farmland stretches on and on, still and vast and now mostly silent.

Yet it doesn't take all that much imagination to picture this land filled with people like John and Kessiah Bowley and Harkless Jolley and James Alfred and Araminta Bowley and all of their brothers and sisters and cousins and other name-changing kin. If you close your eyes, you can almost hear them talking on moon-bathed nights, their words running together and bumping into each other, soft and slurred yet full of purpose. On Madison Canning House Road, travelers can wander past some of Joseph Stewart's endless tracts of land and recall that he helped design a six- or seven-mile-long canal to float cut logs to his shipyard on the west side of Madison Bay, some twelve miles west of Cambridge. From 1810 into the 1830s, enslaved blacks dug the canal through the marsh by hand. Whites and blacks cut, trimmed, hauled, rafted, floated or ox-carted timber to market. Meanwhile, on Stewart's water-bordering land, a black man named John Bowley not only learned to be a ship's carpenter but to think like one, measuring and planning, plotting and fitting pieces together, always looking for the angle that would make everything work.

John and Kessiah Bowley ran away from this land where people lived close to the sea and the land and understood their ways. Yet they returned to it after a Civil War in which thousands died while frying bacon, reading Bibles or shooting at their opponents from lines sometimes only seventy to eighty yards apart. The Bowleys came back to summer heat as fierce as an invading army. They came back to people who clung to and remembered each other. They came back to religious bands that sang without any music except for the anguish and longing of their funeral chants and moans. They came back to the deep waters of the Choptank and to the more shallow waters of the Chesapeake. They came back to an Eastern Shore culture in which people often shifted jobs with the seasons, doing whatever the warm, green lakes seemed to require. They returned to wooden boats and rivers that rose and fell according to the pull—the mood—of the moon. This land was the Bowleys to leave and theirs, they must have decided, to take back. They, after all, had worked it, walked it, farmed it, measured it, dug graves in it and in some way that even they might not have fully understood, loved it. It had given them and so many others the chance to turn trouble into triumph and the tragedy of slavery into the chance to learn and become something new.

TWO

WATERS OF HOPE

. . . all the rivers run to the sea and the sea is not full.

—*The Holy Bible*

He had never helped a slave escape before, yet he agreed to row the girl across the sometimes calm and sometimes raging Ohio River. Hearts, minds and even weather could change overnight on the old Ohio. The river had spells so dry that escaping slaves could wade across it, almost skipping to freedom. Yet when winter thawed into spring, the river roared with the sound of ice cracking and thundering apart. The Ohio was unpredictable and sudden, passionate and, sometimes, impulsive. So, it turned out, was Arnold Gragston.

From the moment he met the young woman he described as "a pretty little thing, brown-skinned and kinda rosy," his life shifted and swung around. Suddenly, the enslaved nineteen-year-old Kentucky man became willing to risk his life helping other slaves heap their plates with something he claimed he'd never craved—freedom.

He became a man who had something in common with Daniel Strawther and Jerry Jones, two black barbers in Marietta, Ohio, who

Fig. 3. If the Ohio River could talk it might describe the tragedies and triumphs of the Underground Railroad. (Photo by Betty DeRamus)

listened carefully to their white customers for information they could sweep up, bag and deliver to the antislavery movement. He became an ally of fifty-year-old Jane, an enslaved, lame and "very fleshy" woman who managed to escape on a foggy night from Wood County, Virginia, with her seven children. He agreed to expose himself to the same dangers as Aunt Jenny of Parkersburg, Virginia, who signaled across the waters to Belpre, Ohio, abolitionists when slaves escaped.

He declared himself willing to risk just as much as Dick Naylor, a free black man who hung around the wharf in Wheeling, Virginia, pretending to be a tipsy bum instead of someone who ferried runaways across the river. And he put himself in the same peril as Harmar, Ohio, Underground Railroad conductor David Putnam, Jr., a man whom a rock-throwing, insult-hurling mob in Parkersburg, Virginia, had forced into the waters of the Ohio in 1839: A steamboat deckhand had to rescue him from drowning.

None of this would have been on Arnold Gragston's mind, though, on the night he took his first step toward joining the freedom movement. He was on his way to court a different young woman, but he ran into an elderly woman who urged him to ferry a runaway slave girl across the Ohio River, the watery boundary separating Kentucky and western Virginia from the free states of Ohio, Indiana and Illinois. At first he said no, but he changed his mind when he saw the girl, who looked as scared as he felt.

He wasn't ready to take her across the river that first night, though. It took another day for Gragston to steel his nerves and smooth away the rough edges of his fears. Slave catchers patrolled the counties along the river, and Gragston, according to his later testimony, couldn't help thinking about what might happen if he were caught: the hounds lunging for his legs, the rawhide whips tearing open his back and his possible sale to another, sterner master. But the brown-skinned girl's face drove out all the other images swimming around in Gragston's head. The Mason County, Kentucky, man showed up the day after meeting the girl, prepared to row her to Ripley, Ohio, a small Ohio River town where free blacks and whites hid and transported fugitive slaves on the secret antislavery network known as the Underground Railroad.

THE RIVER REMEMBERS

Before the West was settled, the Ohio River bore few signs that men had used it, but later it became an eyewitness to history. If the river could talk it would tell many stories about the joy and violence, dangers and desires of the people who came to its shores. It transported such larger-than-life characters as apple-planting Johnny Appleseed and Mike Fink, the brash boatman who once allegedly shot off a black man's heel during a shooting contest with another white man. John Hunt Morgan, the Confederate raider, crossed the river in 1863, bringing the Civil War to Indiana and Ohio's back door. The river also was watching as some thirteen thousand Cherokee passed through Salem, Kentucky, in 1838–39 on the Trail of Tears, their forced relocation from their homes in the southeastern United States to Oklahoma. Accompanied by their black slaves, the Cherokee entered Livingston County at Salem and eventually crossed the Ohio River to Golconda, Illinois. The river became best known, though, for the Underground Railroad stationmasters who crossed it to move hundreds or perhaps thousands of runaway slaves toward Canada. Some freedom seekers called it "the River Jordan," after the biblical river the Israelites crossed to escape Egyptian slavery and reach the Promised Land.

The most famous Ohio River freedom story was the fictionalized tale of Eliza, heroine of the novel *Uncle Tom's Cabin,* who fled to the river with her five-year-old son, Harry, and crossed the ice by leaping from one ice floe to the next. But the river also played a role in the even more dramatic story of fugitive Margaret Garner, who cut her youngest daughter's throat to save her from slavery and then lost her second daughter two months later when the child drowned.

The river had watched as farmers on its free Ohio side sometimes rented or borrowed slaves owned by their friends or relatives on the Virginia side. The river shared the grief of Allen Watkins, a Kentuckian whose first wife committed suicide after being separated from her husband and children. Watkins later fled with his children to the Ohio and hid atop a two-story bridge, escaping, finally, to Canada. The river certainly knew Sam Alexander, a slave taken aboard the riverboat *Thomas Swan* after being sold at the Wheeling, Virginia, slave market. Waving his hands, Sam yelled "good-bye boys" and plunged into the Ohio: He was never again seen by the people on the boat but managed to swim to shore; eventually he was taken on horseback to a free black man who helped him escape.

THE BEAR

The river also was rushing along its 967-mile course on that day in 1846 when sixteen-year-old John Curtis and two younger boys escaped from a plantation in Rockingham County, Virginia, propelled by John's fear that he had killed their master with a farm tool. The runaways fell in with a slave catcher who pretended to be their friend but planned to resell them. However, an innkeeper created a diversion and told them how to escape. With dogs and bounty hunters trailing them, John Curtis and his brothers reached the Ohio River and hid in a nearby cave. Curtis and his brothers stayed in the cave for two months, eating a bear Curtis had killed with a large piece of sandstone and huddling under the animal's warm hide. John Curtis later discovered he hadn't killed his master and managed to borrow the money to buy freedom for himself and one of his brothers. "I heard that story about John Curtis killing that bear [so often] that I know it by heart," says Ohio historian Henry Burke, a Curtis descendant. "Bears still roam around that part of the country."

THE FEUD

The river even inspired legal feuds and bitter courtroom battles. It was the scene of the continuing war between slave owner George Washington Henderson, who owned a plantation in Wood County, Virginia, and Underground Railroad conductor David Putnam, Jr., who lived across the river from Henderson in Harmar village near Marietta, Ohio. George Washington Henderson and Elizabeth Henderson lived in well-polished, slave-assisted luxury. Their house's smaller, two-story wooden back wing was completed by slave labor ten years after Henderson and his sixteen-year-old bride (who stood about four foot eleven but would produce twelve children) arrived as newlyweds in 1826. By 1859, the house had gained a larger three-story front section and become known as Henderson Hall: The hall was the centerpiece of a plantation, horse breeding farm and river port. But it had a dangerous location for a slave-manned plantation, and nothing could change that, not even its lace curtains, hand-painted china, French-patterned wallpaper, daybeds and mammy benches for slave women cradling white babies.

Squatting on the banks of the triangle where the Muskingum and the Ohio River came together, the Henderson plantation stared night and day at the free state of Ohio. Less than a mile from Henderson's plantation, the river was a constant temptation to his slaves. Between June 1837 and April 1849, there are at least seventeen documented cases of slaves' escaping from Henderson's plantation. The runaways included at least one slave who fled to Canada, sent Henderson a letter of apology, returned to Henderson's plantation and then ran again, this time with his family.

The first stop for many runaways fleeing western Virginia was the house of Ohio grocer David Putnam, Jr. More than six feet tall, Putnam was described as a "big-framed, broad-shouldered, long-armed son of nature." He was the great-grandson of Major General Israel Putnam, who reportedly left his oxen and plow standing in the fields when he marched off to fight in the Revolutionary War. David Putnam, Jr., like his great-grandfather, never backed away from a fight—or a chance to help fleeing slaves. Increasingly frustrated by slave escapes, George Henderson slapped David Putnam with a lawsuit in 1847, accusing him of enticing nine of his slaves to run away after they had crossed the river to sell chickens in Marietta. Henderson's debt case against Putnam for each of the nine slaves was dismissed for lack of jurisdiction on October 20, 1852. In the second suit, Henderson requested ten thousand dollars for breach of a lifetime labor contract between himself and his slaves. In 1853, one of Henderson's attorneys asked that the case be dropped after Putnam allegedly found a witness who would testify that one of the fugitives was still in Virginia at the time he was supposedly in Putnam's house. However, even if Henderson hadn't dropped the suit, it would have failed because of a loophole in the Fugitive Slave Act of 1850. Cases pending during the passage of the 1850 act were automatically dismissed because there was no language in the new law keeping those old cases alive, according to a Supreme Court decision in an Indiana case.

Oh, yes, the river knew stories.

ARNOLD

Still, young Arnold Gragston of Mason County, Kentucky, probably would not have known about Sam Alexander's leap of faith into the Ohio or about John Curtis's epic struggle with a bear or about the tug of war between George Henderson and David Putnam, Jr. He also was not likely to have known about a runaway slave named Micah, who crossed to the north side of the Ohio and traveled along the Muskingum River to Owl Creek. Captured by a group that included his owner, Micah fatally stabbed his owner's son during a struggle. The group executed him about six miles west of Cumberland in Guernsey County, Ohio, leaving him in a shallow grave. Arnold Gragston also might not have understood the trancelike power of rivers, their almost hypnotic sway, or how crossing one could become a routine, a ritual, a need that changed a man for good. He simply wanted the girl with fearful eyes to stay safe.

On his first night as an Underground Railroad conductor, Gragston listened carefully to his instructions. He was told to deliver the young woman to the Reverend John Rankin in Ripley, Ohio. Rankin, who had six sons, was so notorious for helping fugitives that the state of Kentucky had offered a twenty-five-hundred-dollar reward for his kidnapping or killing. And for a time he'd headed his own antislavery branch of Presbyterianism known as the Free Presbyterian Church.

Rankin's house, with its hundred stairs of rough stones and wood, sat atop a hill overlooking the entire town of Ripley, the Ohio River and the Kentucky shoreline. It gave him a sweeping view of approaching slave catchers on horseback. The house may have sheltered more than two thousand fugitive slaves on the road to freedom, men, women and children guided by the lantern that Jean and John Rankin kept burning in the upper window of their home. The passage of the Fugitive Slave Act of 1850 had made helping fugitive slaves much more dangerous and difficult. Ex-slaves could be recaptured in free territory and returned to their masters, and anyone sheltering them could be heavily fined. Moreover, despite Ripley's reputation as a slave haven,

Ohio itself, as black leader Frederick Douglass pointed out, was "polluted—she is disgraced by her villainous black laws." He referred to state laws that, among other things, prohibited the testimony of blacks against whites, a product, according to Douglass, of "pandering politicians."

Yet no slave was ever recaptured from the Rankin home, even though the family hid as many as twelve slaves at a time. On one occasion, Rankin disguised himself as a woman and crossed into Kentucky with a group of young men. While bounty hunters armed with rifles and dogs chased him and his group, the true objects of their hunt—an enslaved woman and her children—fled to Canada. Ripley's other famous conductor was John P. Parker, a free black iron foundry owner and former slave who had escaped bounty hunters by, among other things, hiding in coffins and even diving off a steamboat into the river. Parker claimed he had "an eternal hatred" of slavery and proved it by rescuing an escaping couple's baby from the bedroom of the child's sleeping owners.

When Arnold Gragston began crossing the Ohio River, it was 1859, the year of John Brown's raid on Harpers Ferry. It also was the year in which Meredith and Mary Calhoun, owners of seven hundred Louisiana slaves, abandoned America for France and left their estate in the hands of a son who made a black woman his common-law wife and became a radical, antislavery Republican. Also in 1859, a Frenchman named Charles Blondin crossed Niagara Falls by walking on a cable stretched across the water. Later, he made the same crossing while blindfolded, while pushing a wheelbarrow, while walking on stilts and while carrying a man on his back. Blondin could not have been more nervous than Arnold Gragston on his first slave rescue. The river current was strong that night, and Gragston trembled as it rocked him; he was cold and nearly blind in the dark. But then he saw the light of Reverend Rankin's lantern and headed for it. Two men welcomed the girl, and one of them took Gragston's arm and asked if he were hungry. That ended his first trip, but it didn't satisfy his taste for the mingled excitement and fear he had felt on crossing the river.

Sometimes Gragston took two or three people to Ripley and "sometimes a whole boatload," he claimed. He estimated he made three and four trips a month and helped "more than a hundred" fugitives. He never really saw any of the other passengers clearly but always asked them, "What you say," and they answered "Menare," the password he'd been taught. He proceeded with care on his night voyages for fear slave owners might follow him and recapture their slaves.

Yet something—a need for purpose, perhaps, or a relish for risks—made Gragston keep returning to the sometimes green, sometimes blue and sometimes brown-looking river. He "got to liking it," was his only explanation for freeing other people while remaining enslaved himself. He made no money, he added, from rowing people to freedom. He never saw the brown-skinned girl again either and eventually married another woman. All the same, he spent four years helping slaves escape and spending his nights at the river where the water flowed to its own sometimes steady and sometimes rousing beat. Like all great rivers, the Ohio was awash in meanings, most of them contradictory. It represented seagoing adventures and contented fishing, cleansing baptisms and muddy pollution, rescues and drownings, peace and storms, the development of river-facing towns and cities and the need to escape from them. It had currents that could overwhelm a rower but that could save him as he crawled ashore. Gragston suspected that his owner knew about his romance with the river and his slave-freeing activities, but that wasn't enough to make him stop what he was doing or even pause.

When interviewed decades after the end of slavery, Gragston insisted he'd never longed for freedom himself despite living in a state where lawns were sometimes used as auction blocks and where Harriet Beecher Stowe saw naked, chained and shackled slaves sold to the highest bidder. Gragston had been born on Christmas Day on the John L. Tabb plantation in Mason County, Kentucky. According to Gragston, John or "Jack" Tabb "used to have a special slave who didn't have nothin' to do but teach the rest of us . . . how to read and write and figger." Not even the beatings that sometimes occurred when

Virginia-born Tabb didn't feel his slaves responded quickly enough to a summons were enough to turn Gragston against the institution, he insisted. Gragston told the slave narrative collectors who later interviewed him that he believed the beatings might have been a cover to keep Tabb's neighbors from thinking he was too soft on his slaves. Since twentieth-century interviews with former slaves were sometimes reviewed, edited or even rewritten, there's no way to tell if Gragston's interview represents the full range of his feelings about beatings and enslavement.

In the 1860 census, John L. Tabb and his wife, Hannah, owned real estate valued at $7,350 and personal property worth $11,525. Three years later, one important piece of their property bolted and ran. In 1863, Arnold Gragston finally took flight. He had carried about a dozen slaves across the river that night. As soon as he stepped out of the boat on the Kentucky side, slave catchers began chasing him. He hid out in cornfields, in the woods, in a hay pile. Gragston and his wife then slipped across the Ohio themselves, joining the thousands of other fugitives for whom the river bore a number of names, including Canaan and the River Jordan, all whispering of freedom. Eventually, they settled in Detroit but would later return to live in Ripley. When an interviewer for a federal writing project talked to Gragston, he was living in Eatonville, Florida, an all-black town five miles from Orlando. Author Zora Neale Hurston, who lived in Eatonville, would describe it as a place of sand and orange groves, mangrove trees, scrub pine and shiny pride. For Arnold Gragston it might also have been a place where a former slave could eat sun-caressed fruit and sip bittersweet memories of the days when he risked everything for a place in history and a thank-you—however brief—from a pretty girl.

THREE

❖━━◆◆◆━━❖

HE HAD TO HAVE HER

Stand fast, and do not be caught again under the yoke of slavery.
—Galatians, 5:1, *The Holy Bible*

Nelson Gant's life was in the hands of the woman he loved, but nobody could be sure how steady those hands were. The woman was Nelson's wife, Anna Maria, but she was a slave who'd just spent a month in jail. The authorities had battered her with questions and worn her thin with threats. Unless she turned on Nelson, they warned, she'd end up plucking cotton or hacking sugar cane in some soul-sapping patch of the Deep South. One whiff of weakness, one shaky step or blurted-out word and Anna Maria could condemn her husband.

Would she stick to the story that might shield Nelson from prison?

Or would she crack and betray him?

It was December 1846, and Nelson Talbot Gant's third scheduled trial for stealing his wife from slavery was about to begin in Virginia's Leesburg County Courthouse. It was a trial in which things would be

Fig. 4. Lavinia Logan (Lulu) Gee, daughter of Lavinia J. Neal and Nelson T. Gant, a former slave who made legal and economic history. (Photo courtesy of The Pioneer and Historical Society of Muskingum County, Ohio)

said that had never been said in an American courtroom before, and it was a trial that would make history. It also was a trial that could have doomed Nelson to prison for two to ten years, and a case that Nelson seemed certain to lose. His only defense was that he loved Anna Maria and she was his wife, but that turned out to be enough. On his day in court, Nelson's attorneys became magicians, making southern customs disappear, sawing the law in half and even, for a few hours, forcing white slaveholders to see life through the eyes of a former slave.

There was nothing in Gant's early life to suggest he'd be the defendant in a nationally known trial dealing with everything from God's opinion of love and marriage among slaves to witnesses who weren't at all sure who or what they'd seen in the shadowy land between night and day. Nor was there anything to hint that one day an amusement park and stadium would bear Gant's name or that he would own a coal mine or that customers for his produce would crowd his porch, gulping down strawberries and cream.

He had been born a slave on May 10, 1821 or 1822, on the Woodburn estate in the foothills of northern Virginia, some three miles southwest of Leesburg and forty miles northwest of Washington, D.C. Blacks were not newcomers in Leesburg, the seat of Loudoun County: They'd arrived with the first European settlers in the 1720s. By 1840, the low ridge east of the Catoctin Mountain was the home of so many blacks it had become known as Negro Mountain.

JOHN NIXON

Nelson's enslaved mother died giving birth to him, passing away on the path leading from her quarters to the home of her master, John Nixon, according to stories handed down by Gant's descendants. As the son of Nixon or some other white man, the bright-skinned Nelson was raised by Eve or Edith Gant, one of John Nixon's house servants. Nixon was a canny farmer who would one day free his slaves. He also was a man who sometimes seemed able to pick up shifts in the wind and smell changes before they arrived. He built his barn out of brick rather than wood, making it one of the few local barns that didn't burn during the Civil War. Nixon and his more than twenty slaves plowed wheat and corn fields, grew apples, oranges and lemons, kept dairy cattle, sheep, goats, hogs and horses and ground wheat into flour with a gristmill. Eventually, Nelson became a house servant like his adoptive mother, likely cleaning, gardening, marketing, serving food—and paying close attention to everything he saw and heard.

By all accounts, Nelson Gant, even while enslaved, was a man whom people noticed, a man who left large footprints, a man who seemed to fill up a room. His freedom certificate called him a "tall, bright mulatto, with no particular scars or marks," suggesting he had not been beaten or misused by his master. His freedom papers also said he stood about five foot nine and three-quarter inches tall, but some observers would later insist he was a much taller man. Author Thomas W. Lewis, who knew Gant, described him as having "a height exceeding six feet and a frame large and well proportioned." Lewis also claimed that Gant was "a man whom strangers were wont to turn and look at. There was a distinction in face and form. He spoke with weight, and deliberately choosing his words." In photographs of Gant in old age, his strong-featured face resembles drawings of freedom fighter Frederick Douglass.

ANNA MARIA

The life of this tall, or tall-looking, man with no outward scars changed when he met and fell in love with Anna Maria Hughes, a woman with soft ways but a steely will. By all accounts, Nelson's love was no luke-warm, watered-down love. It was love bubbling on a stove, love shouting at the low-slung midnight moon, love yanking a man out of bed so he'd have time to walk around dreaming. Anna Maria was a house servant to Charlaye Ann Elizabeth Jane Russell, who lived on Market Street in downtown Leesburg. She had been born around 1826 and was among a group of slaves that Sarah Elizabeth "Betsy" McCarty gave to her three never-married daughters, Eliza, Sarah and Charlaye Ann Elizabeth, Anna Maria's principal owner. McCarty was the widow of

Thaddeus McCarty, George Washington's cousin. Nelson's stepsister
Winifred likely introduced him to Anna Maria, known as Maria and
described in court proceedings as a "dark mulatto woman" worth four
hundred dollars. Anna Maria and Winifred both attended the Leesburg Methodist Church. According to one source, Anna Maria had
been allowed to attend the colored Sunday school of the Methodist
Church early in life, perhaps when she was as young as twelve.

Romantic love had a tough time thriving in slavery's thin, constantly
shifting topsoil: There was nothing to feed it, nothing to help hold it
in place. Slave owners could choose their slaves' spouses, could breed
them like animals and could separate people who considered themselves married at any time. All the same, slaves did form shaky unions
they called marriages with other slaves or with free blacks. However,
Nelson and Maria took their "marriage" a step further than most enslaved people. They weren't casually "married" by their smiling owners
in a yard or on a porch, nor did they jump over any broom. In 1843,
they repeated their marriage vows before the Reverend Samuel Gover,
a Methodist minister and probably Maria's Sunday school teacher.

However, Nelson Gant became a husband boxed in and betrayed
by love when his owner, John Nixon, of Loudoun County, Virginia,
died in 1844 after a long illness. In his will, the farsighted Nixon
freed "all my slaves of every description, old and young male and female" and directed that his executors move them to a free state as
soon after his death as possible. According to an eastern antislavery
activist who had visited Nixon, the slave owner had been uneasy for a
long time about owning slaves. He was equally uneasy about what his
relatives might do if he decided to let his slaves go. Prospective heirs
often tried to halt or prevent their relatives from freeing slaves. In one
extreme case, a white Virginia planter named George Wythe willed
one-third of his estate to his mulatto cook and another third to her
son and, presumably, his. Wythe's outraged grandnephew, George
Sweeney, poisoned all three. The woman survived but couldn't testify
against a white man in court. As a result, Sweeney was never punished
for his crime.

But John Nixon—a man who was adept at smelling trouble on the way—had been wise enough to do more than simply free his slaves in his will; he provided enough money for one of his executors to move them to a free state and buy land. That would keep them from breaking the law by lingering in Virginia once freed. Under a law passed in 1806 but later modified, all newly freed blacks had to leave the state within a year unless they had special permission to stay. Plagued by bloody dreams since Nat Turner's 1831 rebellion resulted in the deaths of some sixty whites, slaveholders in Virginia and elsewhere worried that independent-minded free blacks might spark and lead revolts. But where did all of this leave Anna Maria Gant?

When twenty-three-year-old Nelson Gant received his freedom on September 9, 1845, he joined the ranks of Virginia blacks who were free on paper but not all that free in fact. At the time, it would have been a crime for him to buy liquor without written permission from three or more judges. It also would have been a crime for him to preach because that might stir up slave rebellions; it would have been a crime to own a dog because dogs would fight for their owners; a crime to learn to read and write in Virginia or to return home after learning to read and write somewhere else; a crime to shave a white man, a crime to run a tavern, a crime to prepare medicines that could cause abortions, a crime in some towns to smoke in public—and, of course, a crime to keep his newly freed self in Virginia. It might just as well have been a crime for him to love since, ironically, his freedom threatened his marriage.

For some of the other slaves freed by John Nixon, the freedom trail led to Zanesville, Ohio, possibly because some antislavery Quakers in the Leesburg area knew abolitionists in Zanesville. But there was no swift, straight-ahead path to a different life for Nelson Gant. He couldn't simply walk, run or ride off into the future and see how it tasted and felt. He had to figure out how to free the woman he claimed again and again that he couldn't live without—and he had to figure it out quickly.

He stayed in Virginia as long as he could, trying to pile up some money. He even took a job chopping wood along the Potomac River near Leesburg, reportedly cutting five hundred cords of wood for forty cents a cord. By the 1830s, lumbering had become an important industry. Large stands of timber were cut down to provide bark for tanning, fuel for fireplaces and stoves and to build homes, barns, canal boats, shops and locks. Wood cutters were in such high demand that, in July 1846, the Potomac Furnace advertised for "one hundred wood choppers." Yet Nelson found it impossible to hold on to any money; by the time he paid for his food and shelter, he had little left. Meanwhile, his wife's owner refused to put a price on Anna Maria's freedom. Apparently she was not moved by Nelson's insistence that he "could not live . . . without the person who was more dear to him than all the world," according to a newspaper account. Around this time, Nelson also was brought before a grand jury for staying in the state longer than twelve months. He was acquitted but ordered to leave Virginia in early September 1846. Before leaving, he promised his wife that he would return for her in six weeks; he also told her where they would meet. His plan was to earn more money, come back and make another offer for his wife's freedom. Yet, like any man in love, he was prepared to go much, much further than that.

Nelson likely took the National Road through Cumberland, Maryland, across the low ridge known as Negro Mountain. He then would have headed east of the Catoctin Mountains into Washington County, Pennsylvania. As the southernmost free state, Pennsylvania was a popular destination for Loudoun County runaways and emigrants. When Samuel Janney, a Quaker and antislavery activist from near Leesburg, visited Pennsylvania in 1845, he was struck by the number of blacks he recognized from his corner of Virginia. In Washington County, Pennsylvania, former slaves from Loudoun County put Nelson Gant in touch with Dr. Francis Julius LeMoyne and his wife, Madeline. LeMoyne was a physician and professor at Washington College who helped start the Western Abolition Society in Washington, and he also was part of the sometimes organized and sometimes spontaneous network of slave-aiding abolitionists known as the Underground Railroad.

It is presumed that Nelson then detoured north to Pittsburgh where he met Martin Delany, whose family had fled their home in present-day West Virginia after young Martin was discovered reading, an illegal activity for slaves. During the Civil War, Delany would be appointed a major in the United States Colored Troops, making him the highest-ranking black officer in the Regular Army. Some historians believe Nelson also crossed the Ohio River into Zanesville where he learned more about the Underground Railroad, probably from other freed John Nixon slaves, and met A. A. Guthrie and other Zanesville and Putnam abolitionists. In the fall of 1846, Nelson Gant returned to Loudoun County, Virginia. By then, arrangements had been made to put Maria on the freedom train and whisk her out of Leesburg.

Gant, however, made one final attempt to buy Maria's freedom. Turned down, he left Virginia. Soon after Nelson's departure, his wife's owner received some jarring news. While Maria was working for her owner's neighbor, county clerk Charles G. Eskridge, she, too, had disappeared. For reasons that aren't known, Eskridge didn't report her absence for three days. Meanwhile, the couple had journeyed to nearby Washington, D.C., where they were directed to the home of a black man who soothed them, sheltered them and then turned them over to the authorities, presumably for a reward. The Gants were arrested and jailed.

THE TRIAL

Before being taken back to Leesburg, Maria spent eight days in a Washington, D.C., jail. Gant spent thirteen days in jail awaiting his first trial, which was canceled when Virginia governor William Smith ordered him shipped back to Virginia for trial. Maria then spent twenty-two days in the Leesburg jail where "every effort known to the master to make the slave confess" was used to pressure her to say Nelson had lured her away. Nothing worked, not even the threat of selling her to a planter who would put the Sunday-school-reared house slave to work slashing sugar cane, planting rice in watery fields or chopping cotton. It turned out she had more spine—and, obviously, more love for Nelson—than her jailers and owner had suspected. She continued to insist that she had run away and then Nelson had followed her.

In Loudoun County, a November court date for Gant's trial was postponed because the prosecuting attorney wanted to wait for the arrival of witnesses. Finally, in December 1846, Gant stood trial in the Loudoun County's courthouse in Leesburg, charged with attempting to steal his wife from slavery.

Nelson's defense team wisely stressed the strength of Nelson and Maria's feelings for each other, pushing members of the judicial panel to put themselves in the couple's tight, slavery-made shoes. In fact, defense attorney R. P. Swann made an eloquent plea for recognizing that Nelson and Maria were as committed to each other as any white couple.

"This man has been united in holy wedlock to a woman for whom he has evinced the strongest feelings of attachment," Swann insisted. "Although his skin wears a different hue from ours, we cannot doubt that the feelings of his heart are the same. Their vows have been registered in the chancery of Heaven; and shall we attempt to set the laws of man above the Divine law, by separating those whom God hath joined? The Ethiopian may not change his skin, nor the leopard his spots, but if it were possible for the prisoner at the bar to step forth in the complexion and lineaments of the Anglo-Saxon race, there is not a man on that bench, nor in this assembly, who would not applaud the deed for which he now stands arraigned as a felon."

Anna Maria was the first witness called. It is not difficult to imagine the mix of feelings that must have all but overwhelmed an enslaved woman who was only twenty, raised on Sunday school lessons and nearly faint from the fear that she would lose Nelson. She must have looked and acted like a terrified but devoted wife, which set the stage for defense attorney J. S. Carper's next startling argument.

If Anna Maria and Nelson Gant's marriage was recognized in heaven, if not on earth, Carper noted, "It was a point well settled in law, that the testimony of husband and wife cannot be taken either for or against each other, because the law regards them as so identified in feeling and interest that their evidence cannot be relied upon." Moreover, Carper noted, the prisoner's wife was a slave, which meant she was under the "power and control of her mistress" who might order her either to give the kind of evidence that would convict her husband "or face being sold to the dreaded slave traders of the Deep South."

Prosecuting attorney Burr H. Harrison loaded his musket and fired back. There was no such thing as lawful marriage for slaves, he argued, making it impossible to apply the common-law rule that spouses in civil and criminal prosecutions could not present evidence that, in the future, might incriminate each other. Slaves, he pointed out, were property, not persons, and could make no contracts that their owners "may not annul."

But defense attorney John Janney refused to back down even in the face of Harrison's harsh nineteenth-century truths. He pointed out that Maria Gant had been married with the consent of her mistress, in her mistress's house, with the implied consent of her master, and joined by a minister of the gospel. Holding that there was no such thing as slave marriage, Janney insisted, would lead to the "general corruption of morals and the most enormous abuses. Can it be possible that the whole colored population of Virginia are living in a state of concubinage? . . . Maria is the lawful wife of the prisoner; and it is a point well established that in a case like this, the testimony of a wife cannot be taken either for or against her husband."

No panel of American justices had heard seriously presented arguments quite like these, and no slavery-era U.S. court was likely to hear them again. They ignored the definition of "wife," which, in nineteenth-century America, didn't include enslaved women, who could be raped or even killed with no consequences. They also ignored all the other black men—and white ones, too—who'd been whipped, jailed, kidnapped, beaten almost to death, sold or hanged for rescuing spouses and other slaves.

However, Virginia courts didn't always render paint-by-the-numbers decisions. Like other southern magistrates, Virginia jurists sometimes insisted on fair in-court procedures to bolster their argument that slavery was a humane and merciful system. In Prince Edward County, Virginia, a freed black man and former house slave named Syphax Brown sued a white man for shooting some of his hogs. He won damages. In nearby Nottoway County, an enslaved man was acquitted of assaulting his mistress with a rock. Even though the alleged victim made her accusations while pointing to a gash in her head, the court still set the enslaved man free. Moreover, as author Melvin Patrick Ely has noted, Virginia was not only a state that surrounded free blacks with walls of laws and strangling restrictions, it also was a state with a tradition of sometimes easy one-on-one relations between individual blacks and whites, who sometimes played cards, drank liquor, ate and even slept together without any consequences.

All the same, there must have been more than one shocked face in the courtroom when a judicial panel decided to allow Maria Gant to leave the stand without testifying. It was an awesome decision. For the first time in the state of Virginia, a marriage involving a slave had been recognized as legitimate. The testimony of a second black witness was rejected, as well, primarily because the man couldn't give a coherent account of whatever he'd seen or thought he'd seen. It had not been quite daybreak, he said, when he saw a man who might or might not have been the defendant in suspicious circumstances. As a result, Nelson Gant, a man who apparently looked taller once he became free, escaped prison for freeing his wife. Even after all these years, it remains a stunning decision.

There were no hard-shelled antislavery men on the judicial panel, whose members included Thomas Saunders, Noble S. Braden, Joshua Pusey, David Reece and Addison H. Clark. Braden belonged to the mostly Quaker Loudoun Manumission and Emigration Society, which had emancipated some blacks to Liberia, West Africa, a move supported by many white Virginians but rejected by some blacks. Pusey not only owned slaves; one had escaped from him by pretending to be the servant of the white woman traveling with him. And eventually John Janney would own slaves, too.

Victoria Robinson, a descendant of the Gants, believes Nelson and

Maria might have benefited from their links to prominent and well-connected people. Defense attorney John Janney, for instance, belonged to one of the most respected families in Virginia. He was a tall, spare man who was among thirty-eight Loudoun County citizens who filed a petition in 1842 calling the laws against free black residency "unjust, oppressive and contrary to the moral sense of this community." When Virginia held a convention to decide whether to leave the Union, Janney would head the convention. He also would be a member of the House of Delegates for a dozen years, an elector in four presidential contests, a candidate for the 1840 vice presidential nomination, a lawyer, an orator and, eventually, a slave owner himself. Maria lived in downtown Leesburg and her neighbor was the clerk of the court. Nelson's friend Samuel Janney operated a girls' school, published several books and wrote antislavery essays aimed at southern audiences; he also was the first cousin once removed of John Janney.

Yet none of this explains why Nelson Gant walked out of the Loudoun County Courthouse a free man instead of spending from two to ten years in prison. For all his influence, John Janney hadn't been able to keep a black man named Leonard Grimes out of prison even though the Washington, D.C.–based Underground Railroad conductor had been tried in the same courthouse as Gant and convicted on purely circumstantial evidence of rescuing seven slaves from a Leesburg planter. Maria and Nelson did indeed have influential friends and connections but so did Maria's owner. The most plausible explanation for Nelson's acquittal was his wife's continued insistence before the trial that she had run away on her own and that Nelson had followed her. There was no proof presented during the trial that this wasn't what had happened, and this particular group of southern jurists had decided to follow the law. The panel's decision not to pressure Maria into testifying is harder to understand—unless the defense attorneys' moving rhetoric did indeed humanize Nelson.

CHARLAYE RUSSELL

Unfortunately, love doesn't necessarily melt, chip or blast away all opposition. Nelson's acquittal changed nothing for Anna Maria, who remained enslaved. The young woman was taken back to her owner's house right around the corner from the courthouse and returned to her old life.

Not content with winning his freedom, Nelson decided to make one more appeal to Anna Maria's owner for her liberty. He couldn't live without his wife, he told Charlaye Russell. He had to have Anna Maria. Within two months of the trial, Russell finally agreed to free Nelson's wife for $775, nearly double what the court had said she was worth two months earlier. Gant's friends in the antislavery movement helped him raise money, and he borrowed about $225 from Thomas Nichols, one of the executors of John Nixon's estate.

At this point, it didn't seem possible that Nelson Gant ever would make it to Ohio, much less become one of the state's richest black men. The money he borrowed from friends had to be repaid; however, every moment he lingered in Virginia he was breaking a law that could return him to slavery. The law ordering all newly freed blacks to leave the state within one year was not always enforced at all times and in all places. Yet the longer Nelson Gant stayed in the Leesburg area, the more likely it was that the ground under his feet could crack open and swallow him. In September 1847, the commonwealth attorney succeeded in getting a grand jury indictment issued for Gant, along with fifteen or so other free Negroes, for remaining in the state of Virginia for more than twelve months after receiving their freedom. That order may not have been served, because in every quarterly court thereafter the bill of indictment was presented again.

For the next three years, the Gants lived in a kind of shadow land in Loudoun County, Virginia, hoping they wouldn't be noticed as they sweated their way out of debt. In 1846, 1848, 1849 and 1850, Nelson shows up on the personal property tax rolls as living with Samuel Janney and Janney's son, John. Presumably, he was working off his debt to Thomas Nichols. In June 1850, the grand jury indictment against Gant was dismissed and the couple, along with their twenty-month-old daughter, Mary, finally left Loudoun for the Zanesville, Ohio, area where family and friends waited. The Gants don't show up in the 1850 census, possibly because their move to Ohio caused them to miss the census taker. Nelson, Anna Maria and their toddler journeyed across the mountains of Virginia until they reached Cumberland, Maryland, and the National Road made of limestone spread thirty feet wide.

The National Road, officially called the Cumberland Road and also known as the National Pike and the Old Pike, was the first and only U.S. road built entirely with federal funds. Drovers walking turkeys, pigs, cows and sheep to market traveled the National Road, and so did farmers carrying wool, tobacco, grain, sugar and cloth to market. Families usually traveled the road in horse-drawn Conestoga wagons, often bright blue and red with white canvas coverings. Others traveled by stagecoach or even on foot. The Gants journeyed 338 miles in all, and it was a dangerous trek: Slave catchers roamed the area, looking out for runaway slaves or anyone they suspected of running off. In case they were questioned, Nelson and Anna Maria carried their freedom papers and their child's papers.

There were no guarantees that people who had spent decades soul-deep in slavery would know how to manage their own lives. However, Nelson and Anna Maria's struggles to become free of both debts and enslavement seemed to have prepared them to chase their own ambitions and desires. Nelson Gant had learned many lessons while working on John Nixon's farm, lessons about planting, fertilizing, protecting crops and also protecting property. He would use all of that knowledge in Zanesville, a city spread over flood plains and hills at the place where the Licking and Muskingum rivers came together.

FINALLY FREE

The couple arrived in the Zanesville area late in the summer of 1850 with only fifty cents. Zane Grey, the Zanesville-born author who wrote many famous westerns, specialized in heroes who had a strong sense of right and wrong and acted on their beliefs. In Zanesville and adjoining Putnam, Ohio, people were as divided as the characters in a Zane Grey novel. Its rivers divided Zanesville into three parts united by the Y bridge, but no bridge could erase the differences slavery had created. Zanesville was generally proslavery, mainly because it had been settled by slavery-supporting people from the southern and middle states. Putnam, which drew more New Englanders, was antislavery. However, blacks and whites from both towns supported the antislavery movement. As a result, some Putnam residents slept with pitchforks to keep proslavery mobs from burning their homes to the ground. Meanwhile, in 1850, black residents of the Zanesville and Putnam area adopted a resolution vowing to "throw the arms of protection around our fugitive brethren and sister, and that we will feed them and clothe them, conceal them and assist them in their escape from the Negro Hounds and bloody men."

The harsh Fugitive Slave Act of 1850 would further arouse Putnam and Zanesville abolitionists: It not only created a federal system for recapturing fugitive slaves, it made it a crime to refuse to help authorities capture a fugitive slave. As a result, more slaves escaped, heading for free Canada. Nelson Gant and other men and women like him would play key roles in the continued life of the Underground Railroad in Ohio. However, Gant first had to figure out how to feed and house his family.

IN OHIO

He found a job as a gardener for attorney Theodore Converse, producing crops for sale and taking care of Converse's land. He also bought a farm just west of Zanesville. When Converse died, Nelson continued raising specialty crops. He was a savvy speculator who bought, rented out and sold parcels of land. At times he employed as many as ten workmen. Through hard work and thrift he saved enough money to invest in more land. Between 1860 and 1900, Nelson bought 140 wooded acres in Falls Township bordered by the Licking River and the National Road and just outside Zanesville and had it cleared of hickory, ash, maple, oak and beech trees. On this land, he built a two-story brick house. Nelson raised vegetables and fruits on his farm, which he named Pataskala, an Indian name for the Licking River. He also owned 160 acres in Springfield Township where he had a strip coal mine and farmland. Sometimes he sold or rented land to others as well.

People from all over the county came to Nelson and Anna Maria Gant's farm to buy strawberries, cantaloupes, beets, rhubarb, tomatoes, carrots, corn and other produce which he sold from the front of his house. It's not likely the couple discussed their past financial struggles, their passion for each other or the Virginia court decision that changed their lives. Fruit might have come up, though. Nelson specialized in raising Dresden melons, cantaloupes that can grow as large as small watermelons and have rough, ridged hulls, juicy, sweet fruit and a strong aroma when ripe. They were named for Dresden, Ohio, some twelve miles from Zanesville, where a number of farmers grew them in the region's low, moist soil. Nelson knew something about promoting products, too: he served strawberries and cream to customers on his front porch. In 1854, he even ran an ad in the *Daily Zanesville Courier* urging people to visit his home west of Zanesville on the National Road "where plenty of fine strawberries and good milk . . . can be found, which will be served to his guests in good style and at reasonable prices." Meanwhile, Anna Maria milked cows and churned the cream, creating the kind of rich, sweet golden butter that has all but disappeared from urban markets. She fed chickens and gathered eggs, sometimes selling chickens at the local market. She also helped out at St. Paul AME Church on Zanesville's South Street, where Nelson Gant was a trustee and steward.

In Ohio, according to oral tradition, Nelson also took up the battle against slavery, becoming a conductor on the Underground Railroad. He was said to have hidden slaves in his wagon, covering them with his fruits and vegetables and taking them to the next stop on the route to freedom. According to some accounts, he may have allowed them to work in his coal mine to raise money for their journeys. If so, he was not the only one in the area who was in the business of helping runaway slaves. Members of the Putnam Presbyterian Church, where Frederick Douglass once spoke, hid slaves in the church basement, and George Guthrie's Greek Revival Home at 521 Woodlawn was a known station on the Underground Railroad as well. The Stone Academy, 115 Jefferson Street, was originally built to serve as the seat of newly created Ohio; that never happened but two conventions of the state Abolition Society were held there.

Nelson and Anna Maria Gant spent the rest of their lives in Ohio and became, according to most sources, the parents of twelve children, although AME bishop Daniel Payne claims Maria bore eighteen children in as many years. Neither ever forgot the extraordinary trial that Nelson survived with Maria's support. In interviews, Nelson credited his wife with "setting him on the Christian path" and for rejoicing with him "when success greeted his efforts" and sympathizing with him "when misfortunes came."

Though there is no evidence that either Nelson or Maria learned to read and write, the couple seems to have valued both education and good times. Nelson T. Gant, Jr., attended the preparatory department of Oberlin College from 1880 to 1885, followed by four years in the college course, where he received an AB degree. The preparatory department was similar to a modern high school. Sadie Gant attended the preparatory department and the conservatory of music from 1869 to 1871. The Gant family also gained an education from their many accomplished friends, including Bishop Payne, famed abolitionist Frederick Douglass and Martin Delany. At the public sale held after Nelson's death, the array of goods for sale included much more than cultivators, buggies, horses, plows, wagons, hayforks and tools. There were mirrors, rockers, armchairs, settees, bookcases, carpets, kitchen furniture, a dining table, two sets of dishes, a punch bowl and a sideboard. These and other items suggested the two story reddish brick Gant house with its winding oak staircase and chandeliers was a place where people celebrated life and shared each other's joys, including weddings. In October 1889, J. D. Hunnicut, a black resident of the Ninth Ward, married Susie Williams at the Gant house.

In an 1866 edition of the *Christian Recorder,* published by the African Methodist Episcopal Church, the editor described a visit to Gant's 160-acre farm one mile and a half from Zanesville. "I spent this day . . . on one of the best farms in Muskingum county, Ohio: it is worth at least fifty-five thousand dollars and is owned by N.Y. Gant, a colored man born a slave, who left Virginia with only half a dollar in his pocket 15 years ago. . . . It has the handsomest grove on it to be found in all this region of country. He is educating his daughters finely, though always looking like as if he was at work, his house presents the evidence of refinement, the finest rosewood furniture and appendages of the drawing room are provided by this sturdy black farmer . . . we spent as happy a day at farmer Gant's as we ever spent in our lives."

While visiting her daughter, Sarah, in Yorktown, Virginia, in 1877, Anna Maria died of complications from malaria. Nelson T. Gant and his children and grandchildren were not the only ones who mourned this woman who had both a giving heart and an unbreakable will. According to Bishop Payne's biography, an Irish woman broke down when told of her death. The woman said that when she needed money to buy a cow to provide food for her children, she had gone from house to house asking for a loan. Everyone turned her down except Anna Maria, who gave her nineteen dollars in gold and told her to repay her if or when she could.

Two years after Anna Maria's death, Nelson married Lavinia J. Neal, of Parkersburg, a wealthy young woman he met while traveling. The *Zanesville Courier* gushed that "the trousseau was extensive and beautiful beyond our powers of description." In Norris Schneider's account of the wedding, the writer felt compelled to mention that it included two cakes weighing "twenty-two pounds with the icing." Gant and Lavinia had only one child who lived, Lavinia Logan (Lulu) Gee, who died at age twenty-four in October 1905, the victim of what was called "tubercular meningitis." An accomplished musician, she had attended the Boston conservatory of music. However, young Lavinia was not part of the Gant legend and neither was her mother.

Nelson Gant died in his sleep on July 14, 1905, in Zanesville and was interred a few days later next to Anna Maria in a section of Woodlawn Cemetery known as Gant Circle. He was survived by his second wife, four daughters and one son. The *Zanesville Times Recorder* claimed the eighty-four-year-old pioneer's heart failed.

So it had. At his death, the *Zanesville Daily News* declared that Gant was "probably the wealthiest colored citizen in Ohio," having a fortune estimated at "several hundred thousand." Yet there was a lot more to his legacy than money. Nelson Gant's trial didn't change the way America viewed slave marriages nor did it set precedents that other slavery-era courts would follow. However, the prosperity and opportunities the couple enjoyed in Ohio changed their lives and the lives of all their descendants, many of them college educated. It even changed the life of "Aunt Sarah Speed," a young white servant girl born in Lincolnshire, England, who lived with the family for many years and was in Gant's will.

Today, Zanesville and Putnam, two communities once divided by the passions that slavery aroused, are one and the same—Zanesville annexed Putnam in 1872. However, the Gant legend lives on in many ways. People still eat Dresden melons just like the ones Nelson once grew on land bordering the Licking River, Zanesville markets advertising the cantaloupes by name when their season starts. Some still remember, or at least talk about, Gant Park. Francis M. Townsend bought twenty-two acres from Nelson in June 1890 and named this land Gant Park. Nelson stipulated in the deed to the land that no liquor be sold on the property: That didn't keep it from drawing crowds. People carried baskets to Gant Park for Sunday picnics and showed up there to watch the Buckshoes, a baseball team outfitted by the Pinkerton Tobacco Company, or Buffalo Bill's Wild West Show. Wendell P. Dabney, a nineteenth- and early-twentieth-century musician, politician and journalist, wrote that Gant Park was "probably the first of its kind" in Ohio. Zanesville also remembers Nelson and Maria with

Gant Street and the Gant municipal baseball and football stadium on U.S. 40 at Townsend Street. The stadium was dedicated on September 20, 1940.

The old Gant house still stands, too, with Nelson Gant's name etched in the glass of one door. Over the years, the two-story brick Gant House at 1845 W. Main St. (once known as the Zane Trace) has had many makeovers and passed through a lot of hands. Nelson T. Gant's son, Nelson T. Gant, Jr., owned it until 1916. It then had a series of owners and roles; at one time it was the Elmhurst Inn, renting out rooms to travelers, and after 1980, it became a chicken restaurant and finally a sports bar and restaurant. In 2001, a local group formed the Nelson T. Gant Foundation. The group plans to transform the old house into a museum and community center that will preserve their story.

But Nelson Gant's heart is on display in Zanesville's Woodlawn Cemetery, the site of his extraordinary tribute to the woman who once—with great care—held his life in her hands. In a cemetery crammed with square headstones, squat mausoleums and pointed obelisks, Nelson's memorial to Anna Maria stands out. Her body rests in a grave topped by a statue portraying a very feminine-looking angel embracing a cross. The delicate-seeming angel clings so tightly to the cross that she seems to merge with it, its strength becoming her strength and its love her legacy. The words etched on one side of the monument make it clear just who Nelson considered his angel. "This monument," it says, "is erected as a tribute of her husband's love."

—◆◈◆—

FOUR

ROMEO MUST LIVE

People crowded insane asylums and churches in 1843, and who could blame them? A comet sped across the world's skies, spreading terror; a mysterious disease destroyed the potato crop around Philadelphia and New York; and record cold weather was said to have wiped out much of Michigan's cattle that winter. Meanwhile, all across America, thousands of people known as Millerites waited to see the Son of God return and turn the world into a lake of leaping flames. In South Carolina, a young and, most likely, white southerner named John L. Brown had reason to expect some stunning sign or shakeup in 1843, too: He was about to be sentenced for trying to free the enslaved woman he loved. In December of that year, Brown (no relation to the more famous John Brown) stood before Judge John Belton O'Neall in Fairfield County, South Carolina, to find out how large a price he'd have to pay for trying to free the woman the judge described as his "mulatto mistress."

"You are to die!" Judge O'Neall told him. "Die a shameful death—the death upon the gallows!"

There is no record of young Brown's reaction to the judge's announcement. Did he tremble? Did he remain stonily silent? Or could

Fig. 5. John L. Brown must have suffered unimaginable anguish being sentenced to hang for trying to free his beloved. (Photo by Timothy L. Hughes)

he already picture himself falling through a trap door with a noose around his neck while onlookers ate their lunches and laughed? All we know for certain is that the same judge who sentenced him to death mocked him for allowing a "strange woman" to lure him into breaking the law. The judge then offered to provide the young man with a minister to help him prepare for death. "You can perhaps read," said O'Neall. "If so, read the Scriptures . . . and pray to God for his assistance. If you cannot read the Scriptures, the ministers of our holy religion will be ready to aid you," the judge helpfully added.

If the *National Enquirer* had been around in the nineteenth century, it might have splashed hundreds of stories about John L. Brown and Hetty, his enslaved lover, across its front pages, especially after Brown's fame—like the comet and the potato blight—reached Europe. The newspaper surely would have had blown-up photos of Brown, the man whom most nineteenth-century newspapers described as white but whom a few, more recent sources claim was African American. *Entertainment Tonight* could have sent a camera crew to South Carolina's midlands to record how the condemned man spent his final hours. Someone also would have interviewed Hetty, a black woman who, according to court testimony, "did not occupy the usual condition of a slave," allegedly coming and going as she pleased until her most recent employer snatched away her privileges. Modern journalists would have camped out on the lawn of Judge O'Neall, the respected jurist, college trustee, railroad company president, militia general and Baptist deacon who had sentenced Brown to death. There might even have been a popular song or two for John L. and Hetty, either a snappy, drum-heavy rap tune or, perhaps, the kind of deep, trancelike blues that made some Charleston slaves sweep their yards before sunup to ward off old Doctor Death.

Yet even without cameras, music, videos, jingles, websites or news bulletins every ten minutes, the story of John L. Brown and Hetty mesmerized much of America and other parts of the world in 1843, 1844 and beyond. A famous antislavery poet slammed Brown's sentence, and preachers attacked it, too. Antislavery groups circulated letters about it. Protesters crowded halls. Newspaper stories bearing the headline "Capital Punishment in South Carolina" ran in scores of northern and southern newspapers. "It makes one's blood run cold to see how amazingly pious this unjust judge talked," noted the *Emancipator and Free American.*

All the same, at least one of John L. Brown's critics insisted the condemned man was no slave emancipator or lovestruck suitor, just a man who planned to sleep with Hetty, use her up and then toss her out. Unfortunately, such comments could just as easily have described South Carolina governor James Henry Hammond, another Brown critic, who had come almost criminally close to molesting four of his teenaged nieces and had nearly lost his wife for sleeping with both an enslaved woman and the woman's young daughter.

Oh, yes, it was a circus, with all kinds of performers juggling the truth and walking on tightropes—and that was only in the United States.

The execution of John L. Brown, originally scheduled for April 1844, was an even bigger cause overseas. It especially aroused the passions of antislavery activists in Great Britain where the sickly but staunch William Wilberforce and other men of conscience had struggled for decades to end slavery in most of the sprawling British Empire. A story about Brown's sentence even caught the eye of Lord Henry Peter Brougham and other members of the British Parliament. If Brown were executed for love, British protesters said, his ghost "would shame American travelers whenever they set foot on the shores of England."

But why so much outrage over one proposed hanging? It was true that New England–born Brown's doomed affair with a hired-out slave echoed *Romeo and Juliet*, Shakespeare's classic drama of young divided lovers struggling to stay together. However, in this case, Romeo was a young man from Bath, Maine, described as "idle" by his sentencing judge, while Juliet was a light-skinned enslaved woman described as "fair herself but born of a slave mother." All the same, hundreds of antislavery fighters had been threatened, tarred, chased, fined, jailed, banished, shot at and even drowned for freeing or trying to free slaves. John L. Brown had tried to rescue only one enslaved woman, not one hundred.

Nor was he the only "slave stealer" scheduled to hang in South Carolina in 1844. A one-eyed, bowlegged man who had freed four slaves in the cotton-rich Sumter District also was slated to hang in the Palmetto State in November of that year. Yet it was John L. Brown's pending death that grabbed the world's attention and raised two questions that must have eaten at the soul of the slaveholding South.

The first question was this: If a white son of the South could break the laws controlling slaves to set free an independent-minded black woman, then what could South Carolina's slave owners expect from the slaves themselves, who already outnumbered them?

But the second question raised by the Brown affair was, perhaps, even more troubling in some places: Could a white man truly love a slave?

In northern South Carolina counties, such as Fairfield, where John L. Brown and Hetty lived, a slave who wasn't a house servant probably worked on a cotton plantation. The slave population didn't grow as fast in the midlands and upcounty South Carolina as it did in the low-lying rice-planting lowlands. But it did multiply upcountry and grow even faster in Charleston and other low-lying parts of the state. Surrounded on three sides by rivers and only a few miles from the Atlantic Ocean, Charleston was the major port of entry for the enslaved Africans who survived the horrors of the transatlantic slave trade. By 1810, it was an African American city. It had 11,568 slaves and 1,472 free African Americans, and blacks were 53.2 percent of the city's population. Along the banks of the Ashley River, thirty-six rice plantations flourished by the time of the Civil War. African slaves who had grown rice in Central and West Africa helped make it one of South Carolina's first cash crops. Although the vast majority of American slave owners were small-scale farmers and workers, South Carolina had at least eight planters who owned more than five hundred slaves. When Nathaniel Heyward died in 1851, the rice planter owned more than one thousand slaves at three plantations and a city home as well. He'd surely heard about John L. Brown.

It's not known how South Carolina's slaves felt about the affair, though. Stooped in rice swamps or dreaming of their own freedom, they might not have known his story—or might have shrugged it off. However, the story had a lot in common with the fantastic tales told by the slaves who lived on islands surrounding the low country, and relished okra soup and rice seasoned with tomato sauce. They created baskets from sweet grass and long-leaf pine needles and palmetto fronds, loved drums and violins, put coins on graves to appease the spirits of the dead and understood the deadly and healing powers of roots and herbs and love. Separated from the mainland, they clung to their native culture, speaking Gullah, a fast-moving blend of English and African languages that often did without verbs and stayed in the present tense. These people spun tales about Africans from Angola who could fly, about conjurers powerful enough to heal or harm for a price and about men foolish enough to make deals with the devil—or fall in love with ghosts or others beyond their reach. If they had known or cared about John L. Brown's dilemma, they might have described it with a Gullah phrase such as "E so tek wid up 'e cyan' rest." (He is so taken with her, he can't sleep.)

Yet both the escape of individual slaves such as Hetty and large-scale slave uprisings apparently dominated the dreams of both small farmers and the planters who lived like English gentlemen, sipping India ale, snacking on small crispy fried turtles known as cooters and sending their children to European schools. This is why South Carolina set up a statewide patrol system in 1721 designed to stop roaming blacks on sight. Charleston enacted a curfew for blacks in 1804, and an 1806 law forbade black gatherings in black churches or elsewhere. A 1743 law required white men to go to church armed so they'd be ready for slave uprisings on Sundays. The state even passed a law that required the imprisonment of black sailors from other states while their ships docked in Charleston. This kept African American sailors from mingling with Charleston slaves and sharing information that could "encourage or facilitate slave uprising or escapes," according to historian James Oliver Horton. Samuel Hoar, an agent of Massachusetts for the assistance of imprisoned colored seamen from Massachusetts, was "forcibly expelled" from Charleston, a New England newspaper declared in December 1844.

Every once in a while, though—as in the Brown case—a room or two in the vast mansion known as slavery would catch fire and burn to the ground.

OTHER REBELS

In 1739, about twenty slaves led by a slave named Jemmy broke into a warehouse near the Stono River, which separates Johns Island from James Island and was named for the Stono Indians. Twenty slaves from the Stono plantation crossed the river in September and armed themselves at a store; they killed two storekeepers and stocked up on firearms and powder. They then marched along the main road, beating drums, shouting "liberty," torching plantation homes and killing ten or twenty whites. A larger group then joined them and began marching to St. Augustine, Florida. Armed whites caught them in a field, simply killing some and cutting off the heads of others. According to some accounts, the heads of some Stono rebels were cut off and stuck on pikes or poles along the road. By sunset, the death toll was forty blacks and twenty whites. Two other abortive uprisings followed the Stono insurrection.

In 1754, a slave woman named Sacherisa was sentenced to burn at the stake for setting fire to her owner's Charleston house. In 1797, two slaves were deported and several hanged for plotting to burn down the city. However, it wasn't until 1822 that South Carolina whites' worst fears took shape.

First a brewing revolt was put down in Camden in the upper part of the state. Then came the famous Denmark Vesey revolt. Vesey, a carpenter, preacher and former sailor who was said to have eight wives, used the winnings from a lottery ticket to buy his freedom in 1800.

He was not only free and black but bold, too. Allegedly inspired by the Bible and by legal documents, he sometimes argued with whites on the streets of Charleston and preached about equality. He enlisted some nine thousand slaves in and around Charleston in a slave uprising set for July 14, 1822. Three conjurers, Gullah Jack Pritchard, Tom Russel and Philip, a blind preacher, played roles in the plot in which slaves were supposed to burn down the city and escape by ship to Vesey's homeland in the West Indies. The insurgents were instructed to put a charm in their mouths before they began their work, and it would make them invincible. Vesey, who belonged to Morris Brown's African Methodist Episcopal Church in Charleston, recruited members of his rebellion at religious meetings.

After three informers betrayed Vesey, he and other alleged conspirators were arrested, Vesey at the home of one of his eight enslaved wives. They stood trial and were convicted, and fifty-five of them were hanged. Large numbers of Charleston's free blacks and slaves stumbled to the gallows after secret trials where they lacked adequate counsel and were unable to confront their accusers. Four white men allegedly involved were fined and imprisoned. The local AME church was burned to the ground and its pastor fled for his life. The AME Church was all but banned in the South, and it became unlawful in 1834 to teach any South Carolina blacks to read or write. Helping slaves run away was one of several offenses that carried a death penalty in the state.

HETTY

All the same, John L. Brown and Hetty apparently dared, as had so many others, to defy southern laws and customs and try to make a life together. Hetty was the property of Charlotte Hinton, of Lexington, South Carolina, not far from Columbia. In its case against Brown, the state claimed that for about a decade, Hetty had been allowed to hire her time out to various people and "do pretty much as she pleased," as long as she compensated Hinton and accounted for her time. For three years before her alleged escape, though, the enslaved woman had been working for John Taylor, Hinton's brother, who lived in cotton-rich Fairfield County in the middle section of South Carolina, a place scented by pine trees and marked by rounded hills and rich pastures and lakes. Fairfield County's first settler showed up in 1740, but others followed in the middle of the eighteenth century, Scots-Irish, Germans, English, Huguenots, slaves. Taylor reportedly had refused to allow Hetty to "act for herself" or make her own decisions. If Hetty did indeed suddenly lose her ability to think and act on her own that might have been enough to spur her to run.

John L. Brown was indicted under the act of 1754 for "inveigling, stealing and decoying away" the enslaved Hetty. At the time, he was living and working with John Taylor and, according to court testimony, was frequently seen "in the morning, just before day, slipping out of the kitchen where the woman lodged." In November 1843, he reportedly borrowed a wagon and asked permission to put some things on it. He placed Hetty's clothes on the wagon and the two were seen following it to Columbia where John left Hetty in the back of a Mr. Crawford's store. Taylor followed the pair to Columbia, but couldn't find Hetty. However, he told the court that he received a letter stating that she had been caught running away and locked up in the Columbia jail. When Brown returned from Columbia to Fairfield County, he admitted he'd taken Hetty and her clothes to Columbia but claimed he had nothing to do with her disappearance. According to witnesses, he'd talked about intending to leave the county and tried unsuccessfully to borrow a horse. It's possible Hetty went into hiding and waited for Brown to show up. If so, their solid plan soon shifted and crumbled.

Brown was convicted of helping Hetty try to escape. His appeal called for a reversal of that conviction and a new trial because, among other things, the names of the grand jurors weren't on the indictment. The indictment also didn't charge that Brown knew Hetty was a slave, and nobody had claimed that Brown meant to help Hetty escape beyond the limits of South Carolina. The appeal even claimed that under the terms of the act of 1754, it was only a crime to help a male slave run away. Given Hetty's independence and her habit of going wherever she pleased, the appeal said, there was no reason that Brown would have thought that helping her move to another place could be considered aiding a slave escape. None of these arguments worked, though, and Brown was sentenced to be hanged.

JOHN L.

The courthouse where Brown was sentenced sat across from the Fairfield County town of Winnsboro's most famous landmark, the Town Clock. Since its arrival from France in the mid-1800s, the clock had recorded minutes and hours through wars and periods of peace, births and deaths. According to an often-told tale, the clock had been hauled to Winnsboro from Charleston in an oxcart and was once used as collateral when a citizen loaned money to the town. However, until the early 1900s, agriculture was the engine that really made the place tick. The early settlers brought cotton into the county and it remained king until soil burnout and forever-hungry boll weevils halted it in the 1920s. Judge John Belton O'Neall mentioned neither boll weevils nor cotton during Brown's sentencing, though he made a number of references to time and how little of it Brown had left.

Brown, according to the judge, was "quite too young" to become a felon but, in the judge's opinion, had come into court acting as if he "thought it was a fine frolic." The young Mr. Brown was said to have come from Bath, Maine, which suggests he might have been a seaman, working as a sailor, stevedore, shipwright, caulker, steward or cook. According to the Reverend Parker Pillsbury, John L. Brown had been "seen walking with a young woman, a slave, to whom it was known he was tenderly attached, and whom, it was farther shown, he . . . aided to escape from slavery." The *Cleveland Plain Dealer,* in 1844, called him a white man. So did the *Emancipation and Weekly Chronicle.* However, the *Vermont Chronicle* described Brown as a "slave in South Carolina" and an 1857 article in the *Charleston Mercury* described him as a "free negro man" convicted of stealing a slave whom he "claimed as his wife."

Years later, Frederick Douglass, the world-famous abolitionist, would tell an even more garbled version of this Romeo and Juliet tale. According to Douglass, John L. had agreed to help his sister escape by writing her a pass and promising to help her in any other way he could. Douglass described Brown as a free man whose "back had not been hardened" by whippings. But author Lindsay Swift claimed that John L. was a "northern white man" who aided in the escape "of a slave woman of mixed blood whom he loved and purposed to marry."

Whether he was a light-skinned black man or a white man—which seems most likely—the relationship between Brown and the woman whom he was convicted of helping must have been more than his white critics claimed. Otherwise, he wouldn't have been willing to risk the death penalty for daring to help her. Under the 1740 code, slaves in South Carolina also could be executed for plotting rebellion, for conspiring to run away, for burning a barrel of tar or a stack of rice or for teaching another slave about the uses of roots and herbs. Between the passage of the Negro Act and the beginning of the American Revolution, at least 191 and possibly more enslaved blacks received the death penalty for a criminal offense. A slave who ran away for the fifth time could receive the death sentence or have the Achilles tendon cut in one leg. A free black accused of helping a runaway could receive a whipping and have his forehead branded—or be fitted for a hangman's noose.

White men guilty of misdemeanors also could be fined, jailed, whipped and, in the years before 1833, pilloried or branded. They could receive a combination of two or more punishments and be expelled from the state as well. White men could be hanged for aiding runaway slaves or stealing them, for treason and for counterfeiting.

ELIZA WIGHAM

Judge John Belton O'Neall sentenced Brown to death under a 1754 South Carolina law that made it a capital offense for slaves or free people "to inveigle, steal or carry away any slave." The time set for his execution was Friday, April 22, 1844, between 10:00 A.M. and 2:00 P.M. News of his scheduled hanging spread quickly, especially in the North. The newspapers also ran stories about meetings scheduled to protest Brown's sentence. Meanwhile, a collective clerical address directed to the governor of South Carolina was circulated throughout Britain. It contained thirteen hundred signatures of ministers and other notables. It was dispatched along with "accounts of the proceedings in Glasgow, Edinburgh and Liverpool" to the United States through the American ambassador in London.

"Public meetings were held, the first of which took place, we believe, in Edinburgh," wrote Scottish abolitionist Eliza Wigham. "The example spread."

In 1807, the British Parliament had abolished the slave trade and began forcing other European nations to abandon the trade as well by using diplomacy and creating a naval squadron to patrol the West African coast. The British Anti Slavery Society first advocated a gradual abolition of slavery. When West Indian planters refused to make concessions, the abolitionists hardened their stance, and by the late 1820s they were demanding immediate freedom for slaves. The great pressure they exerted and continuing slave unrest led Parliament to pass the Emancipation Act in 1833. This began a gradual process of compensated emancipation, meaning slaves were freed but forced to work for their former masters for a time to compensate them for their financial losses.

Not surprisingly, many whites and blacks in both America and Great Britain found the John L. Brown case a perfect vehicle for expressing their feelings about slavery and interracial relationships.

Then, suddenly, everything changed.

JAMES HENRY HAMMOND

Governor James Henry Hammond commuted John L. Brown's punishment to a whipping, ruling that the young New Englander should be lashed thirty-nine times rather than hanged. Thirty-nine lashes was a common punishment, based on the biblical code of Moses, which called for forty stripes "save one." Hammond said his decision came in response to the urging of Brown's neighbors in the Fairfield District and recommendations from the court of appeals. In a widely circulated letter, Hammond then denied that he'd been influenced by foreign abolitionists or even aware of their interest in the case at the time he pardoned Brown.

The foreign abolitionists didn't believe him. "British public opinion prevailed even with the governor of South Carolina," wrote Wigham. "This illustration of the influence of British public sentiment is very striking and must excite a feeling of regret that this power has so often been suffered to remain idle."

Hammond did have a point, though. Not every felon sentenced to death in South Carolina actually wound up swinging from a rope. More than half of such felons were fined, jailed, whipped or banished instead. A felon who was a first offender might be fined and jailed rather than hanged. Whites, though, were far less likely to hang than blacks. Of 331 people executed in South Carolina as a whole, between 1750 and 1800, 277 were described as black or mulatto and 49 as white. In rural South Carolina, 224 of 242 people executed were slaves. Between 1750 and 1775, 38 people were hanged, burned or gibbeted in the city of Charleston. Five cases involved stealing blacks and helping runaway slaves and four were the result of suspected poisonings by slaves of their masters or mistresses. Ten were white. But in 1718, a fearsome white pirate named Stede Bonnet was hanged in Charleston along with twenty-eight crew members, and they were allowed to swing in the breeze for five days.

Governor Hammond's decision not to hang Brown meant the young man wouldn't be the main attraction at a public hanging that would have been advertised for weeks and attended by people from all walks of life. No crowd of curiosity seekers would watch him be escorted to the gallows, hear his last words or see his body jerking and twitching on the rope. Yet Hammond's actions didn't mean he sympathized at all with John L. Brown. Hammond, after all, was a man who believed slavery had rescued millions of Africans from savagery. He also believed that the death penalty was not excessive for Brown's crime, "considering the value of a slave." He was known for proclaiming that all great civilizations needed a class of people who would perform the dirty drudge work and called such people "the very mud-sill of society."

For all his talk about mudsills and savages, though, Governor Hammond could hardly claim the moral high ground. At Silver Bluff, his cotton plantation on the Savannah River, at least one slave had died from a whipping and several slaves had escaped. During an 1837 tour of Europe, Hammond refused to pay his full hotel bill and broke a stick across the head of a servant who tried to stop him from leaving an inn. Hammond was generally believed to have married his wealthy wife for her money. He also had been indiscreet, to put it mildly, with four of his young nieces. Though he denied actually having sex with any of his brother-in-law's daughters, his description of his relationships with them would make almost any reader squirm.

"Here were four lovely creatures from the tender but precocious girl of 13 to the mature but fresh and blooming woman nearly 19 . . . lolling on my lap, pressing their bodies almost into mine . . . and permitting my hands to stray unchecked . . . are there many who would have the self-control to stop where I did?"

After the oldest girl complained, Hammond's outraged brother-in-law became his enemy and used the potential scandal to keep Hammond from winning a seat in the United States Senate.

Wrote Marvin E. Harvey:

> Like Jefferson, Hammond was a great planter and the owner of many slaves. . . . About 1839 Hammond purchased an eighteen-year-girl named Sally and her one year old daughter Louisa. He promptly made Sally his mistress and took Louisa to his bed when she reached the age of twelve.

In Hammond's eyes, then, John L.'s worst offense might not have been sleeping with a slave or even trying to help her escape. It might have been violating the widespread white male southern custom of sleeping with black women to satisfy lust and increase a slaveholder's stock of valuable enslaved babies. Love wasn't supposed to be a part of the equation.

Judge O'Neall, who originally sentenced Brown to hang, also felt the international antislavery community had made a huge mistake in portraying young John L. Brown as a freedom fighter, martyr to the antislavery cause or even Hetty's lover. To the judge, Brown was just "an idle, dissipated young man" who kept the mulatto woman whom he aided "as his mistress." Neither romance nor the desire to assist a runaway had motivated Brown, O'Neall insisted, pointing out that Brown had remained in South Carolina with Hetty instead of running with her to a free state. Sooner or later, O'Neall insisted, the New Englander would have taken the strong-willed woman to another slave state and sold her.

But does a man driven only by easily satisfied lust risk his neck to sate it?

Was John L. Brown's relationship with Hetty no different from Governor Hammond's long-running relationships with both his slave and his slave's daughter?

Did the slave system completely corrupt everyone it touched?

While people pondered—or refused to ponder—such questions, John L. Brown remained in jail for nearly six months, waiting for the whipping that had replaced his death sentence. Judge O'Neall later claimed Brown's long jail confinement was not a punishment but an opportunity for Brown to reform himself and emerge from jail "a better man." Meanwhile, Brown's scheduled whipping seemed to alarm American and British antislavery activists almost as much as his earlier scheduled execution. In one edition, the *Liberator* worried that he might be "so terribly scourged as speedily to consign him to the grave." In another edition, the same newspaper fretted that his whipping "may yet cost him his life." Finally, Governor Hammond granted him a full pardon, and he was freed from prison without being whipped on March 29, 1844, six days after a meeting about it in Scotland.

Unlike Romeo or Marc Antony, John L. Brown didn't die for love.

Nor did his case erase the practice of hanging slave "stealers," a law that Hammond defended as "emphatically British law."

MINA McCOY

In 1844, the same year that John L. Brown was scheduled to hang, a South Carolinian named Mina McCoy was convicted of Negro stealing and sentenced to hang that November. McCoy had taken away four slaves around 1838, spurring then governor Pierce M. Butler to offer a three-hundred-dollar reward for his delivery to "any jail in this state." He was described as nearly six feet tall, slim, with a weather-worn face and his "left eye out." W. E. Richardson, the sheriff of Sumter District, where McCoy had lived, offered a one-hundred-dollar reward for his capture. He was not caught until November 1844, when he was convicted and sentenced to hang. The ever-resourceful McCoy managed to break out of jail a few days before his scheduled hanging.

Yet the protests against John L. Brown's sentence weren't a total loss. They did at least spark thoughts of change. In the winter of 1844, a South Carolina legislator named Christopher Memminger introduced a bill to abolish capital punishment for forgery and other crimes, including aiding slaves to escape. In the Judiciary Committee, the bill was amended to make helping a slave escape punishable with death for the second offense. The bill failed to pass, and the law remained unchanged. All the same, the Brown case accomplished two things: It shone a spotlight on a fearsome law and, for a few years at least, turned two lovers into both folk heroes and enduring symbols of the anti-slavery struggle.

The case even came up during the trial of a former Leesburg, Virginia, slave, Nelson T. Gant, who was charged with stealing his enslaved wife. During the 1846 Gant trial, defense attorney R. P. Swann reminded a judicial panel that America was still recovering from the international shame of the John L. Brown case.

"It must be within the recollection of some now present, that the state of South Carolina was arraigned in the bar of public opinion for condemning a free man to be hung for attempting to carry off a slave woman to whom he was betrothed," Swann noted. "The conduct of the judge in that case, and the character of the law, were denounced by Lord Brougham, in the British Parliament, and the proud State of South Carolina had to employ in her defense [*sic*] the talents of her ablest sons."

JOHN AND HETTY

Even in the twenty-first century, South Carolina—the first state to secede from the Union and the place where the first shots of the Civil War were fired on the man-made island of Fort Sumpter—remains awash in memories. In cities such as Charleston, residents and tourists can still walk on ancient cobblestone streets lit by gas streetlamps, visit grand homes built during the slavery era and cross the bridges now connecting the Sea Islands and Charleston's Gullah people to the mainland. On Johns Island, the major tourist attraction is an oak tree believed to be about fourteen hundred years old and with one limb eighty-nine feet long. The live oak stays green through fall and winter, not losing its leaves until they are pushed off by foliage in the spring. In their own way, John L. Brown and Hetty have been just as enduring.

They are far from household names in modern South Carolina or anywhere else, but they have not been forgotten either. They live on in library archives, in nineteenth-century newspapers, in legal records, in terse references in history books, in doctoral dissertations, in old sermons, in a poem by Quaker poet John Greenleaf Whittier called "The Sentence of John L. Brown" and in whatever part of the universe preserves the shadows and echoes of love.

The world didn't end in 1843 or 1844 as the Millerites had predicted, but the New York State Lunatic Asylum at Utica went so far as to blame the mental problems of about one-third of its patients during that period on the fear that Judgment Day was at hand. Meanwhile, the Mexican-born fungus that hit potato crops in the United States in the early 1840s spread later to Nova Scotia and Ontario, Belgium and Spain, Norway and Sweden, the British Isles and Ireland; it threatened potato-dependent Ireland, especially, with starvation and spurred massive waves of Irish emigration to America. The reason these devastating developments converged remains a mystery.

So do the answers to two questions. What became of John L. Brown after he was booted out of South Carolina? And did he and the woman for whom he risked so much ever see each other again outside their dreams?

FIVE

AUNT SALLY'S COFFEEHOUSE

Freedom was supposed to taste like sweet potatoes simmered in cinnamon or pecan pies baptized with rum. To Sally Williams, it probably was more like cold coffee in a cracked cup. She'd been shipped to New York in the same sort of wagon that delivered letters and medicine, malt liquor and money, parcels, pound cakes and, sometimes, murder victims. Then she was "literally dumped on the sidewalk in front of the dry-goods store of Bowen & McNamee," a northern newspaper claimed. On that day in 1857, the former Alabama slave must have seemed as out of place on Broadway as corn shucks on a dance floor.

It wasn't the only time the Adams Express Company carried human "packages." Adams also would deliver two enslaved black women, "Ann" and "Daphy," to new owners in 1858 and 1861. Both were returned to their old masters, Daphy's new owner deciding she was "unsound." In 1887, someone would try to cover up a murder by shipping a trunk containing a body without a head, left arm and legs to Adams's Baltimore office. In 1913, the body of a week-old infant with a crushed

Fig. 6. Sally Williams's portrait reflects the spirit of a former slave who survived the many hazards of rice farming, ran a business and inspired her son to become a social reformer. (Photo courtesy of Documenting the American South, The University of North Carolina at Chapel Hill Libraries)

head would be found in an unclaimed package at the Adams Express office in Sterling, Illinois. And, of course, Henry "Box" Brown, a Virginia slave, had become famous for having himself nailed inside a three-foot by two-foot wooden crate and shipped by steamer to Philadelphia in 1849.

But Sally Williams was no slave, no pound cake, no envelope of powdered quinine and no concealed murder victim. In 1857, according to some estimates, she was sixty-nine years old. In her raw leather plantation shoes and stiff-brimmed secondhand hat, she looked very much like someone who had spent part of her life leg-deep in stagnant, mosquito-thick rice fields and the other part of it in kitchens. None of that mattered, though. She was waiting for Isaac, the son she hadn't seen for decades. He was the son who'd become educated enough to preach in half a dozen states, pen letters to newspaper editors and raise money for the black trade schools he hoped to set up.

He also was the son Sally Williams had carried on her back while slogging through mud in North Carolina rice fields. The son she'd inspired by running a profit-making business while still enslaved. The son for whom she'd managed to buy books. The son who'd tracked her down by following a trail of clues from one person, one memory, one decade to the next. And the son who would be more than a week late meeting her in New York.

By the time Isaac Williams finally came face to face with his mother at the home of a store employee who had befriended her, she'd been wealthy and poor, lost and redeemed, loved and abandoned, a woman in trouble and, finally, a woman triumphant. It was a shattering moment for them both. A contemporary account of that meeting describes it this way: "All at once, the truth flashed upon her, and she sprang forward. . . . She held him tightly to her . . . as if he had been an infant; and when he could not speak, but only wept, she would say, 'Don't cry, Isaac, don't cry. I prayed to de Lord dat I mighn't cry.' And he could only answer . . . 'the Lord be praised.' "

According to New England poet Edna Proctor, who wrote the only known account of Sally Williams's life, Sally was born around 1796 on a plantation "not many miles from Fayetteville," North Carolina. However other sources say she was born in 1770, 1788 or 1790. No slave really knew his age, claimed slave-born educator Booker T. Washington, who drily pointed out that "I am not quite sure of the exact place or exact date of my birth, but at any rate I suspect I must have been born somewhere and at some time." Frederick Douglass, the foremost black leader of his day, was just as blunt: "By far the larger part of the slaves know as little of their ages as horses know of theirs," he wrote.

All the same, Sally likely was born near Fayetteville, in Cumberland County, one of half a dozen towns that served as the state capital until Raleigh was chosen. North Carolina, with its shallow and narrow waterways and relative isolation, never ranked high among the major slaveholding states, but it had about one hundred thousand enslaved people by 1790. In Fayetteville, which sits on the west bank of the Cape Fear River and sixty miles from Raleigh, slaves were sold in the town market, the center of commerce and festivals. On most farms, slaves received one pair of coarse shoes and enough rough cloth to make a jacket and trousers or a dress every year. If the women had any underwear, they had found it or made it themselves.

However, Sally worked on a rice plantation, Proctor claims, and rice wasn't grown in Fayetteville. In 1840, Fayetteville's major products were wheat, cotton, corn, turpentine and lumber. Sally Williams and her family must have moved farther south to the rice-growing Lower Cape Fear area of New Hanover or Brunswick counties, where South Carolina's Geechee or Gullah culture had spread to North Carolina. Gullah people spoke a language that combined English and various African languages and had preserved some African customs and beliefs. This culture gave area slaves some protection against total white control, especially during the months when slave owners and their families abandoned their steamy rice plantations for towns. But the swampy land, stagnant water, parasites and air- and insect-borne diseases drastically raised death rates among rice-growing slaves and their children.

At thirteen, Sally married her first husband, a man chosen by her owner. She married Abram Williams before a "colored Methodist preacher," according to the account of her life originally published in 1858. After a severe whipping, she ran away from her master and hid with a friend who lived near Abram. When she learned her angry master had decided to hire out all of his slaves to other temporary owners and collect monthly payments, she showed up at the hiring-out and boldly joined her master's other slaves. The man who hired her agreed to let her do whatever she wished as long as she paid him six dollars a month. That would enable her to earn wages for her owner and herself.

Her own mother had taught her to pour all of her energy into whatever she did, even if the work seemed pointless or designed only to produce wealth for others. She decided to open what would be known today as a coffeehouse. She didn't serve anything approaching what is usually called "soul food," dishes often thought to have been the specialty of every black cook in eighteenth- and nineteenth-century America. Her establishment did specialize in coffee, home-brewed beer and gingerbread. She also took in washing and developed a reputation as a seamstress.

She was an instant success. She earned enough to buy furniture and even hire a girl to help her in the house. She also hired Isaac away from his master, bought books and persuaded her master to teach Isaac to read. She sat transfixed while her oldest son read the Bible to her. Tragedy entered her life, though, when the husband she loved and who returned her love developed a taste for gambling. After disobeying his master's orders to stop making bets, he eventually was sold away to New Orleans.

His departure tore Sally apart, but she eventually married again, this time to a free man, no doubt thinking they would be able to stay together. There were fewer than five thousand free blacks in North Carolina in 1790. Yet they would face increasing restrictions by the mid-nineteenth century and find themselves resented by wealthy whites who believed they helped slaves run away and poor whites who felt they competed with them for jobs. Sally never loved her free husband as deeply as she had Abram but the match apparently satisfied her. However, the early death of her son, Lewis, taught her one more bitter lesson about the fragility of slave relationships. She was soon to learn another. Her neighbors became envious of her business and began pressuring her master to shut her down. She had more hustle and shine than her neighbors, white and black, figured a slave should have. She was too popular, they said. Her house was too tidy, and rumors even circulated that some of her furniture had come all the way from Europe. She should have known they'd find a way to stamp out her fire. Bowing to pressure from his neighbors, her owner finally closed Sally's business and sold her to a trader taking a group of slaves to Alabama.

Her sin was not simply achievement, though. At times, blacks even more exceptional than Sally had prospered in North Carolina. By 1820, the town of New Bern had 2,188 blacks of whom 268 were freedmen, several of them well-to-do or slave owners themselves. Those well-off freemen included bricklayer Dunum Mumford, butcher Sylvester Pimborton, barber John Carruthers Stanly and his son, John Stewart Stanly. John C. Stanly had been born the enslaved son of an Ebo slave woman and reputedly a privateer or pirate merchant. After he gained his freedom, he became a barber and, at one time, was one of the largest slaveholders in the state and known as a hard taskmaster. John Chavis, born free around 1763, conducted schools in Granville, Wake and Chatham counties, his students including the sons of prominent white families. He was considered the best in the state.

Thomas Day, who was born free in Dinwiddie County, Virginia, in 1801, became North Carolina's most sought-after furniture maker, a man whose bedsteads and posts, cradles and sideboards, stools and bookcases filled the homes of planters eager to see themselves as gentlemen. One newel post in a Caswell County, North Carolina, home resembled a wooden African statue with sharp angles cut into the wood and a large head, oversized feet and bent knees, all carved from one large piece of wood. Day also created staircases with exaggerated S curves, church pews, and a set of twelve mahogany chairs bought by Governor David Settle Reid in 1855 for sixty dollars, the equivalent of slightly more than one thousand dollars today. Day was held in such high regard that after North Carolina passed an 1826 law barring any more free blacks from entering the state, white citizens successfully petitioned the legislature to make an exception for Day's wife, Aquilla Wilson, so she could move there from Virginia.

Yet there was a world of difference between tolerating or even celebrating the accomplishments of presumably light-skinned and slave-owning free blacks and accepting the success of an enslaved woman such as Sally Williams who had Africa in her eyes, hair and heart. When she was herded into a slave pen before being taken to Alabama, Sally longed for death but found herself unable to pray, unable to hope, unable to believe in the future at all.

When her son, Isaac, heard that she'd been sold, his life with his mother flashed before his eyes, according to Proctor's book, and he vowed that one day he'd free both himself and her. Isaac was then a young man in his twenties. Meanwhile, according to Proctor's story, her second husband, Lewis Beggs, offered the slave speculator three hundred dollars for her, but the man refused the money. Another black man who admired Sally also tried to head off the sale. He crept to the slave pen where she was being held before being shipped to Alabama and urged her to climb the fence and escape. She tried several times but kept falling and then it was too late: The slave trader had returned. Meanwhile, Beggs brought her a new dress and begged her to find someone to write to him from Alabama, telling him if she thought it wise for him to join her there.

Once in Alabama, however, Sally sent word to Beggs to stay in North Carolina. But he had already started to walk to Alabama with a bundle slung over his shoulder; on the way, he ran into a man who had seen Sally, and this man warned him that hostility toward free blacks in Alabama was worse than anything he'd experienced in North Carolina. He was not lying: North Carolina was among the last southern states to take the vote and the right to carry firearms away from free blacks, and some less-populated border sections of North Carolina were actually havens for escaped slaves, especially skilled ones. The man also told Beggs that Sally had sent him a letter urging him to stay at home. Beggs returned home, but never recovered from the loss of his wife and the death of his son. He reportedly sank into an alcoholic daze, drinking more and more until he died.

In her new home, Sally regained her faith and spent more than twenty years shouldering the burdens of slavery. At least one nineteenth-century writer urged "refined" and "elegant" white women to try their hand at bread-making and other domestic arts to prepare for such emergencies as the absence of a cook. It's not likely many refined and elegant women who owned slaves took her advice. Enslaved women took care of children, prepared meals for their owners and guests, sewed, washed, ironed, cleaned and coped with their owners' moods. Sally had to deal with a jealous cook who sabotaged her cooking and lied about her, causing her to be whipped for a theft she hadn't committed. And she had to endure a fault-finding mistress who often whipped her or lashed out at her in fits of brandy-spurred rage.

But Williams still had two secret weapons. One was the intense religious experience she'd had as a girl. Since Sally's story was dictated to Proctor, there's no way to separate Sally's own beliefs from those of the obviously religious white woman who wrote her story, which was originally published in 1858 by the American Reform Tract and Book Society, a group that had issued many publications denouncing slavery, infidelity, drinking, breaking the Sabbath and dressing extravagantly.

Slave narratives are not always completely reliable guides, and some were edited or rewritten. However, the religious conversion Sally Williams experienced echoes many other published stories about the trances, visions and religious revelations of nineteenth-century black men and women who found hope in their inner lives and visions. Jarena Lee, a free-born black woman, was propelled by visions when, in 1827, she journeyed more than two thousand miles alone and gave nearly two hundred sermons. There are countless stories about enslaved men, women and children who heard voices while plowing, who believed they had been carried off by angels or who felt they had grown new feet and hands when they accepted God. Many also reported being ushered to the gates of heaven, visiting hell, following Jesus through snowbanks or seeing Satan in chains. Sally's conversion came when she was about ten and her best friend, Mary, suddenly became ill and died. Sally's grief eventually drove her to a camp meeting where she fell into a trance that lasted for three days. She later said she'd seen Jesus standing before her with outstretched hands. Her young master had told her again and again that there was no afterlife, no heaven, but his words no longer swayed her. She chose to decide for herself what to believe.

SNAKES AND ALLIGATORS

Sally Williams's other secret weapon was the bond she'd developed with her sons while working in North Carolina's rice fields. Converting acres of land into rice plantations was dangerous and hard labor, which required people to work for weeks in mud and water and ninety- to one-hundred-degree heat. They also had to repair embankments and ditches during the cold, wet winters and deal with rice-threatening hurricanes and floods. Slaves on rice plantations usually performed one specific task, which could include chopping and burning trees, clearing jungle-thick brush, killing weeds, digging ditches or building sluice gates to drain the water from the field for sowing and flood it for cultivation. If they completed their tasks on time and had any energy left, they might work on their own gardens or, perhaps, earn money for doing additional work.

Women like Sally usually took infants or very small children with them when they trudged into the slushy fields, sometimes leaving a little child to guard them. Some mothers would lay their children under trees or by roadsides or at the ends of rice rows while they worked. A white carpenter from Waterford, Connecticut, who spent eleven winters working on North Carolina plantations, claimed a six-year-old on one of those plantations had accidentally drowned a two-month-old child left with her. But Sally Williams kept her children close while she sloshed around in squishy mud.

"The same labor is commonly assigned to men and women—such as digging ditches in the rice marshes, clearing up land, chopping cordwood, threshing," according to the carpenter. Sally dropped the seed rice into holes and covered the holes with her hoe, work done while stooped over in boiling heat and all too often wading through water.

Yet Sally couldn't eliminate all of coastal North Carolina's dangers—or even its discomforts.

The rice birds didn't choke, bite or smother, but their noise could be scary just the same. Every August, those God-blasted bobolinks swooped down on rice plantations throughout the South, stealing the ripening grain. They sang as they flew, and these choirs of black, white and gold birds produced a loud and crackling kind of bebop that no banjo or field chant could match. People stood on river banks and shouted and shot at the birds. Some tried to run them off by pounding on drums or even thumping on old tin pans. Still, they came, descending on fields, moist meadows and marshes.

Alligators with bad tempers and yawning mouths patrolled the waters, too, and they called for special caution. Alligators lie almost motionless for a good part of the day, soaking up warmth from the sun and then seizing prey and swallowing them in one gulp or tearing them apart. Nowadays, adult alligators are usually ten or more feet long but some male alligators might have been over fifteen feet long in Sally Williams's time. They could be snappish when injured or disturbed. Moreover, they stirred up the age-old fears buried in fables about fire-breathing dragons.

Yet the snakes were an even bigger worry as they sunned themselves in North Carolina's marshes and meadows. The experts say an eastern diamondback rattlesnake, possibly the most dangerous species of rattler, attacks only when it feels threatened. Such knowledge might not have been much comfort to someone who stumbled upon a diamondback and heard its menacing clatter or who came across poisonous copperheads, timber rattlesnakes, pigmy rattlesnakes or a yellow, black and red striped eastern coral snake "capable of retaining its hold after it strikes." And Sally Williams's narrative notes that a snake had strangled a baby whose mother left him alone.

Snakes and alligators weren't the only dangers on swampy, heat-soaked rice plantations. Even in an era when some people believed that watermelon, cabbages and cucumbers spread cholera and that drinking too much whiskey caused meningitis, it must have been clear that conditions on rice plantations were especially unhealthy.

Diseases spawned by filth and stagnant water struck the very young especially hard. They often perished at more than twice the rate of enslaved children on cotton, tobacco and other kinds of plantations. Babies died from dysentery, spread by sewage-fouled water. They died from typhoid fever spread by the lice in their unwashed clothing. They died during epidemics of cholera, another disease linked to contaminated drinking water and marked by cramps, intense vomiting, profuse watery diarrhea and, all too often, death within six or eight hours. They died from mosquito-borne yellow fever. They died from malaria. They died from pneumonia. They died from hookworms and lockjaw. And they died from what one writer described simply as "puniness." Meanwhile, the disease-spreading mosquitoes were so relentless in the heavy air that owners of rice plantations spent late summer in towns while their slaves and employees harvested rice.

But Sally kept her children safe, creating memories that bound her to them. When she was sold away from her family, from her coffeehouse and from her history of rice field toil, her son, Isaac, vowed he'd never forget her. And he didn't.

"Somehow she instilled something in her son, Isaac, that put him on a life long mission to free Sally," says Dale Rich, who designed and researched a 1995 exhibit at the Detroit Public Library on Williams and three other black female pioneers. "She kept the faith, so did Isaac."

ISAAC

After gaining his own freedom, Isaac had come to understand that the fight for liberty in a slave society had no endpoint. It was a struggle that had to be waged again and again. Isaac fought with his faith, which he spent most of his life spreading. His name shows up in city directories and newspaper articles in at least six states. He became a free man and a traveling minister for the African Methodist Episcopal Church. The institution, vital with thousands of members even up to now, was established in 1787 as a protest against segregation in a predominantly white Methodist church in Philadelphia. It was a religion emotional enough to appeal to former slaves who needed an outlet for their feelings and a belief in the personal and protective God who spoke to Moses and delivered his people from chains. In both traditional Methodism and the AME Church, circuit-riding preachers moved from settlement to settlement, farm to farm, plantation to plantation, baptizing, performing weddings and burials and spreading the gospel. Isaac Williams, the boy who once read the Bible to his mother, would preach in the South and the Midwest. He also would become a man capable of writing letters to newspaper editors about his plan to set up trade schools for black youths. In a March 5, 1885, letter to the editor of the *Mobile Register*, he wrote: "The plan which will succeed is easy. It will cost money and in large amount, but it can be got. A high school for colored boys and girls can be established in every city in the South, and if the matter was undertaken in the proper spirit, men at the North, and women too would help pay the running expenses. A few hundred dollars spent by the city for schools of a better grade would save the colored boys who are going to ruin."

They were prophetic words, and Isaac was determined that as many people as possible would hear them. At various times, he would live in Detroit, Michigan; Indianapolis, Indiana; Nashville, Tennessee; Mobile, Alabama and Jackson, Mississippi, all cities with AME churches. After marrying a woman named Harriet in 1833, he, following his enslaved mother's example, found a way to prosper. In 1838, his wife's father bought her freedom; Isaac worked as a hired-out carpenter in New Orleans until he could purchase his own liberty. Yet he was still searching for the mother he'd vowed to find.

Finally, he learned through an acquaintance that his mother's cousin lived in Mobile, Alabama, a city that had a whipping house where hired hands lashed slaves with thick whips for breaking ordinances, violating curfews, committing petty theft or being accused of insubordination or improper contact with whites. Slaveholders in Mobile also were sometimes fined for allowing their slaves too much liberty.

However, as literary critic Veta Tucker points out, "Oral communication and memory functioned to maintain ties in slave communities where there was nothing else to rely on." In some cases, the tragic separation of slaves from family members also helped transfer "personal information from one slave family to another in distant communities," Tucker added.

JOSEPH CONE

Isaac's mother's cousin, Mary Ann Williams, heard about his search through the combination of gossip, overheard conversations and passed-around letters that prominent former slave Booker T. Washington called the grapevine telegraph. She eventually sent word to Isaac that Joseph H. Cone owned his mother. Cone lived in Dallas County, Alabama, part of the cotton-rich west-central part of the state. For years, Isaac wrote to Cone, asking how much he wanted for his mother's freedom, and for years, Sally's owner refused to answer Isaac's letters, presumably because he feared his wife would oppose such a sale.

It was 1852 before Cone finally wrote to Isaac, offering to free his mother for four hundred dollars. Cone might have agreed to this because he doubted Isaac could come up with such a sum: Four hundred dollars in the 1850s would be the equivalent of nearly ten thousand dollars today. However, Isaac was not only free but also a man who was developing a national reputation as a preacher. In 1852, news about him even appeared in the celebrated antislavery newspaper, the *Voice of the Fugitive*, noting he had been selected to attend an AME conference held for ten to twelve days in Cincinnati. Finally, in March 1856, Williams, described as "pastor" of an African Methodist Episcopal Church, began traveling the country collecting money for his mother's release. He succeeded.

Veta Tucker calls Isaac's campaign to free his long-absent mother "a testament to the remarkable bonding and memory of slave family ties in spite of slave owners' disregard for family ties and forced separations, prohibited movement and long term isolation-incarceration on backwater farms."

Yet getting his mother to the North was almost as difficult for Isaac as persuading her Alabama owner to sell her. The former slave didn't dare return to the Cotton Belt himself during the slavery era "for fear that his free papers would be disregarded," a newspaper noted in 1889. In fact, an 1834 Alabama law included a clause stating that if a freed slave should return to Alabama after leaving, he or she would be re-enslaved and sold. Not only would it have been dangerous for Isaac to linger in Alabama; it would have been equally dangerous for his recently freed mother, whose very presence might spawn discontent— or so many slave owners feared.

For reasons that aren't clear, the Adams Express Company didn't want to make direct arrangements to ship Sally Williams to New York. The company referred Isaac to another business that paid for his mother's freedom with a bank draft and then arranged to have Adams carry her to the North.

When Isaac didn't show up at the Adams office, Sally went home with a friendly store employee and cooked for the family. She spent the next few days waiting for her son, her anxiety sliding into despair and then resignation. Finally, after nearly two weeks, Isaac returned from New Haven, where he'd been collecting money. At the Adams Express office, he met the store employee who'd taken in his mother.

Isaac M. Williams quickly introduced his mother to her new life by taking her to the homes of some of his New York friends and to Plymouth United Church of the Pilgrims in Brooklyn. At Plymouth, Minister Henry Ward Beecher didn't wear clerical garments or stand behind a pulpit. Customarily, he stood before his audience. God, he would often say, had created a rich and beautiful universe for his people and wanted them to enjoy the testaments of his love—the kind of sermon that would have brought particular joy to a former slave. Finally, Sally and Isaac traveled by ferry to Lake Erie and to Dunkirk by rail. People crowded around Sally on the train, drawn by her rough dress and simple dignity and entranced by the story of a son who'd managed to free his mother. In Buffalo, a reception for them drew more admirers and raised more money.

DETROIT

At 11:30 P.M. on February 2, 1857, they reached Windsor, Ontario, which sat across the Detroit River from Detroit. There they boarded a ferry. From there a carriage took them to the house where Isaac and his wife and children lived. Sally's home was now 135 E. Fort in a neighborhood known as Shannon Alley in Detroit, a city that, in 1860, would have a population of slightly more than 45,000, including 1,403 blacks.

Under the Northwest Ordinance of 1787, slavery was forbidden in the entire old Northwest, a region that included what would become the states of Ohio, Indiana, Illinois, Wisconsin and Michigan, which had been admitted to the Union in 1837 as a free state. It took a while, though, for freedom to sink in and take hold. Once the territory became American, residents who had owned slaves under the French and then the English kept their slaves. As a result, during the 1830s, the *Detroit Gazette* kept on running advertisements for runaway slaves.

In 1833 black Detroiters rioted in protest of a court verdict returning a fugitive slave couple to Kentucky. Wayne County sheriff John Wilson, who was assaulted during the melee, died within a year. But with the assistance of the rioters, the fugitive slave couple escaped. After 1834, so-called whorehouse riots broke out frequently in Detroit, too, with stone-hurling white mobs attacking brothels catering to black men in mostly German neighborhoods. In most cases, the rioters would order out the prostitutes and their customers and then smash the furniture and sometimes burn the buildings. Despite such flare-ups and frictions—as well as a seldom-enforced law requiring blacks entering the state to post a five-hundred-dollar bond guaranteeing their good behavior—most Detroit blacks would have found the area friendlier than many American towns.

"Slaves felt generally that if they could reach Detroit, all would be well," wrote early twentieth-century journalist Ulysses W. Boykin.

Detroit's small black population was very much a part of the life of a bustling port city where steamships and sailing ships, carts, wagons and trains moved in and out, bringing in needed goods and taking farm and manufactured products to other parts of the country. From 1845 to 1846, the city even was home to Robert S. Duncanson, a black painter who specialized in portraits. He would become the first African American artist to gain international fame, but he couldn't make a living. So he returned to Cincinnati after being evicted from his Detroit quarters. Alexander D. Moore had better luck. A black Virginian who came to Detroit in the late 1850s, he played with the Moore and Curtis String Band, owned a barbershop, had a dancing school and a group that played for dances on the steamer *Hope.* All the same, Detroit would be most celebrated as a major endpoint for the Underground Railroad.

The city was home to William Lambert, tailor, abolitionist, close friend of John Brown and head of Detroit's black antislavery network. He sometimes distracted bounty hunters while his colleagues slipped fugitives across the Detroit River. George DeBaptiste, an African American entrepreneur, steamship owner and former valet to President William Henry Harrison, was just as bold. By 1860, DeBaptiste owned the *T. Whitney* steamboat and ran it on the Detroit-Sandusky-Amherstburg route to freedom, transporting fugitives to Canada. Other black abolitionists included barber John Richards, Reverend W. C. Monroe, an Episcopalian minister, and Joseph Ferguson, Detroit's first black doctor. The local abolitionist movement had white allies, too, including Seymour Finney, who didn't mind living dangerously. Finney owned a stable that sheltered runaway slaves, and he also owned a hotel that sheltered slave catchers searching for runaways. When Shubael Conant, another white abolitionist, died in 1877, he left a will directing that blacks could purchase or build new homes on his southeastern Detroit property. Before that, blacks could only move into new areas when whites deserted them. John Sabine, a British-born saddler and harness maker, had a shop near William Lambert's and was his friend and ally.

Sally Williams reportedly never left home without her free papers, enjoyed hearing her son preach and made many visits to people in the

Detroit area. Despite her apparent contentment, though, she had no idea whether her first husband and enduring love, Abram, was living or dead. Her son Daniel, she'd learned, had been jailed in Virginia after escaping from a cruel master in North Carolina and fleeing for the North. Moreover, Detroit would not be her final home or freedom her only hope.

Was Isaac Williams a part of the Underground Railroad? As a clergyman with the deeply antislavery AME church, he certainly fit the profile. He also had a reputation as an antislavery activist. In 1855, two years before he freed his mother, Williams's name was used as a reference by a Missouri fugitive who raised money in Detroit for his own mother's freedom.

Isaac McCoy Williams would continue moving from city to city, state to state, and taking his family with him. In fact, Williams, who was fifty-one in the 1860 census and married to forty-year-old Harriet, remained an extremely active county-circuit-riding preacher all of his life, although it's not clear if he was a traveling deacon or elder or an exhorter who explained and interpreted the Scriptures and held prayer meetings. The AME Church relied heavily on traveling preachers to set up churches and return now and then to preach. Lay preachers and local ministers kept their congregations alive.

By 1870, Isaac was living in Indianapolis with Georgiana, a new wife, and a child named Abraham Lincoln Williams, who had been born in Indiana in 1869. Georgiana's place of birth was said to be Louisiana. The household also included Sarah (Sally) Williams, said to have been born about 1770 in North Carolina. That household lost its heart, though, when Sally Williams died on January 3, 1876, in Marion County, Indiana, of what was called "pleuritis."

"Indianapolis has lost a colored woman, known as Aunt Sally Williams, 106 years old," noted *Inter Ocean,* a Chicago newspaper. "She had a very large family, all the members of which, so far as she could learn, had died of old age, excepting one still living in Lexington, Ky."

At the time of his mother's death, Isaac Williams was indeed alive and still driven to spread the gospel of religion, education and self-help. His name shows up in the 1880 city directory for Nashville, Tennessee. According to census data, he was then sixty-seven, though that contradicts earlier estimates of his age. He was living with thirty-year-old Georgiana and their three children, ten-year-old Abraham Lincoln Williams; seven-year-old Rebecca J. Williams and a five-year-old son named Greely Sumner Williams. Rebecca and Abraham were Indiana-born, but Greely's birthplace was reportedly Kentucky, suggesting Isaac might indeed have been there when his mother died.

Isaac's crusades for black uplift didn't always please other blacks. In 1883, "colored citizens" of Canton, Mississippi, apparently met to voice their anger at a pamphlet published by Reverend J. L. Tucker that they felt portrayed them in a way that was "unwarranted and untrue," according to a Methodist publication. The group slammed Isaac, then apparently in Jackson, Mississippi, for endorsing Tucker's "attempt to degrade us in the eyes of the world."

Around this time, Isaac left the AME Church and joined the Protestant Episcopal Church. In 1884, he was identified as the rector of the Church of the Good Shepard [sic], a Protestant Episcopal Church in Mobile, Alabama. In 1885, he taught school in Mobile. In 1885, according to the *Alabama Review*, he also founded the Widows and Orphans Mutual Aid and Building Association to establish a home, school and house of worship for "the poor and friendless" in the black community.

His fame was growing. Saluting nineteenth-century black progress, the *Southwestern Advocate* newspaper noted the growth of "colored" churches, the rising number of black students and the emergence of prominent black preachers and politicians such as the "venerable and well-known Isaac M. Williams." "Mr. Williams represents the best class of colored people," *The Daily Picayune* in New Orleans commented in 1887, noting that he was in town soliciting aid for his church. He was identified as pastor of "St. Luke's Protestant Reformed Episcopal Church." Throughout this period, he also kept hammering away at his plan of establishing industrial schools for blacks. He'd become determined to create trade schools preparing poor, friendless black vagrants and small-time offenders to earn honest livings. In 1889, he collected money for his project in Boston and, according to a New York newspaper, was headed to Philadelphia to do the same. "The white people in the South have aided me greatly, but they cannot do all and so I ask the aid of those charitably disposed in the North," he told the *New York Age*. In a letter to the *Mobile Register* he added: "Aid can be given and ought to be given to raise the Negro to the dignity of true manhood."

SALLY AND ISAAC

There's no record that Isaac Williams ever opened any of the trade schools for which he labored so long and about which he wrote and spoke so often. However, like countless other slaves and former slaves, he and his mother had managed to create something from nearly nothing. Faint echoes of their story seem to show up in other works. Mark Twain wrote a story published in the *Atlantic* in which he asked a cheery black woman he called Aunt Rachel how she'd managed to live to the age of sixty without experiencing any trouble. She stopped him in his tracks by telling him how she'd watched her husband and seven children sold off at an auction in 1852 but had later accidentally run into her youngest son during the Civil War. He was the son who'd promised his mother he would escape, and she was the mother who had threatened to kill anyone who bought him off the auction block.

But there are more direct accounts of Sally and Isaac's lives. Poet Edna Dean Proctor's version of the life and times of Sally and Isaac was entitled, *Aunt Sally: or, The Cross the way of freedom; a narrative of the slave-life and purchase of the mother of Rev. Isaac Williams of Detroit, Michigan.* It appeared one chapter a week in an antebellum newspaper called the *Independent* . . . "Devoted to the Consideration of Politics, Social and Economic Tendencies, History, Literature and the Arts." The book records a deeply felt history of triumphs and losses, disappointments and joys.

She "was like a pop-up doll," says Dale Rich. "You knock the doll down and instantly it pops up again. Sally managed to pop up time and time again. . . . She lived as a slave but managed to gain a kind of quasi freedom—knowledge. . . . All this during a time when slaves lived and died and did not move an inch."

Proctor's book also contains portraits of Sally and Isaac Williams engraved from daguerreotypes. Although historian John Blassingame asserts that Williams's overtly Christian narrative doesn't really provide that many day-to-day details about slavery, the picture of Aunt Sally Williams tells us a great deal. "Aunt" was an honorific term for older black women who never could be called Mrs. or Miss in the old South. In her portrait, Williams wears a head wrap, but no one would ever mistake "Aunt Sally" for the distorted images of bug-eyed, plantation-loving mammies and kindly uncles that America would eventually create. She was not what one so-called southern cookbook described as "a jovial, stoutish, wholesome personage." Her face, so serious, so strongly drawn, would never appear on toys, games, trading cards, tablecloths, syrup pitchers, piggy banks, restaurant fronts, salt and pepper shakers and coffee mugs. Nor would it show up on chewing tobacco wrappers, black thread, washing powder, pancake and cornmeal mix boxes and movie screens. Though she squeezed as much achievement as possible from her life, Sally Williams was never at home with slavery. She may have baked ginger cakes and ridden a delivery wagon to freedom, her picture reminds us, but she also had visions, longed for purpose, cultivated dreams and understood love.

———◆———

SIX

THE PREGNANT PILGRIM

Jane was nine months pregnant when John Brown's men came to free her. All kinds of questions must have swarmed around her that day, buzzing and biting. Should she stay behind or run? Take a leap of hope or keep swimming in the same old stagnant, mud-choked creek? Then one of the raiders gunned down Jane's master, David Cruise, leaving him bleeding away his anger on the floor of his cabin. He'd been shot, some said, to keep him from grabbing his gun. Meanwhile, Cruise's young son, Rufus, rushed out into the snow, half-naked and risking frostbite. By then Jane's heart must have been thumping almost hard enough to burst through the bony cage locking it in. Should she stay or leave? Run or stand still?

If she fled with John Brown's raiders while howling winds and mile-high snows battered the midwestern plains, she would have had no idea what might become of her and her baby. Maybe Brown's men could outrun and outwit the posses on their trail, and maybe they couldn't. But pregnant or not, Jane didn't have a lot of reasons to remain enslaved in Missouri. The alleged father of her child either ran

Fig. 7. Former Missouri slaves Samuel and Jane Harper survived a three-month trek to freedom with John Brown and his men. (Photo courtesy of the Kansas State Historical Society)

and hid from the raiders or was away courting another woman, depending on which source you believe. Jane either wept that day or, as David Cruise's son later claimed, she grinned and began packing. Either way, she decided to join ten other runaways on a long, treacherous march that would change her life and theirs.

Slave rescues were "the most romantic and exciting amusement open to men who had high moral standards," historian Albert Bushnell Hart once wrote. That was true enough if you defined "romantic" as running for your life. Hart might have used less high-toned words if he'd tramped, ridden and stumbled from Missouri to Michigan with Jane and her fellow fugitives in the winter of 1858–59. During the slavery era, not many black fugitives could leap aboard a train or wagon and ride safely to a free state or, after 1834, free Canada. Sailing or galloping to California, the Bahamas, Mexico, Nicaragua or southern ports without being caught was not an easy thing, either. The quest for fredom was no frolic, no bright-eyed amusement.

THE KANSAS-MISSOURI WAR

This story, though, is not only about thirty-five-year-old Jane, who would find love as well as liberation and labor pains on her bruising slog to freedom. Nor is it just about a young white boy named Rufus Cruise whose feet nearly froze as he ran from the sight of his slain father. Nor does it focus on the plea for help from an enslaved black husband and father named Jim Daniels that spurred John Brown and his band to rescue eleven slaves from Missouri and take them to the gateway to Canada.

It is, first of all, about the war between Kansas and Missouri, which was the first stage, the bloody dress rehearsal, for what would become the Civil War. By letting Kansas Territory settlers decide for themselves whether they wanted slavery, the 1854 passage of the Kansas-Nebraska Act sparked the conflict between Kansas and Missouri. The lack of any natural barrier between Kansas and slave-owning Missouri prompted thousands of slave supporters from Missouri to cross into

Kansas and vote in an 1855 election. That election installed a legislature that legalized slavery, but many people rightly considered it a fraud. Meanwhile, antislavery emigrants from New England began flocking to Kansas, too, hoping to make it free. A group of antislavery Connecticut citizens who moved to Wabaunsee, Kansas, in 1856 became known as the Beecher Bible and Rifle Colony. They gained that name after the Reverend Henry Ward Beecher raised the money to buy twenty-five rifles and donated twenty-five Bibles from one of his parishioners. On both sides of the border war, tempers, axes and guns erupted, and Kansas became known as "Bleeding Kansas." "There's death in every open window as you pass along at night," the poet Juvenal wrote nearly two thousand years ago when describing ancient Rome. The Kansas-Missouri border wars weren't quite that terrifying, but they often came close.

"Murders without number have been committed, innocent women, in the dead of night, have been driven naked from their homes, and their houses burned in their presence," asserted a letter published in the *Newark Advocate* in 1856. "There are two leading parties here, with a third hanging like camp followers upon the skirts of both. These parties I will term the Pro-Slavery party, the Free-State party and the Plunderers."

JIM DANIELS

This was the history that laid the foundation for the escape of eleven Missouri slaves, including the very pregnant Jane, from various Missouri owners in the winter of 1858–59. But none of it would have happened exactly as it did if not for a Missouri slave named Jim Daniels. It was Daniels who sought out John Brown, a steel-spirited man whose unrelenting push for black equality convinced some people he was mad and others that he was one of the few men who saw nineteenth-century America as it was.

The most frequently told version of the story is that Daniels got permission from his owner to sell slave-made brooms. He then took the brooms to the area where Brown was thought to be camped. It was a season of deep snows and even deeper anxieties. John Brown had left Kansas headed east in January 1858, in search of backers for his planned attack on the federal arsenal in Harper's Ferry, Virginia. The drillmaster training Brown's men deserted him and told part of what he knew about the planned raid to a senator and others. Brown had returned to Kansas to let the air clear. He camped in a rude defensive structure on the north side of the Osage River, some seven or eight miles from the Missouri border. He had the thinness of someone who is not quite strong enough to carry his own weight, and he had grown a full beard. He looked like what he was, a man recovering from typhoid fever. By that winter, though, he was as much a myth as a man, someone who could serenade a child, recite every chapter of the Bible and order slave masters and their supporters killed.

On Sunday, December 19, Jim Daniels, described as a handsome "mulatto," met with one of Brown's men and then came to the Osage River settlement.

The trip must have taken all of his courage, his resolve, his nerve. Trembling, he fell to his knees and told his story. He and his family were part of the estate of James Lawrence, a Tennessee native who had moved to the Missouri farm in 1855 and died in February 1858; his daughter and son-in-law, Harvey G. Hicklin, were running the farm in December 1858. Daniels believed that he and his family were either about to be moved to another part of the state or sold and probably divided at an administrator's sale. Lawrence's son-in-law, Hicklin, had become uneasy about the safety of his servants and decided to allow the administrator of the estate, Peter Duncan, Esq., to take all the slaves on the plantation up into Jackson and Lafayette counties, Missouri, and hire them out or keep them there until peace returned to Kansas. Hicklin had control of the slaves until March 1859 but arranged to let the administrator have them on the first of January. It's likely that neither Daniels nor any of Lawrence's other slaves had any desire to be divided, moved or taken to the hemp fields of Jackson County, Missouri. Typically, hemp workers had to cut, haul and pound open eighty to one hundred pounds of hemp stalks per day to make the stalks suitable for rough cloth and ropes.

Now what happened to them was up to John Brown.

But there was no way a man who thought of himself as the wrath of God come to life could say "no" to Jim Daniels. In fact, the enslaved man's plea must have seemed heaven-sent, the perfect beginning for the armed rebellion, the battle of battles, that Brown believed would soon consume the country and burn away its sin of slavery. So he said "yes" to Daniels and "yes" to rescuing pregnant Jane and "yes" to freeing young Sam and the other slaves. The very next day, Brown and his men embarked on one of the most incredible adventures in the history of the antislavery movement, an eighty-two-day trek in the heart of winter through eleven hundred miles of territory, much of it proslavery.

On the evening of December 20, 1858, Brown divided his group into two raiding parties to free the slaves owned by three Bates and Vernon County, Missouri, farmers. He led one group, and John Kagi and Aaron D. Stevens, or Whipple, as he called himself, led the other. At about midnight, Brown's group arrived at the James Lawrence plantation in Henry Township; they surrounded it and removed Jim Daniels, his wife, Narcissa, their two children and Sam Harper, a young slave. Hicklin had hidden fifty-two dollars in gold and silver under the feather ticking of his children's trundle bed. The raiders searched his house but apparently never found the money.

Young Sam along with Jim Daniels and his family were listed in the Lawrence family's probate records, along with a featherbed, two candlesticks worth twenty-five cents and a two-year-old gray filly worth $95. Those records stated that Sam was believed to be eighteen and worth $1,000. Jim was said to be thirty years old and worth $1,200. Brown, according to historian Richard Hinton, felt the personal property on the estate belonged to the slaves whose labor created it and that it should be used to finance their escape. Two raiders stayed behind with Hicklin for an hour or two, threatening to shoot him if he tried to escape. The goods taken from the Lawrence estate included cattle, two horses and harness, one yoke of oxen, pork, lard, tallow, a saddle, shotgun, books, blankets, overcoats, a large old Conestoga wagon, beds and bedding. The confiscated property was later sold to defray the expense of a long journey.

Brown's party also took slaves from another plantation, the John La Rue farm, on Duncan's Creek, half a mile north of the Osage. The occupants may have considered fighting but quickly surrendered. There, the raiders took five slaves, six horses, one wagon and some pork. John La Rue and Dr. A. Ervin were taken prisoners temporarily.

JANE

There are several versions of what happened when the raiders reached the farm where Jane lived, the stories clashing as violently as the free-staters and proslavery men in Bleeding Kansas. In some stories, Jim Daniel's wife is pregnant, not Jane. Depending on which account you accept, the group under Kagi and Stevens either burst into or asked for accommodations for the night at a farm between what is now Stokesbury and Hume, Missouri. Kentucky-born David Cruise, about sixty, lived there with his second wife, Lucinda, and his sons, Ralph and Rufus, but Ralph wasn't at home that night. Cruise owned several hundred acres and had been a judge of elections in the presidential elections of 1856, in which the antislavery Republican Party received not a single vote in Henry Township. In Wilbur Siebert's account, Cruise's wife became suspicious of the men and handed her husband his gun. Other historians claim the "old gray-headed pioneer" himself grew suspicious and reached for a gun his wife was holding. According to the *History of Vernon County,* Cruise's revolver had a loop of ribbon tied around its handle; when he reached for it, the ribbon allegedly caught in the cylinder and he couldn't fire. Still others say Cruise was unarmed. Nobody, however, disputes this: One of the raiders shot Cruise to death. It might have been a man named Al Hazlitt or Bill Beckford or Aaron Stevens, a man whom a North Carolina newspaper would describe as "impatient of restraint and the source of . . . anxiety to his family." When the shot crackled, Cruise's thirteen-year-old son, Rufus, began running. He ran through the snowy Missouri woods barefoot and in his nightclothes, not stopping until he reached a relative's house a few miles away. The snow, he would later write, was at least six feet deep, but he was numb to the cold and numb to all of his pain and discomfort even though his "feet felt as big as bushel baskets." And Jane, too, had her own version of events. One day she would tell historian Wilbur Siebert that her master, David Cruise, "would certainly have fired upon the intruders had not Whipple (Stevens) used his revolver first, with deadly effect."

One Missouri writer speculated that Jane was pregnant "presumably by Cruise's manservant George, who hid from the raiders and stayed with his slain master's family." This writer also claimed that Jane didn't want to leave George and go off with the raiders and that "she cried and resisted." In another piece, though, Jane is described as laughing when she saw the raiders coming and starting to gather her things. Rufus Cruise would later claim that when the raiders first entered his house and began warming themselves at the fire, Jane "came and looked through the window at them and laughed and then went back to the kitchen and began to pack up. She told my mother 'goodbye' and said 'I wish George was along.' " Also according to Rufus Cruise, Jane took sixty dollars, some of it hers and some of it his mother's, her and George's clothing and her bedding. Cruise also insisted George was away from home, courting a black woman named Charlotte who lived about a mile and a half away.

Any enslaved woman willing to run away only a few days before her baby was due had to be dazzled by freedom and desperate for a taste of it. But it happened sometimes. A pregnant Louisiana woman named Lucille successfully escaped in 1833, according to historian John Hope Franklin. Eighteen-year-old Martha Ann was nearly eight months pregnant when she fled Virginia in 1850. And Margaret Garner, the Kentucky fugitive who killed her daughter to save the child from slavery, was pregnant when she escaped, pregnant when she was captured, pregnant when she was jailed and pregnant when she was shipped to Arkansas.

Yet some observers found it difficult to believe that black women like Jane—women who ran away from their masters—really craved freedom.

"To approximate the ease of their former mistresses, to wear fine clothes and go often to church were their chief ambitions," James W. Head of Loudoun County, Virginia, would write in 1908. "Negro women had never been as well-mannered, nor, on the whole, as good-natured and cheerful as the negro men."

Not good-natured? Not well-mannered? Not cheerful? Jane likely felt a whole range of emotions on the day she left her home in Missouri: elation, confusion, weariness, fear of the unknown and fear at embarking on an arduous journey. Nine months pregnant, she already might have experienced nausea, fatigue, vomiting, backaches and mood swings. She would have had a chance to feel her baby move around and then drop, ready to squirm and scream its way into the world. To make matters more perilous, Jane, at age thirty-five, was past the black female life expectancy in some states. She also was an enslaved woman who might have been underfed. As a result she was more likely to suffer such pregnancy complications as puerperal sepsis, convulsions, fever, premature labor and infections. And like all nineteenth-century women, white or black, she surely knew that her child stood a good chance of dying at birth or before it reached its first birthday.

After the Cruise shooting, the two groups of raiders marched back to Brown's Kansas headquarters at Bain's Fort, including the eleven slaves and two white hostages. Kagi and his party reportedly took two yoke of oxen, mules, horses, a wagon laden with provisions and clothing from Cruise. At the fort they reunited with Brown's party. Brown reportedly asked the slaves if they wanted freedom and when they said yes, he promised to take them to a country where they could have it. In the meantime, the white captives were released.

For the next month, Jane and the other escaped slaves would lead lives totally different from the small, well-organized routines of their years in Missouri. They were fugitives, and they were traveling with one of the most notorious men in America, a man for whose capture

President Buchanan had offered a $250 reward. (Brown had offered a $2.50 reward for the capture of President Buchanan!) On the night of December 21 they set out for Osawatomie, Kansas, some thirty-five miles to the northwest. When they reached it, they were hidden in an abandoned cabin on the south fork of the Pottawatomie Creek. Brown stayed for a time near Fort Scott and Trading Post to see whether the Missourians would counterattack. The group spent some time with Susan and Augustus Wattles, reformers who had moved from New England to Ohio and Indiana and finally to Kansas in 1857, setting up a small community called Moneka just north of Mound City, Kansas. Brown and his companions arrived at the Wattles's home in the middle of the night, freezing and hungry. James Montgomery and some of his free-state men were already there, sleeping in the loft.

"Allow me to introduce to you a part of my family," John Brown announced. "Observe I have carried the war into Africa."

Men in the group spent the night outside Wattles's home in wagons. Jane and Jim Daniels's wife and the children in the party reportedly were taken to the home of Wattles's son, John Otis Wattles. It was around this time that Jane had her baby. It's quite likely she had it while hidden and shivering on the dirt floor of an abandoned cabin outside Osawatomie about two miles northwest of Greeley, Kansas, in Anderson County. According to some contemporary accounts, she and her newborn baby may have stayed for a time under or near a cabin built by German-born Valentin Gerth, who had arrived in the area in 1854. Gerth, like Jane, had come from Missouri, arriving in Kansas with a friend named Francis. The two friends pitched a tent in an old Indian field, planted corn and built the log cabin. However, Gerth's friend, who supported slavery, fled Kansas in the summer of 1856.

Jane would not have known any of this history, but she would have been grateful for even a sliver of shelter. She also might have been grateful for—or at least startled by—the presence of James Blunt, a physician who practiced in the area about one-half mile west of Greeley, known as Mount Gilead. At a time when midwives usually delivered the children of both black and poor white women, Dr. Blunt delivered Jane's baby. An admirer of John Brown, Blunt would later become a major general in the Union Army, the highest rank of any Kansan fighting for the North; however, the baby he delivered in December 1858 didn't bear his name. The child was named for John Brown. Because of the high infant death rates in the nineteenth century, both enslaved and free mothers usually waited a while before naming a new baby. The prompt naming of Jane's baby suggests that the child's mother had changed already, becoming a woman who believed in the future, a woman with plans, a woman who felt that after receiving the miracle of freedom, she could expect other miracles as she crossed prairies and raced whirling storms.

FLORELLA

On Christmas Eve, 1858, Brown's raiding party stopped at a home whose inhabitants would have welcomed Jane, her baby and the other fugitive slaves and seen them as human beings, not symbols of a struggle. The group's hosts in Osawatomie, Kansas, were Reverend Samuel and Florella Adair. Florella was John Brown's half-sister, and the Adair home was a stop on the Underground Railroad. Florella's husband, Samuel, was one of several nonviolent and nonresistant agents of the Tappanite American Missionary Association. Samuel Adair preached to free-state supporters about the humanity of blacks, trying to touch the hearts of people who opposed slavery but did not necessarily welcome blacks.

"Many of them wanted not only to keep slavery out of Kansas but to keep Negroes out, too," noted historian Carlton Mabee.

Something else made Samuel Adair stand out in a region rife with conflict: He used words as weapons but carried no guns. "In all ordinary cases I feel much safer without them," he said. He was so scrupulous about keeping his conscience clean that he had refused shelter to one of John Brown's sons who helped hack to death five proslavery men on Brown's order at Pottawatomie Creek, Kansas. The victims, it was said, had urged attacks on the free-staters and on members of

Brown's family. Adair, on the other hand, did shelter two other Brown sons not involved in the murders. On Christmas Eve, 1858, the peace-loving Adairs opened their home to Brown and Jane and the other runaway slaves—there were twelve now, counting the newborn. Flo-rella Adair might have been especially sympathetic to the plight of a woman who had given birth in a troubling time. Florella herself had been seven months pregnant when she learned that her nephew, Fred-erick Brown, had been shot by proslavery men. Florella also knew what it was like to live in a war zone filled with violence that far ex-ceeded the Old Testament call of an eye for an eye. At the height of the Kansas-Missouri conflict, some people lost their lives merely for voicing an opinion. Also, Florella and her husband, like John Brown, believed in black equality, a rare thing even among abolitionists.

When John Brown and the fleeing slaves came to the Adair house, the men hid among corn shucks or husks, and the two black women, Jane and Narcissa, hid in the house. The raiders had horses, mules, cattle, wagons, tools, clothing and food taken from the farmers whose slaves they had taken.

In late January 1859, Brown and the twelve fugitives came out of hiding and set off northward toward Nebraska with the fugitives in an ox-drawn wagon and an armed guard of fifteen abolitionists. What-ever reluctance Jane might have felt at the beginning of her journey she might have overcome by then and, perhaps, embraced the adven-ture. No one knows how she managed to keep her baby quiet at key moments when an infant's squall might have doomed them all. The baby might have been a quiet infant or Jane might have had to drug him at times with Mrs. Winthrop's Soothing Syrup, a popular morphine-laced concoction, or some similar potion, to keep him from crying. Yet Jane and the others—whether or not they knew it—were in the vanguard of the coming war between the Union and the Con-federacy. They also were extremely lucky to have avoided the trap that already had ensnared one of Brown's friends, John Doy, a homeopathic doctor originally from England. Brown and Doy were supposed to start out together, Brown delivering eleven slaves to freedom and Doy taking thirteen. However, at the last moment, Brown decided to strike out alone. By following his instincts, he avoided Dr. Doy's fate. When Dr. Doy and his son Charles left Lawrence, Kansas Territory, for Nebraska with thirteen slaves on January 25, 1859, they were captured just twelve miles out of Lawrence.

In a January 30, 1859, letter to her brother, who was studying at Phillip Exeter Academy, John Brown's wife, Mary, noted: "There were only ten men who knew when they were to start, and one of those ten must have told the Missourians all about their plans. . . . It is queer how the Missourians knew every thing about it: as soon as any change was made they knew it instantly. There are a many spies all around."

Now, John Brown and his men and twelve fugitive slaves were about to cross the Midwest, passing through states where they had friends and states where they had enemies; they would encounter stalkers and saviors, bounty hunters and benefactors. Most of the slaves in the Brown party seemed supremely confident that things would work out, according to historian Richard Hinton. Brown, after all, had already set them free, already changed their lives by making their futures important. According to Hinton, however, Jim Daniels, the man who'd requested Brown's help, seemed more thoughtful than the others, perhaps dwelling on some of the dangers they faced. The group deliberately avoided traveling in a straight line. They would have known that the governor of Missouri had offered three thousand dollars for the arrest of John Brown and one thousand dollars for each of the killers of Jane's former owner, David Cruise.

SAM HARPER

Samuel Harper, who was only eighteen in 1858 and would become an important part of the lives of Jane and her baby, later talked about his thousand-mile trek, which defied both fugitive slave laws and the weather: "It was mighty slow traveling," he said. "You see there were several different parties amongst our band, and our masters had people looking all over for us. We would ride all night, and then maybe, we would have to stay several days in one house to keep from getting caught."

On January 24, 1859, Brown's party received a friendly welcome, provisions and clothing for the escaped slaves in Lawrence, Kansas, which had been settled by free-state men. After Brown's party passed through Lawrence, they moved on to Topeka. The Daniel Sheridan house was the headquarters for Brown when he was in the Topeka area; it was a small stone house from which Brown could see approaching officers of the law in time to escape. Brown and the slaves arrived in a prairie schooner, a kind of wagon used by freighters and drawn by four horses. Shoes and clothing were collected for the fugitives, including Jane's newborn. The group then pushed on to Holton where danger waited.

This time they stopped at the log cabin of Albert Fuller on Straight Creek, a station of the Underground Railroad. There they decided to spend the night. Because of rising creek waters, they had to stay for several days. One evening after the runaways were safely in the cabin, Aaron Stevens went down to the stream to water his horse. Two deputy U.S. marshals on horseback stopped him.

They asked if he had seen any slaves and he admitted that he had, offering to take them to the house where the runaways were hidden. Only one went with him. Stevens lingered near his horse long enough for the men in the cabin to see who was with him. Then he threw open the door and said, "There they are, go take them."

As the slaves watched the marshal approach the house with Stevens, they wondered if their daring journey had ended, according to Sam Harper's recollections. They feared Stevens planned to turn them over to bounty hunters. If Jane was watching the marshal approach, she might have taken special care to slip the baby some soothing syrup. But the incident was not what it seemed. Instead, Brown's lieutenant had tricked the marshal into stepping into an ambush.

The group took the marshal prisoner, but that didn't solve their problem. He was part of a posse led by John P. Wood, a deputy U.S. marshal from Lecompton who hoped to collect the three-thousand-dollar bounty on John Brown's head. Supposedly, a traitor from New Hampshire named Hussey had put Wood on Brown's trail. The Wood posse included armed and presumably resolute men. Wood drew up near the creek and sent for reinforcements. One of the men in the cabin crept to the home of an antislavery farmer and asked him to ride to Topeka and let Colonel John Ritchie know that John Brown was surrounded at the Fuller cabin. About a dozen men left Topeka and came to Brown's rescue, some making the trip on foot. They reached Holton the next afternoon, which was January 31, 1859.

A BATTLE WITHOUT BULLETS

Meanwhile, John Brown made preparations to cross the ford in the face of a posse poised to confront them on the other side. He led twenty or thirty men to the crossing, and there something amazing happened, something that must have sent a signal to Jane, Sam and the others that they had nothing to fear after all. Though the posse might have contained as many as eighty men, they didn't fire one shot. Confronting both John Brown the man and John Brown the legend, they either feared a trap or lost their nerve and fled. As the first of the free-state group reached the creek, some of Wood's men "ran back towards and mounted horses and within a short time nearly the entire posse was retreating in wild panic." In some cases, two men leaped aboard one horse. One rider flew into the air as he put spurs into his horse.

The newspaper *Freedom's Champion* described it this way: "One unfortunate fellow . . . caught hold of the tail of the horse of one of his companions and held on lustily, bounding over the ground at a terrific speed. . . . How far they ran, we can't tell, but it is supposed they never stopped until their horses were exhausted or they reached home." Three or four prisoners and five horses were captured, but the prisoners soon were set free.

The Brown party next crossed the frozen Missouri River to Nebraska City, Nebraska, where thawing ice halted their flight. Brown's men cut down trees, flung logs from the shore to firmer ice and

dragged their wagons across by hand, just hours ahead of their pursu-
ers. Traveling east into Iowa, with its landscape of timber and seas of
grass and flat but fertile soil, they took an established Underground
Railroad route. They reached Tabor by the first week in February.
Tabor, Iowa, should have been just the sigh of relief that Jane and the
others needed. It was not just a station on the Underground Railroad.
It was a place where, according to the *Palimpsest Journal,* "The entire
population was in sympathy with escaping slaves and practically every
family was ready to do something to help the fugitives." Sometimes
the slaves were escorted to the next station on foot, sometimes they
were driven in buggies or oxcarts and wagons. However, this time the
people of Tabor called a public meeting where a deacon denounced
slave rescues as robbery and urged fellow Christians to follow suit.
Disgusted to the core, Brown stalked out of the meeting.

Not all Iowans had turned against Brown, though. His followers
discovered that when they reached Grinnell, Iowa, on February 20.
This was a town where United States congressman Josiah B. Grinnell
had a room in his house called the "liberty room," which harbored
Underground Railroad passengers. This is where Brown's band of fugitives and his men hid in the winter of 1858–59, and this is where his
group's guns were stacked.

They hit Springdale, Iowa, on February 25. By then, Jim Daniels
and his wife would not have been the only couple among the fugitives.
Sam Harper and Jane had become not just close but in love. Apparently, it didn't matter that Jane, at thirty-five, was almost twice
eighteen-year-old Sam's age. Sharing danger or facing what feels like
imminent death can create incredibly strong bonds, of course. For Jane
and Sam, a mixture of fear, need and hope had pushed them into each
other's arms. In a country divided between friends and foes of slavery,
two chased, weary and displaced former slaves found something like
comfort as they and Jane's baby trudged toward a future they could
not quite imagine.

According to a note Brown sent to a friend, the whole group and
their teams were housed for two days free of charge in Springdale.

People cheered the runaway slaves at meetings and donated clothing, bread, cakes, meat and pies for their journey. The group journeyed six miles from Springdale and hid overnight in Keith's Mill, an old grist mill. With the help of William Penn Clarke of Iowa City and J. B. Grinnell, a boxcar was held for the fugitives in West Liberty; it was headed for Chicago on the Rock Island Railroad. Brown had the twelve fugitives put in a freight car attached behind the locomotive. A passenger recognized Brown but was persuaded to keep silent. At Davenport, Iowa, U.S. marshal Laurel Summers boarded the train with a posse but failed to look in the freight car. In Chicago, Allan Pinkerton, the country's most famous detective and a relentless foe of slavery, arranged rail transportation to Detroit for Brown's group. He also had raised some five hundred dollars to transport the slaves to Canada.

John Brown didn't try to conceal what had happened in Missouri in the cabin of Jane's former owner, David Cruise. He believed the details surrounding the shooting would feed his movement and bring the country closer to a mass slave uprising. He also believed it was his role, his mission, to provoke the conflict that he expected to end slavery in a burst of gunfire and blood. During his march through the American heartland, Brown wrote a piece for the *New York Tribune,* justifying his raid into Missouri. After noting that many free-state men had been killed and wounded, he added: "Eleven persons are forcibly restored to their natural and inalienable rights, with but one man killed, and 'all hell is stirred from beneath.' "

JANE AND SAM

On March 12, 1859, John Brown saw the runaways safely board a Windsor-bound ferry in Detroit. That night, Frederick Douglass, the great black antislavery leader, delivered a lecture in Detroit. Afterward, he and local black leaders met with Brown at the home of a local abolitionist. There John Brown is believed to have revealed his plan for the ill-fated but momentous raid on Harper's Ferry, Virginia.

The story of what eventually happened to John Brown and his small band of white and black followers, five of them his sons, is well known. In early July 1859, Brown, now calling himself Isaac Smith, rented a large farmhouse in Washington County, Maryland, and he and twenty-one men moved in. They holed up there for months, Brown reading the Bible and others reading Hugh Forbes's manual, drilling in the loft and shining their weapons. He could see but one course for himself, the one he believed God had chosen. By the time he established a base in Washington County, Maryland, it was late spring of 1859 and close to the time when he would try to trigger a widespread uprising of blacks by raiding the federal arsenal at Harper's Ferry, Virginia, in the Blue Ridge Mountains where the Potomac and Shenandoah rivers meet. That raid failed, possibly because Brown moved up his timetable after learning that his former lieutenant Hugh Forbes had leaked the details of the planned uprising.

A Tennessee woman named Mahala Doyle was glad to hear that John Brown would hang. Brown and his men had killed her proslavery husband, William, and her twenty-year-old son, Drury, in retaliation for attacks on antislavery men during the Kansas-Missouri wars. But when Mahala Doyle pleaded for the life of her fourteen-year-old son, John, Brown had let him live. She wasn't impressed. In November 1859, she sent the imprisoned Brown a letter from Chattanooga saying she wished she could be in Charlestown for his execution and that the son whose life he'd spared would like to "adjust the rope around your neck."

Yet on December 2, 1859, the day of Brown's execution in Virginia, the Syracuse, New York, city hall bell rang sixty-three times, one stroke for each year of Brown's life. One hundred minute guns were fired that day in Albany, New York, at half past noon, commemorating his execution. Prayers were offered for Brown and his family in Philadelphia, too.

John Brown and his slain raiders were eventually buried in a plot at North Elba, New York, not far from the site of a small rural black colony funded by abolitionist Gerrit Smith and known as Timbuctoo.

Most of the twelve slaves who were part of John Brown's final cross-country adventure—people who surely were among his chief mourners—disappeared from the pages of history after reaching Canada. Samuel Harper, on the other hand, shows up in the 1871 census, where he is identified as a black male laborer and a Baptist who was living in "Windsor Town, Ontario." He also was said to be the head of a household. The 1901 census of Canada records that Jane Harper was living in Essex County, Canada, and had a spouse named Samuel. The attachment that had sprung up as they ran away turned out to be lasting.

In 1895, historian Wilbur Siebert interviewed and photographed Jane and Sam. They were living on Bruce Street in Windsor, Ontario. They told Siebert they had a son living in Detroit. In their photograph they no longer resemble the couple that crossed America on foot, on wagons and on a train during their life-changing adventure. Jane Harper is gray-haired but straight and sturdy. Samuel Harper, once referred to mostly as Sam, is no longer a young man but does not seem to have aged much. He was (now) a distinguished-looking man who wore well-shined shoes and both a coat and a vest. Did he mourn John Brown? His words leave no room for doubt.

"I wish, I was in a position to pay John Brown Junior, one half what I owe his father, for what he did for us," Harper told essayist James Cleland Hamilton. Harper claimed his former owner sought him out in Windsor and tried to talk him into returning to Missouri. The man promised he'd treat him better, but Harper wasn't impressed. He said his owner must have thought him a foolish man, indeed; otherwise, why would he have come "all dis way to ask me to go back to slavery."

Harper said it took him, Jane and the others three months to reach Canada. But if he had known slavery would end so soon he said he might never have left Missouri, where he could have scooped up land after the war for twenty-five cents an acre and lived in a climate milder than Canada's.

He expressed no regrets, though, for marrying Jane. They, after all, had shared both doubts and desires, nightmares and dreams on their journey to the land where they made a life together.

Fig. 8. This sketch of three people represents a historic struggle between six armed white men and six armed runaway slaves at Hood's Mill, Maryland, in 1855. (Drawing by Timothy L. Hughes)

SEVEN

THE SIX-GUN
SOLUTION

If the bounty hunters' rifles were supposed to frighten a band of slaves fleeing through Maryland, they failed. If the long guns were meant to make the runaways blink, rethink, sweat, shiver and back down, those weapons were a waste.

By all accounts, there was something inside these particular runaway slaves—especially the two couples—that wouldn't bend. Something that was both chimney-hot and icebox cool. Something that believed in the future but knew how to grab hold of the moment and squeeze. Something that was miles past anger and right next door to rage.

Surrender? Let strangers turn them around and march them back to Loudoun County, Virginia? Clearly, these weren't options for Frank Wanzer, also known as Robert Scott; Barnaby Grigsby or Grigby, alias John Boyer; Barnaby's wife, Mary Elizabeth, and her sister, Emily Foster, also known as Ann Wood, who was Wanzer's fiancée; and two men from a neighboring county who trailed their wagon on horseback. If they had believed in surrender, the two couples in the wagon wouldn't have stood and faced half a dozen armed men prepared to return them to the farms they'd just fled and collect rewards. If they had been willing to trudge back home, one of the enslaved women wouldn't have urged her companions to fight just as a slave hunter pointed a rifle at her. If these runaways had been prepared to acknowledge failure, they wouldn't have drawn their own weapons and gone to war on Tuesday, December 25, 1855, in the snowy Maryland woods.

Runaway blacks came in every size and shape and state of mind: no simple, one-size garment could fit them all. A recently freed black man named George McCoy refused to leave Boone County, Kentucky, without an enslaved woman named Mildred Goines. In 1837, the pair escaped together to Canada. Eventually, they became Underground Railroad conductors in Ypsilanti, Michigan, and had a son named Elijah McCoy, who became a world-famed inventor. While still a young enslaved boy in Lexington, Kentucky, Lewis Hayden became a rebel, too. His defiance started when General Lafayette, the French hero of the Revolutionary War, tipped his hat to the boy. The show of respect changed young Lewis Hayden's whole idea of who he was and who he could become.

"I date my hatred of slavery from that day," he explained after he had become an Underground Railroad conductor in Boston with a reputation for threatening to blow up his house rather than let slave catchers inside.

And there were runaways like Wanzer, Foster, and the Grigsbys, people who had their own particular roll call of fears and hopes and who were willing to risk whippings, wounds and even death for a chance to learn how it felt to be truly alive.

The six Virginia slaves using false names had run away together on Christmas Eve, 1855, in a carefully planned and timed escape. The leader of the group was Wanzer, a fair-skinned and reddish-brown-haired widower of about twenty-five with two children. He lived near Aldie, Virginia, a little mill town about eleven miles south of Leesburg, Virginia, and resting in a gap between hills. Few blacks lived in Aldie itself, but the surrounding area included black communities such as Bowmantown, one of Loudoun County's oldest black enclaves, Stewartown, whose residents shared a Baptist church with Bowmantown residents, and a town with the colorful and, perhaps, accurate name of Back-in-the-Hollow.

Wanzer's owner was Luther Sullivan, a man he later would call the "meanest man in Virginia." Wanzer claimed that Sullivan begrudged his slaves every crust and scrap of food and in 1851 had sold Wanzer's mother and two siblings to a Georgia slave trader. Frank Wanzer's motivation for running away was the well-founded fear that Sullivan's financial troubles were about to swallow him up, pushing him to sell Frank and separate him from his loved ones. Sullivan owned several properties near Middleburg; however, as a result of a chancery case, he put his farm up for sale in 1854 and eventually sold it. By 1860, forty-five-year-old Sullivan and his family were living in Washington, D.C., and Luther Sullivan was a "clerk," according to census records. His household at that time included twenty-eight-year-old Eliza, twelve-year-old Mary, ten-year-old Luther, nine-year-old Ann, eight-year-old James and two-year-old Emma.

Barnaby's owner was a farmer named William Rogers, whose home was halfway between the towns of Aldie and Middleburg, Virginia. Rogers owned about a dozen slaves and, in Barnaby's opinion, sometimes drank more than he should, but wasn't the kind of man who loved to have his slaves whipped. His home still stands today and is now known as Pheasant's Eye at Dover. Grigsby told Pennsylvania Underground Railroad activist William Still that he hadn't fled to escape any cruelties. He simply wanted the chance to earn his own living and make his own choices.

Emily and her sister, Mary Elizabeth, were both slaves of Townsend McVeigh, who had lived at Valley View Farm near Middleburg. McVeigh bought the property in 1833 and greatly expanded the house, which one document called a "mansion." There is no record of what McVeigh thought about his slaves. However, Mary Elizabeth claimed he was a harsh man who barely allowed his slaves to talk, forbade them to raise chickens to supplement their diets and allowed her only three dresses each year. She could not find anything good to say about her mistress, either, claiming she was hard-edged, had a crushing spirit and showed no mercy to a slave. According to census records, McVeigh owned thirty-one slaves in 1850. In 1860, he had nineteen mules or horses, twelve slaves over sixteen and thirteen between the ages of twelve and sixteen; the number under twelve isn't known. By 1870, McVeigh, sixty-nine, still lived near Middleburg. The names and the owners of the two other members of the Wanzer group aren't known but they are thought to have come from nearby Fauquier County, Virginia.

No matter how high a slave's pile of grievances, the decision to run away from a plantation or farm was a risky and often agonizing one. Some or all family members and friends might have to be left behind, possibly forever. Fugitives would have to trade familiar tasks, tastes, smells and voices—the rhythms that had awakened them every morning and rocked them to sleep every night—for new realities they could barely imagine and that might, in some cases, disappoint them. They had no guarantees that their escapes would succeed either. Spouses escaping together or people fleeing in groups drew more attention than slaves traveling alone, especially if they rode horses, walked together or tried to board boats. There were many cases documenting the dangers of escaping in groups. In the early hours of May 21, 1855, eight or nine slaves boarded a small boat on the North St. Louis, Missouri, side of the Mississippi River, led there by a free black man and a black female Underground Railroad conductor named Mary Meachum. On the Illinois banks, police agents and slave owners greeted them. Shots were fired, five slaves were caught, Meachum was arrested and the man waiting to transport the escapees to Alton, Illinois, was wounded.

Runaway slaves also might be trapped by snowstorms, weakened by hunger or tracked down and tackled by slave catchers or slave-hunting dogs. They might be confused by incomplete or contradictory directions, betrayed by supposed friends, spied on by enemies, worn down from wandering around in circles or just plain unlucky. It took an enslaved man named Harry Thomas fourteen tries before he succeeded in escaping from Mississippi. Thomas's punishments for running away included whippings, smacks with two-by-fours and being dragged by a horse; by the time he successful escaped to the Buxton settlement in Ontario, he had become an expert at treating wounds.

The 1850s was an especially perilous time for people of color—free or enslaved, young or old, fair-skinned or dark—to roam America alone. The Fugitive Slave Act of 1850 further strengthened laws already allowing bounty hunters to capture runaway slaves in free states without giving suspected runaways any chance to defend themselves.

"New York has become as Virginia," complained black leader Frederick Douglass in an 1852 edition of *Frederick Douglass' Paper.*

Aware of the possible dangers, Frank Wanzer and the five who fled with him in the winter of 1855 didn't make an impulsive dash for freedom. Instead, Wanzer plotted and mulled over every aspect of their getaway. Since owners typically gave their servants a week off from work for Christmas, the holiday season was the perfect time to run away. During Christmas week, enslaved people usually were allowed to travel longer distances from their plantations to visit family members, some staying away for as long as six days. According to the memoirs of former slave Booker T. Washington, the holiday week also might feature a dance or frolic and "a good deal of whiskey."

Temporarily liberated, slaves might spend their holiday making corn-brooms, mats or baskets. They might hunt rabbits and raccoons, run races, gorge on roast pigs, savor chicken, dance to fiddle music or chug whiskey. In North Carolina, the Caribbean and at least one southern Virginia county, Christmas Eve and other holiday celebrations featured a ceremony known as Junkanoo, John Canoe or John Koonering. The ritual showcased a slave wearing rags, a well-dressed slave and a half-dozen other costumed performers playing instruments and parading to their masters' houses. After the two leading characters danced, spun, kicked, sang and clapped, the celebrants would ask for and receive money from the white gentry.

No wonder Wanzer and the rest of his group believed their absences might not be noticed amid all the hand-clapping and toe-tapping and scurrying back and forth that marked the Christmas holiday among slaves. But waiting for the right time was only the first step of the group's elaborate plan. Wanzer was so trusted by his owner that he was often sent alone in a farm wagon on errands in nearby towns. So he must have reasoned that it wouldn't alarm local whites to see him in a wagon on Christmas Eve. The wanted poster for the runaway slaves stated that the fugitives' stolen wagon had the name E. C. Brown painted on the side, likely a reference to prominent Middleburg merchant Edwin Conway Broun [sic]. Edwin Broun ran the Virginia community's main store and post office until his death in 1879. One of the escaping slaves may have worked for Broun and perhaps made deliveries for his business. It's not known how Edwin Broun's wife, Catherine, felt about Wanzer and the other Christmas Eve runaways, but Mrs. Broun, who had buried five of her children, took it hard when her servants fled during the Civil War. "Poor things, they think they are going to their friends," she noted. "How disappointed they will be."

On Christmas Eve, the Wanzer-led group's journey began, but it didn't follow any of the Underground Railroad routes leading directly from Loudoun County, Virginia, and across the Potomac River into Maryland and then Pennsylvania. Rather than take the obvious path from Loudoun to Columbia, Pennsylvania, Wanzer guided his friends through an area that was mostly country roads and paralleled the tracks of the Baltimore & Ohio Railroad. Frank, Emily and the others took this longer, more secluded and time-consuming path to minimize their chances of running into large numbers of people who might include unfriendly strangers or bounty hunters. Under ideal road conditions, a coach driven by a fresh team of horses could travel at the speed of nine miles per hour. But biting December snow and frost would have made conditions far from ideal for the Christmas Eve fugitives. Away from the smoother main roads, they also might have encountered whorls of mud and horse dung and treacherous potholes.

All the same, they managed to reach Conrad's Ferry, which would take them across the Potomac River. At the time, Conrad's Ferry was operated by the son of Bazil Newman, later documented as an African American businessman, farmer and Underground Railroad conductor. The extended Newman family included some enslaved and some free blacks, some people who married whites and some who claimed to be white. In times of drought or scanty rainfall, the Potomac was shallow enough for runaways to swim or wade across: Peyton Lucas, a Loudoun County blacksmith, swam across the Potomac after escaping from the Baptist minister who owned him. At other times, people crossing the river needed boats. It's not known where the Wanzer party spent Christmas Eve night, which was a Monday, but Underground Railroad Free Press publisher Peter Michael believes they could have stopped at Cooling Springs farm and spring house, a Maryland safe house owned by his great-great-grandparents, Margaret and Ezra Michael, and their children.

THE SHOOTOUT

Once across the Potomac and into Maryland, Wanzer eventually detoured sixteen miles to the west of his route and came to Hood's Mill, some thirty-five miles west of Baltimore. It was now Christmas Day, and Emily, Frank and their friends had become fugitives from Virginia's grain mills and mountains and from people to whom they had many connections, including family ties. Also by December 25, 1855, wanted posters describing Emily Foster, Mary Elizabeth Grigsby and Barnaby Grigsby—but not Frank Wanzer—were circulating, though they had escaped only the night before. This suggests they were such highly valued slaves that they had been missed even during the Christmas revelry. However, the posters provided only physical descriptions of the young runaways.

They noted that Emily was about twenty-two years old and Mary twenty-four. Emily was said to be "heavier built" than her "delicate" sister, Mary Elizabeth, and had "a full face and (was) very black." The poster offered a fifty-dollar reward for Emily, Mary Elizabeth and

Barnaby Grigsby if they were captured in Virginia and one-hundred dollars if they were caught outside of the state "and so secured that we can get them again." Barnaby Grigsby or Grigby was described as about twenty-five or twenty-six and having a "yellow color" and black whiskers and standing about five feet nine or ten inches. The poster didn't mention the cunning and leadership skills of Frank Wanzer, the planner of the escape, noting only, "It is probable several others left with" Emily, her sister and her brother-in-law. Most important, the poster circulated by Virginia slave owners William Rogers and Townsend McVeigh failed to say anything about the boiling point for these particular escaped slaves, especially the two women. That was a serious omission.

When trouble struck, the runaways had journeyed some one hundred miles or so and just reached Cheat River, Maryland. There they ran into six white men and a boy who, despite Frank's nearly white appearance, challenged the group's right to be traveling through the woods of a slave state. It's not known if the men who demanded to see the runaways' travel passes were professional slave catchers or people who helped protect the slave system by questioning any roaming blacks they met. Under prevailing slave codes, slaves found more than a certain distance from their masters' houses could be stopped and asked to show written permission from their owners or overseers. If they didn't have passes, they could be arrested. Blacks were especially likely to be stopped as they neared the Pennsylvania border and prepared to make their last rush to freedom.

But this was one of the crises for which Frank Wanzer had prepared. He first informed the white men bristling with questions that "no gentlemen would interfere" with travelers such as them. The Maryland men ignored Frank's appeal to their pride and ordered the runaways to surrender. According to Underground Railroad conductor William Still's version of the encounter, the runaways responded by shifting to Plan B: they pulled out their weapons. One of the Maryland men then raised his long rifle, pointing the muzzle at one of the young women and threatening to shoot.

"Shoot!" she shouted, clutching her own double-barreled pistol and a long pointed dirk or dagger—the kind of knife sometimes called the California or Missouri toothpick. "Shoot! Shoot!" she continued to yell as her equally well-armed companions stood their ground.

It's not clear if that defiant young woman was Emily or her sister. Neither had anything in common with the frail, self-doubting heroines so often depicted in nineteenth-century novels, the kind of young women who might twist their ankles or tumble into canyons just as villains closed in. Nor did either of the sisters seem resigned to being whipped until their backs became so sore and bloody they'd have to sleep on their knees and avoid bathing for weeks while their stink drew flies. They must have been more like those pioneer women who hoed corn in their nineties, kneaded bread with guns resting beside them and sneaked into the dense woods to pray to the God who freed His people from their chains. There's no record that either Emily or Mary Elizabeth wept on December 25, 1855—or trembled or moaned or pleaded for mercy.

Meanwhile, Wanzer had cocked the hammers of his pistols and was about to fire. The white men suddenly pulled back. They retreated to the side of the road, realizing, no doubt, that the balance of power had shifted right there near the line separating the slave state of Maryland from the free state of Pennsylvania. Finally, the Maryland men rode off, not bothering to try to search or challenge a wagonload of armed fugitive slaves.

"Seeing the weapons, [and] the unflinching determination . . . to kill or be killed, the patrollers backed down," says Allen Uzikee Nelson, the great-great-grandson of Frank Wanzer.

As the two enslaved couples drove off, gunshots crackled behind them. The two runaways from Fauquier County, Virginia, who had been following the main group on horseback might have been so far behind they weren't aware of the threatening standoff between their friends and the Maryland posse. One fugitive behind the wagon was fatally shot in the back, according to a newspaper account, and the other presumably captured.

An apparent story about this shoot-out appeared in the February 2, 1856, issue of the *Provincial Freeman*, an African American newspaper. It had been reprinted from the *Syracuse Chronicle*. "Those with the females escaped, but the men who [were] alone were probably captured, as they have not been heard from," the newspaper claimed.

But after traveling so far and making up their minds to snatch freedom, Frank, Emily, Barnaby and Elizabeth refused to turn back. They abandoned their wagon in the woods and fled on horseback so they could travel faster. By December 26, they had made the journey from Hood's Mill, Maryland, to Columbia, Pennsylvania, in Lancaster County, an area considered "a big hub in the Underground Railroad," according to Uzikee Nelson.

"Four of the group arrived safely on Wednesday at one o'clock in Columbia, Pennsylvania on the Susquehanna River," he said. "They were welcomed by William Whipper."

WILLIAM WHIPPER

Samuel Wright had laid out the town in 1787, named it Columbia and set aside the northeast corner for freed slaves. Informers and spies watched its bridges and an antiblack riot had erupted there in 1834. Yet Columbia was so near the slave state of Maryland's border that it became the avenue for many slave escapes. And the young Virginia runaways couldn't have found a better defender and champion than William Whipper, a black lumber, real estate and fuel magnate.

One of four known children of a wealthy white man and his servant, Whipper had helped found the American Moral Reform Society, believing that blacks would win freedom through elevating their morals. But he had come to believe that freedom was an inborn right, not something that had to be earned. He had inherited a number of businesses from his white father, including a lumber mill, a coal yard, twenty-six railroad cars, stock in the bridge and bank and a lumber yard. His wealth enabled him to help many freedom seekers. By 1860, his property was worth $23,800, nearly half a million in today's dollars. From 1847 to 1860, he donated about one thousand dollars a year to aid runaway slaves passing through Pennsylvania.

He was a deep believer in nonviolent resistance, and though one of his obituaries would question whether he had ever "connected himself with any church," he obviously believed in helping his oppressed neighbors. He also carried around a considerable load of slavery-induced anger. In a letter published in *Frederick Douglass' Paper* in 1852, he described the shooting of a slave in Columbia: "The alleged slave moved but slow, and the officer shot him in the head to quicken his step . . . I am desirous to know whether it is constitutional for slaveholders and their officers, when they shoot down . . . slaves on the soil of a free State, to leave them to be food for vermin."

Once the Wanzer group recovered somewhat from their travels, Whipper arranged for the young people to journey to their next stop. He put them inside the false end of one of his Smith and Whipper Lumber Company freight cars and shipped them to Philadelphia. By New Year's Day, 1856, they had arrived there. Uzikee Nelson believes Whipper sent them to his wife's brother, Stephen Smith, another wealthy black lumber and coal merchant who had moved from Columbia to Philadelphia following Columbia's racial troubles in the 1830s. In Philadelphia, the escapees also met Underground Railroad conductor William Still and received false identity papers. They then rode on to Syracuse, New York, a stop on the Erie Canal that was not far from the Canadian border.

CALEB DAVIS

In Syracuse, antislavery men had passed resolutions declaring that they never would allow a fugitive slave to be taken from them—and they meant exactly what they said. In 1851, Syracuse freedom fighters, white and black, put muscle behind those words during the Jerry Rescue, one of the most daring events of the antislavery movement. After slave catchers captured fugitive slave William "Jerry" Henry in Syracuse in 1851, the red-headed slave was taken before William H. Sabine, U.S. commissioner. Jerry broke away and ran into the streets in handcuffs but was caught near the railroad tunnel. He then was shackled with leg irons and locked up, but that wasn't enough to hold him. On the evening of October 1, 1851, a rescue party of two to three thousand whites and blacks gathered around the police office, throwing stones and timbers at walls and doors and forcing their way into the station. One official, his arm smashed by someone wielding a club, leaped from a window. Finally, the official guarding Jerry "fairly pushed him out and into the arms of his rescuers," according to an 1891 account of the incident. After the abolitionists took him away, Jerry hid in one house after another in the black community for more than a week. Cloaked in a dress, hood and shawl, the disguised Jerry also spent four days at the home of a sturdy sixty-year-old white butcher named Caleb Davis who had fought in the War of 1812. Davis was a proslavery man from Vermont, a "butcher of rough exterior and great physical strength."

"One would have thought his roof would have been the last on earth to shelter the hunted slave," the *Sunday Morning Herald* noted. Yet for four days Caleb Davis hid Jerry while continuing to fling curses in public at his antislavery neighbors and complain about Jerry's rescue. Some sources suggest that Caleb Davis hid Jerry because he was upset over the possibility that the militia might be called out to suppress a slave rescue. It is also possible that his support for slavery was only a pose: At least one newspaper article claims his wife was an abolitionist. Most likely, Davis resented the Fugitive Slave Act, which mandated fines and jail time for citizens who refused to help federal marshals chase or jail fugitive slaves. That much government poking and prying into the lives of ordinary citizens was too much for Caleb. He apparently preferred helping a slave escape to being forced to help slave catchers.

Jerry finally boarded a schooner for Kingston in Ontario, Canada, and, as the *Sunday Morning Herald* noted, the people of Syracuse breathed a deep sigh of collective relief. But his rescue became part of the town's identity, an event recalled every year during celebrations of

Syracuse's history. The arrival of Frank Wanzer, Emily Foster and the Grigsbys four years after Jerry's rescue no doubt stirred up memories of that incident. In fact, the Reverend Jermain Wesley Loguen, a fugitive slave, an African Methodist Episcopal Zion minister and one of the men who rescued Jerry, became the two Virginia couples' protector and guide.

"The seven arrived at Loguen's last, where they were cared for, and are probably now on their way for the Land of Free," the *Provincial Freeman* predicted, getting the number of persons in the Wanzer group wrong but capturing the spirit of their continuing adventure.

It also was Reverend Loguen who finally married Frank and Emily, two good-looking and bright former slaves who had shown their true selves to each other during their flight from home and their do-or-die struggle in the Maryland woods. By plotting his and his friends' escape, Frank had shown how careful and cunning he could be, and by standing up to armed men in Maryland, Emily had displayed the kind of raw, uncut courage that, in William Still's opinion, probably "added not a little to her charms." After Frank and Emily married at an Underground Railroad station in Syracuse, the Wanzers and Grigsbys traveled on to Canada, reaching its shores by January 28, 1856.

FRANK

When the two families arrived in Toronto in the middle 1850s, the city had about fifty thousand residents, including some twelve hundred blacks. By 1851, the AME church on Richmond Street, east of York, had 128 members. Though black immigrants experienced discrimination in Toronto, the city's public schools and colleges were open to black and white students, making it unique among Canadian cities. Most Toronto blacks owned homes and some had valuable property. They included people like washerwoman Deborah Brown, a former Maryland slave who fled with her husband, Perry, when he was about to be sold away from her in the middle 1800s. It also included free black people like Massachusetts-born Peter Long, who moved his family to York (Toronto's original name) in 1793 and began raising and selling produce. It was a peaceful segment of the population, too. Of 5,346 persons arrested by Toronto's police in 1856, only seventy-eight were black.

For a while, Frank seemed comfortable in the freedom of Toronto and in the company of his new bride and his good friend and fellow runaway, Barnaby Grigsby. But his ghosts—those memories he couldn't bury, shake or cut loose—had followed him. Like many other escaped slaves, he couldn't forget the people he'd been forced to leave behind, especially his two young daughters. He also might have been inspired by the open antislavery work of William Whipper and Reverend Jermain Loguen and even a big, burly and profane Syracuse butcher named Caleb Davis who had helped a runaway slave named Jerry elude jail. Frank decided he couldn't walk away from the unfinished job of saving his loved ones. So several months after he and Emily settled in Toronto, Frank Wanzer decided to return to his old Virginia plantation. He told no one what he planned to do. Was he afraid Emily might want to return with him and risk being captured? Did he feel he could move faster if traveling alone? All the historical records tell us is that he took off one day in August 1856, carrying three pistols, twenty-two dollars in cash and his knowledge of geography and escape routes.

Some slaveholders claimed that runaway slaves suffered from "drapetomania," a disease that nineteenth-century psychiatrists insisted gave slaves an uncontrolled urge to run away from their masters, answer disrespectfully and refuse to work. The only cure for this alleged disease was said to be severe whippings and hard labor, which "sent vitalized blood to the brain." They would have had even more bizarre names for an escaped slave such as Frank Wanzer who insisted on crossing slave territory again to return to the scene of his escape.

Wanzer took a train from Toronto to Columbia, Pennsylvania, and then traveled by foot back to Virginia, moving in the shadows and sleeping in the woods. His journey took two weeks. This time he managed to avoid slave catchers, sheriffs and constables, not to mention slave owners. It's not known how he engineered the escape of his family and friends, but on August 18, 1856, Frank returned to Toronto with his sister, Betsy Smith, about twenty-seven and also known as Fanny Jackson; her husband, Vincent Smith, about twenty-three and also known as John Jackson, and a friend named Robert Stewart, about thirty, who traveled under the name of Gasberry Robison. Betsy and Vincent settled in Hamilton, Ontario. Frank returned to his life in Toronto with Emily, knowing that he had done what he could to make his family whole.

"It definitely made me proud to know that this man would escape and then go back," said Wanzer descendant Uzikee Nelson, ". . . very proud."

HARRIET ANN AND MARY ETTA WANZER

However, according to Nelson, Wanzer never could rescue the two baby daughters he'd left in Virginia: Harriet Ann, then one, and Mary Etta, two. Their deceased mother, Harriet Johnson, had been Frank Wanzer's wife until 1855 when the nineteen-year-old woman died of typhoid fever.

"Frank Wanzer hated that he had left his two daughters . . . and his sisters behind in Virginia," says Nelson. "Frank knew that plantations made money . . . selling cash crops, selling children of slaves and hiring their slaves out to others for money."

Frank couldn't rescue his daughters because they were living in their master's Big House with their grandmother, Harriet. The 1870 census showed the two girls still living with John T. and Nancy Lynn of Aldie, Virginia. Mary Etta was then sixteen and Harriet Ann was fourteen. Both were listed as mulatto housekeepers for the Lynn family. When the girls married, the official records listed their parents as Frank and Harriet Wanzer. Uzikee Nelson is a descendant of Harriet Ann, who later married Benjamin Franklin Allen.

The Wanzers and Grigsbys spent the rest of their lives in Canada. According to Frank Wanzer's great-great-granddaughter, Winona Nelson, Frank was a gardener. No matter what memories might have followed Frank and the others of Virginia's red oaks and tumbling rivers, crossroads and mills, high ridges and bridges, woodlands and villages, people and events, the two families did their best to fashion new lives in Toronto. In 1861, the Wanzers and Grigbys shared a one-story frame house on half an acre of land in Ward Three of York Township West, the Toronto district with the highest number of African Canadians and African American immigrants in all of York Township. The Wanzers owned a horse and four pigs, all of them valued at fifteen dollars. Both were Wesleyan Methodists, a group that, in its early years, was staunchly antislavery. Frank Wanzer was thirty and Emily was twenty-eight in 1861; Barnaby Grigsby was thirty-three and Mary was thirty. The Wanzers had added two children to their family by that year as well, Mary Wanzer, two, and one-year-old George, both born in Canada. Unfortunately four of their children died, three while still infants and a daughter at fourteen. The Grigsbys had no children. By 1871, the Grigsbys had moved to St. John's Ward and been joined by Smith W. Grigsby, aged fifty and likely a relative who made the trip to Canada following the end of slavery in America.

ALLEN UZIKEE NELSON

The Wanzers and the Grigsbys don't really come alive, though, until Allen Uzikee Nelson talks about them inside his high-ceilinged Washington, D.C., row house—a house crammed with brooding West African masks, patterned textiles, carved throne chairs and ancestral memories. The lanky native of Tupelo, Mississippi, is a descendant of Frank and Harriet Wanzer, the wife Frank married before he wed Emily Foster but who didn't live long enough to taste freedom. A retired professor of engineering technology at the University of the District of Columbia, Uzikee Nelson now creates monumental freestanding outdoor sculptures that he says are "intended to rejuvenate our ancestral memory" and "improve the self-esteem of African Americans." His huge sculptures of weathered steel and stained glass stand guard over parks and other public places around Washington and in front of the Smithsonian Anacostia Community Museum. Some sculptures also enliven the leafy street where he and his wife, Januwa, a fiber artist, live amid hundreds of books.

Nelson was an adult before his late mother, Sarita Emily Allen Nelson Nunnelee, told him about Frank Wanzer and urged him to read Wanzer's story in William Still's classic book, *The Underground Railroad*. Nelson later learned more about his daring ancestors from the stories spun by his great-aunt, Elizabeth Allen Hanson, who was born in 1882 and died in 1992. The more he researched the Wanzer-Grigsby story, the more intrigued Nelson became, realizing how much creativity and planning it took to bring together slaves from different plantations and steer them safely to Pennsylvania.

That's when the Underground Railroad stopped being something he'd heard about and became something he could feel, something he could trace from one documented site to the next, something he felt he almost could jump aboard and ride. He and other relatives have visited and erected a marker at Frank Wanzer's grave in Toronto, Ontario, and wandered through the area where he might have lived and worked. Meanwhile, many of Uzikee Nelson's outdoor sculptures echo the shapes and the spirit of African masks, those ceremonial disguises that prepared people for everything from circumcisions to weddings to deaths and that linked Africans to their ancestors. Some Nelson sculptures also honor the North Star, which guided so many fugitive slaves to the free or freer North.

"It was kind of mind-blowing," he says in describing how he felt once he became aware of his ancestor's creativity and courage. "They did plan," he says, "even when [Frank] came back a second time."

Some former American slaves returned to America to fight in the Civil War or came back after the war to search for the people who still haunted them. Others might have returned because they missed the steamy heat of Georgia and Mississippi or, in some part of their souls, felt bound to a land whose fields they had watered with sweat and whose rivers had baptized so many bleeding backs. However, Frank

Wanzer was not among those who returned to Virginia while the war raged to fight with the U.S. Colored Troops, nor did he return to Virginia's familiar hills after the war. Though some of his relatives stayed with him for long periods in Canada, his trip to rescue family members in 1856 was the last time he set foot in the past. Yet it could be argued that he had already fought and won the battle to create his own identity and give at least some of the people he loved that same choice. Frank Wanzer passed away on August 13, 1911, and was buried on August 15. He was eighty-two. His body lies in Prospect Cemetery, Section 15, Grave 1683, but Emily's final resting place isn't known. Uzikee Nelson believes it's dangerous for people to forget the pathfinders in their families, the people who did what must have seemed nearly impossible at the time, the ancestors who kept putting one foot in front of the other and trusting that those feet—aided by a rough map, a whispered name or memorized directions—would lead them to new lives. "If you don't know your history . . . you have no idea where you may be going," says Nelson. However, the headstone for Frank Wanzer and his sister-in-law Mary Elizabeth Grigsby, who both died in 1911 and were buried together, contains an equally moving message. Simply, sweetly and for all time, it reads, "Resting in freedom."

EIGHT

THESE FEET WERE MADE FOR WALKING

I walk slowly but I never walk backward.

—Abraham Lincoln

Yea, though I walk through the valley of the shadow of death, I will fear no evil.

—Psalm 23:4

When the Civil War erupted, James Henry Cole rushed to enlist, but the Union Army slammed its iron doors in his face. Why take black recruits who lacked the spunk and smarts to stand up under fire, military officials grumbled. The Civil War was going to be a white man's war, most Americans agreed. It was going to be a war for small-town boys hungry for something besides cornfields and cows. It was going to be a war for men worried that the excitement might end before they could see, hear or even smell it. So James Henry Cole

Fig. 9. James Henry Cole walked from Mississippi to Michigan in the 1850s but didn't become wealthy until the outbreak of the Civil War. (Photo courtesy of the Burton Historical Collection of the Detroit Public Library)

took his unwanted skills and energy home, created a war-related business and, by and by, got rich.

He had been only fifteen or sixteen in 1853 when his white father freed him down in Yazoo County, Mississippi. That's when he began his three-year walk from the muddy, cotton-heavy Mississippi Delta to the unknown chill of the North. His wealthy father was a planter who owned about 150 slaves. He made it his practice to free all of his mixed-race children by Jim's enslaved mother—apparently his favorite—as soon as they could care for themselves, Jim would later tell a newspaper reporter. Once the youngster learned to work with horses, he was freed.

Though many slaves went barefoot in summer and sometimes all year, Jim likely left home wearing boxy, brogue-style plantation shoes, the kind of shoes that could fit either foot and didn't require oiling and waxing. The kind of shoes for which a North Carolina planter named Ebenezer Pettigrew had paid $1.20 a pair in 1847.

Jim put on his shoes and walked away from the pine-smelling Delta where sweet gum trees grew as wide as a man and lightning bugs flirted in the dark. He left a land where more than half the population was enslaved. He turned his back on a region where people customarily settled scrapes with dueling pistols or bare-fisted brawls in dirt-floor taverns. He said good-bye to his family and friends. He abandoned a way of life where each plantation was a kingdom with its own laws and mobs dealt with suspected criminals. In three years of walking, he would have taken more than two million steps and traveled at least one thousand miles.

"The journey to the north must have been frightening," wrote his great-granddaughter, Leontine Cole-Smith. "The Fugitive Slave Laws of 1850 permitted runaway slaves to be returned to any state." After leaving Mississippi, he passed through Tennessee, probably following the route of the Mississippi River, according to Cole-Smith. By 1850, Tennessee had 239,459 slaves, 23.9 percent of the population. Most were in the western portion of the state, which had the right kind of soil for cotton plantations. If Jim had veered east while crossing Tennessee, he would have found something altogether different—people who mostly consumed whatever they grew and antislavery Quakers who had formed the Tennessee Manumission Society to work for the end of slavery. He drifted from farm to farm, working for food and a place to stay. According to family lore, a judge named Cole had suggested that Jim take his name when the former slave applied for his freedom papers. But, in another version of the story, a Tennessee farmer named Cole suggested that Jim adopt his name. Jim immediately embraced the idea. At the courthouse, he became James Henry Cole, beginning his transformation from "slave to freed slave to identifiable person," according to his great-granddaughter.

After leaving Tennessee, James Henry Cole stopped in the western Kentucky town of Salem, a green valley spread between tall craggy bluffs and flanked by the Cumberland River. Trained to work with horses, the black youngster would have encountered plenty of horses in Salem; in fact, grass grown in the Bluegrass State's limestone-rich soil, soil with a high level of calcium, produced superior, stout-boned horses. He also might have run into merchants, grocers, hotel keepers, law students, plasterers, blacksmiths, a carpenter, a physician and many farm laborers. The most important person he met, though, was a beautiful young free black girl named Mary Belle Thompson or McCroskey who was apparently literate but not quite old enough to marry. Cole, for his part, wasn't economically solid enough to marry, but he promised Mary Belle he'd return for her. Then he moved on. He might have been apprehensive about staying too long in Livingston County, Kentucky, where free black people were occasionally seized as slaves. One black stranger remained in jail for a year before officials discovered he was free. Another suspected runaway spent ten months in jail before being sold at the courthouse door.

Cole headed north, probably crossing into either Indiana or Ohio before entering Michigan. In 1856, he finally reached Detroit, where he joined the antislavery Second Baptist Church, the spiritual home of 15 percent of the city's black population. "Because of great-grandfather's tender age, the ladies of the church took special interest in him," his great-granddaughter wrote. "They showered him with motherly aid and comfort."

Determined to live up to his new name and new prospects, he began working in the stables of a Detroit hotel. But after learning how many more opportunities he'd have as an educated man, he decided to go to school. His ignorance so bothered him that Cole, who'd already walked at least one thousand miles, took another walk, this time to Farmington, Michigan, some twenty miles west of Detroit. There, he must have been told, he could attend school. Along the way, a farmer gave him a ride. Learning of the young black man's quest for learning, the farmer agreed to hire Cole for the summer and pay him with a winter's worth of education.

Cole spent two years in Farmington, attending a country school and beginning his habit of continually learning new things. Farmington had been founded by Arthur Power, a twice-widowed antislavery Quaker from Farmington, New York. His son, Nathan, was one of the vice presidents of the Michigan State Anti-Slavery Society. Cole would have found a welcoming atmosphere in a place known for a time as Quakertown and a likely stop on the Underground Railroad. After returning to Detroit, he spent five years working as a chore boy and hostler at the Franklin House. During this time, he rediscovered the Thompson/McCroskey family from Salem, Kentucky, which also had moved to Detroit. Since blacks lived only in Wards Three and Four, Cole had no trouble finding Mary Belle and renewing his courtship.

After Cole tried without success to enlist in the Union Army, he quickly found another way to become involved in what would become as much a war for black freedom as it was a war to save the Union. His skill with horses was extremely valuable at a time when people bred and sold horses, hitched them to plows, wagons and sleighs and used them to blaze trails through the wilderness, pull hay rakes, drag logs, hunt, fetch doctors, stage races and, of course, wage wars. In Detroit, Cole began raising feed and caring for the horse teams of local farmers. He built two barns and received a government contract to stable the horses of the First Cavalry and Artillery based in Michigan. He cared for the horses until receiving orders to send them to areas where the Union Army needed them. The fact that the Confederates had more cavalrymen who were riding their own horses probably gave the South an initial advantage in the war, but in the long run having soldiers supply their own horses hurt the South.

In 1863, the secretary of war authorized Michigan governor Austin

Blair to raise one regiment of black volunteers to fight for the Union. Blacks flocked to Detroit from all parts of the state and country and from Canada, soon filling the regiment with black volunteers. The First Michigan Colored Infantry Regiment made its first appearance in October of that same year, armed with muskets and walking tall. Later known as the 102nd U.S. Colored Infantry, its fourteen hundred black volunteers would serve in the Union ranks from Michigan as the 102nd United States Colored Troops. They would see action in South Carolina, Georgia and Florida, and 10 percent would lose their lives, including a ten-year-old drummer boy.

James Cole would not be among them. On September 23, 1863, he finally felt substantial enough to marry his beloved Mary Belle. As he so tersely put it, "couldn't go to war, so I got married." Later when black recruits were needed, he was drafted for military service but never called into active duty, according to relatives. But his work as an Army contractor laid the foundation for the fortune he would create with the same patience he'd shown while studying and working his way North. For a time he owned an express and delivery business, which evolved into a livery business. Later he opened a moving business with his sons. He saved his money and invested in public halls, stores, houses and other income-producing property on what is now Detroit's near east side.

By 1902, James H. Cole and his son, James Cole, Jr., both made the list of forty men and women mentioned in the *Detroit News-Tribune* Sunday edition, April 27, 1901. The feature article was entitled, "Detroit's Most Exclusive Social Clique, the Cultured Colored '40.'" He also belonged to a black Republican Club, to the Union League Council No. 1, a group devoted to improving conditions for working men through labor unions, and the local chapter of the colored Knights Templar, a fraternal organization. In an interview, Cole said the reason young people didn't make more progress was that they failed to save money, focused on buying fine clothes and lived beyond their means.

"Things come to them too easy," he told the newspaper. "Many of the older colored men saved and accumulated some property which, since their death, their children have run through. The young people think they must dance and wear fine clothes and would rather live in fine rented houses and entertain their friends in great style than to own a little home of their own. They only seem to have an ambition for a gay time. Oh, yes, there are some amongst us that are getting along pretty well."

MARY BELLE

But James and Mary Belle Cole, like other early black entrepreneurs, wanted to do more than pile up dollars. They wanted to become whole people, to peel off the stereotypes that still clung to blacks and hobbled the race. And Mary Belle Cole was as much a striver as her husband.

"She was quite a woman in her own right," says Gabrielle Bradby Greene, a descendant, pointing to Mrs. Cole's service on various civic boards. Leading women of the black elite in Detroit did more than bear children, raise gardens and prepare food, clothing and household goods. They founded clubs and organizations designed to ease the sufferings of the aged, the poor and the infirm and orphaned, sponsor lectures on scientific and literary subjects, organize and host musical performances and improve the image of black women. Mary Belle Cole joined the Banneker Literary Circle, named for the famed black eighteenth-century mathematician and astronomer Benjamin Banneker. The circle, which discussed poetry and the Bible, met at the homes of members, including Mary Cole's home on Beaubien Street.

Newspaper descriptions of the Cole home don't mention how many shoes he owned once he reached Detroit. But the stories do note that the Cole home resembled an old southern homestead, with wide arches, large rooms opening up to each other and a large "well-thumbed library." Nothing could shield them from the most common of all nineteenth-century tragedies, though. Five of their ten children died, four before the age of sixteen. However, the legacy of James H. Cole the long-distance walker who found a name in Kentucky—survived all of this and more. When Cole died on May 24, 1907, in Detroit, the former slave was said to be worth over two hundred thousand dollars.

That sum, of course, could not come close to the fortunes of white captains of industry such as John Jacob Astor, who left an estate worth at least $20 million when he died in 1848. Still, it was enough to make headlines. "Richest Negro in Detroit Is Critically Ill of Pneumonia," declared the *Detroit News* a week before Cole's death. "Born in Slavery, by His Own Exertions He Won Education and a Large Fortune," said another. James H. Cole left a widow and four children who organized the James H. Cole Realty Company.

"His generosity to his church, his contributions of over $20,000 to the Underground Railroad, and his donations to other charitable organizations to help the underprivileged Negro were his legacies," according to Cole-Smith.

James H. Cole's donations to the Underground Railroad would have helped countless runaways obtain food, clothing, medicine, transportation and even land. Yet the success of a man such as Cole in the nineteenth and early twentieth centuries is not an isolated story. The James H. Cole Home for Funerals founded by Cole's descendants in 1919 is still in business in Detroit.

Nearly every community in America has discovered stories of former slaves and freedmen who were agile enough to slip around barriers, sneak through the holes in the system and take what seemed like very little and turn it into more than enough.

OTHER NINETEENTH-CENTURY BLACK SUCCESS STORIES

When Thomas Downing, the son of parents who had been freed, arrived in New York City in 1819, the Virginian brought only one salable skill with him. He knew just about everything there was to know about oysters. He had been born in Chincoteague, an island village in an Atlantic Ocean inlet just south of the Maryland-Virginia border. He grew up fishing, trapping terrapin, digging clams and raking oysters. When he moved to New York, he decided he wanted to become an oysterman with middle- and upper-class clients. He succeeded, catering outside events, launching ships, catering the elections of bank and insurance directors and other official occasions. He also served on the executive committee of the local antislavery society and fought for equal voting rights. His Oyster House became such a staple that when he died, he was mentioned in the *New York Times*.

At the age of ten, Richard Potter sailed to England as a cabin boy and wound up becoming the apprentice to a Scotch magician. The son of a slave, he learned to swallow swords, throw his voice into a dummy, and burn a hundred-dollar bill on a candle flame, then cause it to become whole again. He also learned how to pile up cash. He charged $250 an act, and by the time he died in 1835 had become the owner of a 175-acre estate in New Hampshire and a millionaire. He was not only the first black magician but also the first magician born in America. If that's not enough, he had a son named Henry Potter—most likely nicknamed Harry.

Andrew Jackson Beard, born a slave in Alabama in 1849, designed plows, invented an automatic coupler for railroad cars and used his profits to develop a thriving real estate business. In 1883, nineteen-year-old C. H. James started a business in West Virginia by bartering household goods for vegetables and selling the produce for cash. His business grew from one wagon to a department store on wheels, selling cotton, pots, thread, sugar and other goods primarily to white coal miners. Meanwhile, former slave Clara Brown piled up ten thousand dollars by scrubbing and boiling shirts in Central City, Colorado, the site of gold discoveries, and investing in mining claims. After the Civil war, she found thirty-four relatives and brought them West.

Charles Shearer, like James Henry Cole, gained something besides wounds from the Civil War. Born in 1854 in Spanish Oaks, Appomattox County, Virginia, Shearer was rescued from a barn by Union soldiers who found him beaten and chained. A skilled hunter and fisherman, he joined the regiment and managed to feed the group. After the war he attended Hampton Institute, married and became a waiter in Boston hotels. Eventually he and his wife opened a laundry and a summer inn on Martha's Vineyard, a tradition carried on by family members. Malinda Russell, a free black woman, ran a boarding house and pastry shop on Chuckey Mountain in Green County, Tennessee, until 1861 when southern guerillas robbed her of her savings and forced her and her crippled son to flee to Paw Paw, Michigan.

A black man known as Free Frank McWhorter hired his own time from his owner and set up a saltpeter manufacturing company on the Kentucky frontier during the War of 1812. Saltpeter was the principal ingredient in the manufacture of gunpowder. He earned enough from producing saltpeter to purchase his wife's freedom and his own. In 1836, the former slave known as Free Frank had established his own town, New Philadelphia, Illinois, some eighteen miles from the Mississippi.

Robert Gordon, a Virginia slave, managed his owner's coal yard and managed to produce a high grade of coal from the leftover slag his owner gave him. He purchased his freedom in 1846 and later invested in a Cincinnati coal yard. By 1820, James Forten, who invented a sail making device, had some 40 employees, black and white, in his sail-making business. Pierre Andre Destrac Cazenave, a Louisiana merchant and commission broker, was worth over $100,000 by 1860.

Another unlikely entrepreneur was Elleanor [sic] Eldridge, the Rhode Island–born daughter of Robin Eldridge, a man who had gained his freedom fighting in the American Revolution. After the death of Elleanor's mother, the ten-year-old girl went to work for a family, spinning, weaving, cleaning house and studying arithmetic. At fourteen, she was weaving bedspreads and rugs and at sixteen she was making premium cheeses. Eventually, she and her sister, Lettise, went into business together, weaving, nursing and making soap. By 1822, she had saved enough money from a painting and wallpapering business to buy land and property.

These stories, some smudged by time and some still bright, help illuminate the saga of black entrepreneurs in America. So do tales of James H. Cole's three-year journey in search of love, learning, a last name and, no doubt, better shoes.

NINE

A PENNY FOR
YOUR PAIN

Early in the nineteenth century, an enslaved Missouri woman named Tempe sued for her freedom in court and won. So did Polly, a free black child who had been kidnapped in Illinois and sold into slavery in St. Louis. So did Winny, Rachel and Ralph, Charlotte and Jerry, Milly and Matilda, Julia and Celeste and many other Missouri slaves and slave couples—all in a period stretching from the early 1800s to the 1840s. In 2003, archivists from Washington University in St. Louis were startled to find nearly three hundred original documents of trials spawned by "freedom suits," many filed by people desiring to maintain family connections.

These suits and other documents were discovered stashed away in metal filing cabinets that hadn't been touched since the Civil War. They didn't challenge slavery itself. They only claimed that the person bringing the suit was being held illegally in bondage. Slaves suing under the law had to prove they were free, and that they had been physically abused while being held in servitude.

During the period, many slaves won their freedom based on the

Fig. 10. Tempe and her husband, Laban, stood together when the enslaved woman sued for her freedom on the grounds that anyone who has tasted freedom once deserved to remain free. (Photo of Underground Railroad sculpture by Timothy L. Hughes)

doctrine that anyone who had once lived in a free state deserved to live in such a state forever, even if that person had been brought back to a slave state. Missouri became the most famous testing ground for "once free, forever free" cases, which did nothing to weaken slavery, but brought the human side, the yearning, dreaming, complaining and aggrieved side of the institution into the courts.

The plaintiffs in these cases couldn't read or write, but they had voices and they were willing to use them. They had heard about these freedom suits paid for by taxpayer money; they knew about the lawyers who could help slaves sue for their freedom. Slave owners who were defendants in such cases had to put up a bond, which they would lose if they failed to appear in court or if they sold their slaves downriver before their cases could be heard. The slaves filed suits that spoke for them in court and passed on their stories to white juries. They signed their Xs to complaints. They dared to say again and again, "I am somebody, and I count."

The spirits of a Missouri slave named Tempe and her free husband, Laban, come to life in the forty-one neatly handwritten pages in Tempe's court file. She did more than make vague, foggy statements about mistreatment. She got her state-paid lawyer to write down every injustice she felt she'd suffered. She told the court in her initial pleading that her master, Risdon Price, "wounded and ill-treated" her on August 31, 1817, assaulting her to the point where she was in danger of losing her life. In 1818, she filed a complaint about her lack of decent clothes. In another affidavit she complained that her duties were harder than those of other servants and that she was often verbally abused. Laban, a free man of color, backed her up, saying that he had "great reason to believe" that Price was about to sell his wife downriver. Tempe argued that she should be free because she had worked for years in the North for another master before Price took her to St. Louis. She demanded five hundred dollars in damages.

Tempe's case took three years to make it through the court, but in 1821 she won her freedom. The jury awarded her damages of one cent for years of apparent anguish, but, no doubt, freedom soothed her outrage. Dozens of other Missouri slaves won freedom suits as well. Some claimed they were free men or women who had been kidnapped into slavery. Others insisted they had bought their freedom or been emancipated by a master. In 1830, an army officer purchased a slave named Rachel in St. Louis, and she remained with him until the following year when he took her to the free territory of Michigan. In 1834, he took her back to St. Louis to be sold. A Missouri court found in favor of her owner. Later, the state supreme court overturned that decision. In a new trial, she won her freedom. The most common and effective argument was that people ceased being slaves once they had tasted and become accustomed to freedom.

Then this window of opportunity slammed shut.

One of the last "freedom suits" in Missouri was the infamous Dred Scott case. The enslaved man, who had a wife, Harriet, and two young daughters, had run out of options by the time he decided to sue. He had not been allowed to buy his way to freedom and evidently didn't want to run with a family. His freedom suit was filed in 1846, appealed several times and finally settled in 1857. An all-white jury awarded Scott his freedom in his second trial because he once had lived in the nonslave territories of Wisconsin and Illinois. When Scott's owner, Irene Emerson, appealed, the state supreme court overturned that decision and returned Scott to slavery. Supported by lawyers who opposed slavery, Scott then filed suit in the U.S. Supreme Court. The high court decided that blacks weren't citizens, couldn't sue in courts and had no rights whatsoever that white people had to respect. This ruling and the hardening of racial lines across the country ended the freedom suits that had recognized the claims of people like Tempe and Laban—as well as Dred and Harriet Scott and their two daughters.

It also confirmed the claims of states' rights believers that only the states, not Congress, could enact laws regulating slavery.

In Missouri and elsewhere, the lines separating slavery from freedom became more difficult to cross.

The two concepts, the two conditions, had become stark enemies, facing each other on battlefields without any possibility of a truce.

Many conditions and events helped set the stage for the Civil War. The deep social, political and economic differences dividing North from South certainly helped.

So did the Fugitive Slave Act of 1850. Congress had passed it as part of a compromise bill designed to make it harder for slaves to escape. A tougher bill, legislators believed, would discourage runaways and soothe slave owners who were grumbling about seceding from the Union. But the act did just the opposite of what Congress intended: More slaves than ever ran away. The legislation denied fugitives the right to a trial by jury. Instead, they had to rely on commissioners who received ten dollars for deciding a man was a slave and five dollars if they set him free. The act also required citizens to help federal marshals capture fugitives. Citizens who refused could face up to a thousand-dollar fine and six months' imprisonment. As a result, people who hadn't cared one way or the other about slavery resented a system that forced them to become involved. Meanwhile, more and more slaves escaped and kept running till they reached free Canada.

The South's heavy reliance on slave labor to raise cotton also helped make the Civil War inevitable.

So did the 1852 publication of Harriet Beecher Stowe's best-selling antislavery novel, *Uncle Tom's Cabin*, which made millions of people weep at the murder of a saintly black man and identify with an enslaved woman's daring escape with her son.

So did Abraham Lincoln's election to the presidency with less than 40 percent of the popular vote, much of it from non-slaveholding states.

So did John Brown's raid on Harpers Ferry, which ended in failure but gave the antislavery movement a martyr and prophet.

And so did the death of Missouri's freedom suits.

Fig. 11. Well-to-do white North Carolinians so prized Thomas Day's furniture that they petitioned the state legislature to make an exception for Day's Virginia-dwelling wife after the state decided to close its doors to free blacks. However, Day, who owned slaves under circumstances that aren't clear, may not have had as much in common with his slave-owning neighbors as they believed. By 1851, all three of his children were enrolled in a private Massachusetts academy that posted notices of antislavery meetings and was believed to be a stop on the Underground Railroad. (Photo courtesy of the North Carolina Museum of History)

Fig. 12. Elijah McCoy was the son of a freed slave who ran away with the enslaved woman he loved. Inspired by his antislavery parents, McCoy became one of America's most famed inventors. Born in Colchester, Ontario, and educated in Edinburgh, Scotland, he couldn't find a job as an engineer in the nineteenth century. Working as a locomotive fireman on the Michigan Central Railroad, McCoy was frustrated by frequent stops to manually oil the trains' moving parts to keep them from wearing out prematurely. In 1872 he invented and patented a lubricating cup that supplied drop after drop of oil to moving parts while the trains kept on rolling, saving companies millions of dollars in lost production hours. McCoy's best-known invention, the cup was used on ocean liners, steamships, railroad locomotives and many other manufacturing machines. However, he frequently assigned all or part of his patents to other individuals or companies to raise money for research. Variations of his oil cup are still used on naval boats, in mining and construction machinery, in factories and even in space exploration vehicles. (Photo courtesy of the Burton Historical Collection of the Detroit Public Library)

———◆———

BOOK II

TRICKS AND TRAPS ON THE ROAD TO FREEDOM

INTRODUCTION

My education in Underground Railroad traps began in 2000 in Professor Kimberley Davis's Adrian, Michigan, home. I had gone there to hear a story about her late grandfather's house, a place Davis believed had been a stop on the Underground Railroad and a place that she also believed her grandfather and others haunted. I wasn't sure I believed in the kind of ghosts you could see and sense, not even if they were the shadows of escaped slaves.

But the sounds and smells of the past really did seem to seep through the walls of that house.

Sitting in Davis's kitchen, I could feel myself sliding back in time. I could smell the raw onion that a runaway slave might have rubbed on his back to throw off the hounds on his trail. I also could smell the biscuits and macaroni pies a fugitive might have munched on the road.

I could hear the scary howls of slave-tracking hounds and sense the fear leaping from the men and women who fled slavery on foot, in false-bottomed wagons and in boats. I could even imagine the clip-clop of horses that knew the roads to freedom as well as their riders, the clatter of their hoofs muffled by bits of carpet.

But Davis didn't really jolt me until she mentioned that some runaways wound up seeking help from fake safe house operators. Bounty hunters pretending to be antislavery fighters would take them in for the night and turn them over to the authorities the next morning. People traveling on the road to freedom, I quickly learned, had more to worry about than harsh weather, hunger, relentless bloodhounds, geographical confusion or persistent slave catchers. They had to worry about being betrayed by people they'd considered friends. In fact, as another acquaintance noted, relations between supporters and opponents of slavery in some ways resembled the old Cold War between America and the Soviet Union. Both sides used spies and counterspies. Both sides had a grab bag of tricks and traps. Both sides also knew a thing or two about stitching together a complicated plot and assuming a false identity.

Actually, it wasn't all that hard for eighteenth- and nineteenth-century Americans to reinvent themselves and become someone new. That was what the country was all about. In a new, open and seemingly endless land, people often roamed from town to town, shedding the past and staking out a future. Runaway slaves surely did it. So did runaway criminals, indentured servants and people just weary of who they'd always been. There were no credit agencies to keep track of people's debts, and no internet on which to verify someone's credentials. People were presumed to be who they said they were until something they said or did stirred suspicion. That was especially true in black communities, where people often had reasons to mask the past. Around 1868, a fourteen-year-old black youngster named Charles Henry Darden showed up in Wilson, North Carolina, and began to fashion a new life, according to his granddaughters, Norma and Carole Darden, authors of a family memoir called *Spoonbread and Strawberry Wine*. No one in the town ever knew where he came from, who his family or friends were or whether he had been a slave. Yet he managed to hammer out a new life, becoming a blacksmith, opening a repair shop and finally winning the hand of one of the town's most popular young ladies.

George DeBaptiste, a Virginia-born Underground Railroad conductor who worked in Indiana and Michigan, knew men who forged counterfeit papers that enabled slaves to pass for free men. He also knew runaways who had shaved off their curly hair to pass as Quakers and pale-skinned fugitives who had pretended to own their darker mothers and siblings. He could tell stories about a man who had tried to betray fellow slaves planning to escape but wound up traveling to Canada with them, tied up and gagged all the way.

In a December 22, 1843, open letter to "The Colored People Residing in the Province of Canada," Henry Gouins [*sic*] cautioned blacks to be wary of con men, including black ones. He talked about how a black man named George Wilson had urged him to come to Ohio "upon pretence of his rendering me a service." Agents of a slaveholder met him when he arrived in Perrysburg, Ohio, and arrested him as a runaway slave. Only the "kind interference of two professional gentlemen" who investigated the charge kept him from jail. He fled the town after promising to compensate his rescuers for their troubles. He cautioned his readers against "placing too much confidence in any person."

Con men could put on some compelling performances, though. Private Palmer Sherman, a member of the 22nd Wisconsin Infantry, certainly did. He belonged to a Civil War regiment so protective of runaways that it became known as the Abolition Regiment. However, two slave catchers paid him to betray an enslaved man named George who had taken refuge with the unit. After George accepted Sherman's invitation to join him on a wild turkey hunt, the enslaved man was captured and jailed. Colonel William Utley, the regiment's commander, promptly sent a detachment of soldiers to rescue George.

Around 1858, John Brodie, a teamster, duped two escaping slaves into returning to Covington, Kentucky, with him, promising to help them set free several relatives they'd left behind. As soon as they crossed the Ohio River, a white mob met them. The two runaways were lashed one hundred times and sold farther south, making it difficult for them to run off again.

To add to the confusion, a gang of desperadoes called the McKinscyites would steal slaves from a plantation and sell and resell them several times before setting them free. According to William Lambert, a leader in Detroit's antislavery network, the antislavery movement did a lot of soul-searching over whether to accept such a group.

"It was a long time before we could make up our minds to use these scoundrels," he said, "but we at last concluded that the end justified the means. Indeed, we went further than that before we got through with our work and held that any effort to secure liberty justified our means. . . . Our associations with the McKinseyites were from the very necessities of the case of short life. They were sure to be caught sooner or later, and at last some more daring robbery than usual brought some of them to prison and dispersed the rest."

But the con games rolled on.

Sylvester Atwood, a white steamboat captain, was tricked in the 1840s into sailing some white men to Amherstburg in Ontario, Canada, a favored destination for runaway slaves. The men claimed they just wanted to enjoy sea breezes and soak up sun, yet once they reached their destination, it became clear they were hunting slaves. Two days later, the angry Atwood placed an ad in a newspaper announcing that he'd been fooled. For the next twenty years, he took his revenge, sailing runaways from the northern Ohio borders to Detroit and Canada.

All the same, the smell of treachery was as much a part of the abolition movement as African Methodist Episcopal churches and Quaker meetings.

In the following stories, the con games range from the incredible to the almost amusing and involve U.S. Army regiments, cooks, Quakers, ministers, judges and a Pennsylvania raftsman who stood nearly seven feet tall.

TEN

——◆◆◆——

THE BREAKFAST
OF GENERALS

How about a rousing breakfast of thick-cut country ham with eggs, grilled chicken, fish, grits, biscuits, griddle cakes, apple butter, honey and jam? Or how would you feel about a dinner featuring turtle soup, leg of lamb, macaroni pie, oysters, turkey, bread pudding and ice cream? Welcome to the world of nineteen-century plantations staffed by enslaved cooks and cooks' helpers. Runaway slave Althea Lynch's name doesn't appear on any list of famous Big House cooks but she must have been a Dutch oven, fireplace, tea kettle and skillet sensation. Her skills are said to have freed her from a wartime Washington, D.C., jail.

Bizarre? Oh, yes. Funny? No, not really. Caught in the middle of an escalating battle between the U.S. Army and Washington, D.C.'s civilian officials, Althea Lynch's mealtime relationship with Major General James S. Wadsworth was strong enough to spring her from jail. But in the early days of the Civil War, President Lincoln and his military commanders kept slow dancing around the deeper problem that Lynch's arrest highlighted: how to deal with runaways seeking federal

Fig. 13. The Civil War unleashed a flood of runaway and newly liberated slaves who crowded Union Army outposts. (Photo courtesy of North Carolina Museum of History)

protection without offending slave owners in states such as Maryland and Kentucky that remained, at least on paper, loyal to the Union.

Many officials and soldiers dealt with the problem by allowing slave owners to stride into Union camps, snatch up their servants and drag them off. Others protected the fugitives. In November 1862, a young female runaway slave sought refuge with the 22nd Wisconsin Infantry at its camp north of Lexington, Kentucky. Recently sold, the eighteen-year-old woman claimed her new owner intended to hire her out as a prostitute. The presence of a single and highly attractive runaway created a dilemma for Colonel William L. Utley, commander of a regiment known as the Abolition Regiment. Utley feared the young woman would distract his men or spark conflicts, but he wasn't about to return her to enslavement. Finally, the girl was disguised as a Union soldier. Two volunteers from the regiment then drove her to Cincinnati, leaving her with abolitionists who promised to send her farther north.

In Washington, D.C., Colonel Utley's counterpart was General Wadsworth, who was equally determined to protect runaways at all costs. But the Fugitive Slave Act of 1850 was still on the books, giving federal marshals the right to pursue and snatch runaway slaves anywhere, any time, and return them to their owners. In the winter of 1861, Washington D.C.'s county jail, known as the Blue Jug, contained sixty fugitive slaves, as well as horse thieves, confidence men, and suspected traitors. Congress had tried to fix this problem, passing two confiscation acts in 1862 that prohibited returning runaways to their masters and freed slaves who had fled to federal camps. But these laws didn't protect slaves with masters who remained in the Union.

The laws did put slaves under U.S. military protection, but that didn't stop D.C. authorities from jailing them. In theory, though, soldiers could have retaliated by arresting city police who went too far. Only under such tense and murky circumstances could the jailing of a young mulatto cook trigger a crisis that involved one military governor, two posses and a U.S. marshal.

Nobody recorded what kind of breakfasts Althea Lynch cooked for Brevet Major General James Samuel Wadsworth, military governor of the District of Columbia. They probably were not super-lavish spreads. Despite his wealth and his head-turning wife, General Wadsworth had simple tastes—too simple, some people thought. William O. Stoddard, one of Lincoln's private secretaries, was crushed to discover this in the fall of 1861 while inspecting the Army of the Potomac. Stoddard had heard rumors that Wadsworth "would not postpone a meal on account of anything of less importance than an attack." He was let down when he saw that Wadsworth's headquarters was just a little "old paintless frame farmhouse," he wrote, and he was even more distressed that the general's dinner was "regular army rations" well cooked and served on a pine board table without a tablecloth. Still, Stoddard entertained himself with "the passing thought" that he and the general might share a champagne toast sipped from glasses.

He had to settle for "weak whisky and water" sipped from tin Army cups.

On the other hand, Althea Lynch likely was one of those cooks who could transform almost anything, including rough Army rations, into the kind of meals that could haunt someone for hours. If her master posted a runaway slave ad for her, the ad likely pointed out (as did an 1828 ad for a runaway named Barbara) that she was "one of the best female cooks in the county." And for a brief time, Lynch's cooking made her at least a minor player in the all-American game of what shall we do with the slaves.

The Civil War had caught Washington, D.C., half-dressed and needing a lot of cosmetics. The swampy town was very much a southern place but suddenly it was the heart of the Union, too. When the war started in 1861, Washington didn't seem quite ready for its new roles. On one side, the slave state of Virginia, which sided with rebels, flanked it. On three other sides, it was bordered by the slave state of Maryland, which remained in the Union, but just barely. Meanwhile, Washington, D.C., was filled with people whose favorite song was "Dixie," a lamentation for southern cotton fields and the way of life those fields had spawned, including the slaves still being bought and sold in the nation's capital.

In her escape from slavery, Althea Lynch might have had help from the District of Columbia's Underground Railroad network. At various times, that network included such people as John Allen, who had been brought before the district's circuit court in 1833 for forging freedom papers for an enslaved man and helping him escape. It included Harriet Anderson, who challenged Washington's curfew laws in 1830. It included James Beckett, who was said to have helped a group escape from slavery in 1855. It included the people who masterminded the attempted escape of seventy-seven men, women and children aboard the schooner *Pearl* in 1848. It included Gamaliel Bailey, who helped buy people out of slavery and edited an antislavery newspaper. And it once included Leonard Andrew Grimes, driver of a horse-drawn cab that transported politicians, professionals and others in the Washington, D.C., area. An Underground Railroad conductor, Grimes went to prison in 1840 for rescuing a woman and her six children from slavery in Leesburg, Virginia, and driving them to D.C. He later became an antislavery activist in Boston.

The war, though, created its own Underground Railroad, one that did not really need conductors. The advance of Union armies into slave territory pushed more and more escaped slaves into Washington, D.C.'s already overcrowded black neighborhoods. In the beginning, most Union soldiers didn't see themselves as slave liberators. There wasn't, after all, a whole lot of freedom in D.C., where black codes allowed an unclaimed fugitive to be sold to pay for his imprisonment charges. Black people found on the street after 10:00 P.M. could be locked up until morning and fined as much as ten dollars. The census of 1860 recorded only eighteen hundred slaves in the city but over nine thousand free blacks worked as servants, hack drivers, bootblacks, barbers, waiters and, of course, cooks.

Yet long before the government decided the war would be about black freedom, slaves such as Althea Lynch had already smelled the coming changes. In the meantime, the infighting continued over who had actual jurisdiction over D.C. runaways—the U.S. military, as represented by Wadsworth, or the deputies, represented by Ward Hill Lamon, a young lawyer and Virginia native who issued warrants for the arrest of fugitive slaves.

The gulf between these two groups kept growing. The Army became more and more inclined to distrust all slaveholders. But Lamon and his deputies seemed equally likely to return the slaves of slaveholders who pledged their loyalty.

Military provost and abolitionist Wadsworth soon moved fugitive slaves from their prison cells to the nearby houses of Duff Green's Row. To avoid congestion, some runaway slaves were placed in private service in Washington and other cities. Each fugitive was questioned about his master's loyalty. Those whose masters were deemed traitors received military protection papers signed by Wadsworth. Wadsworth seemed bent on doing whatever he could to keep the Fugitive Slave

Law from working in the District of Columbia. Yet civil authorities may not have respected the general's power at all times.

The arrest of Althea Lynch seemed to prove that. Even though she was said to be Wadsworth's cook and carried his protection papers, D.C. constables seized her anyway. She was locked in the Blue Jug until district commissioners could examine her.

It's safe to say that Wadsworth wasn't pleased when he heard about Lynch's arrest. He ordered Lynch's release, but her jailor refused. Eventually Wadsworth sent an officer and a detachment of a dozen soldiers to force the jailor to give up his keys. The cook was released and the jailor and a deputy marshal were in turn tossed into a military guardhouse.

Once Marshal Lamon heard about this, he rushed to the White House but couldn't reach President Lincoln. He then gathered a posse large enough to make the military guard at the jail yield and become prisoners themselves. Later in the day, though, the Army and the marshal exchanged captives. If this sounds like an old comedy routine with the same punch line repeated again and again, that's a pretty fair description. Nobody was laughing, though. The bottom line was that Althea Lynch remained free and, presumably, Brevet Major General Wadsworth continued eating the kind of meals he enjoyed, at least for a time.

Wadsworth died in 1864 of wounds received in central Virginia's two-day Battle of the Wilderness, a conflict in which regiments became confused and disoriented in the tangled underbrush. Althea Lynch vanished from the pages of history, but one hopes that she remained in the profession that not only shielded her during the war but was one of the few always open to blacks.

From the beginning of this country's history, enslaved and free blacks grew, peppered, oiled, diced, boiled, stewed, fried and fricasseed food. They also invented ice cream molds, biscuit cutters, lemon squeezers, an egg beater with two compartments, a rolling pin, a lunch pail, a bread-crumbling machine and a dough-kneading machine. They cooked in the White House, cooked in plantation Big Houses, cooked for small farmers, cooked for restaurant owners and cooked for themselves. They might even have created that all-American delicacy, potato chips. (Actually, potato chips are credited to three possible inventors. One of them, George Crum, is sometimes described as a Native American and African American chef at a Saratoga Springs, New York, resort.)

Food even played a role in the freedom struggle. In the early 1800s, Alethia Tanner started a small garden in the District of Columbia near the President's Square. By 1810, she had earned enough to purchase her freedom and eventually bought the liberty of twenty-two relatives and friends. Underground Railroad conductor George De-Baptiste, a free black Virginian, worked at various times as a barber, baker, caterer, boat steward, ice cream parlor owner, presidential valet, ship owner and salesman in several states. In 1836, he worked as a steward on Mississippi riverboats, buying provisions and supervising the kitchen and dining service. This might have been when he learned to cook. William Henry Harrison, a future U.S. president, was so impressed by DeBaptiste's stories and swagger that he hired him to manage his North Bend, Indiana, farm. When Harrison was elected president in November 1840, DeBaptiste accompanied him to the White House. Unfortunately, the inauguration took place on a bitterly cold day in March and Harrison spoke for nearly an hour without his hat and warm green cloak. He quickly fell ill and died of pneumonia.

Though we don't know which of Althea's dishes so captivated General Wadsworth, it's not hard to imagine the kind of postwar food she might have served. Here are a few modernized possibilities suggested by contemporary cooks:

BATTLEFIELD BISCUITS

2 medium-sized sweet potatoes
3 or 4 level teaspoons of baking powder
2 cups of flour

2 tablespoons sugar
1 stick of sweet unsalted butter, melted
⅔ cup milk

Preheat oven to 400 degrees F. Boil potatoes until tender. Peel while hot by holding potatoes under cold running water. Pull strings out of potatoes and then mash with potato masher. Sift dry ingredients together. Beat melted butter into sweet potatoes. Add dry ingredients a little at a time, alternating with milk. Mix just enough to moisten. Shape into patties. Put patties on cooking sheet. Turn down oven to 350 degrees F. Bake biscuits ½ hour to 45 minutes. Cook on top oven shelf so the biscuits don't burn on the bottom (Barbara Wynder).

ANNIE WYNDER'S CONTRABAND COD

1 pound of cod
6 medium white potatoes, peeled and diced
1 medium-sized onion
Salt and pepper to taste
1 egg
Flour
¾ cup oil

Boil a pound of cod for about 15 minutes. Pour off hot water through a strainer. Hold cod in strainer under slow running cold water and work with fingers to get the bones out. Boil potatoes until done, then strain and mash them. Dice a medium-sized onion and add to potatoes. Add cod to potatoes and onion, season with salt and pepper and mix with one beaten egg. Form mixture into balls with a big spoon. Heat oil in a frying pan. Roll balls in white flour. Fry until brown in hot oil. Serve with tomatoes and peas (Barbara Wynder).

CONFEDERATE CLAM CAKES

1 pint of larger-sized clams
1 onion
Flour
2 teaspoons baking powder
¾ cup cooking oil

Chop up clams really fine. Chop onion fine. Mix enough flour with clams and onion to make a patty with the consistency of a pancake. Then add baking powder to that mixture. Put cooking oil in hot skillet. Using a mixing spoon, pour batter into hot oil, fry like pancakes, browning on both sides. Serve with boiled potatoes (Barbara Wynder).

ELLA MCDONALD'S IRRESISTIBLE EGG CUSTARD PIE

2 tablespoons room temperature butter
Sugar to taste
1 cup milk
2 large beaten eggs
2 tablespoons cornstarch
1 teaspoon vanilla
I pie shell

Cream butter and sugar, then add milk and other ingredients. Fold into a pie shell. Bake at 325 to 350 degrees F. for 45 minutes to an hour (Janice Berry).

PLANTATION PIG

8 pig ears
8 pig snouts
4 pig feet, split

3-pound piece of pork shoulder
Salt
Black pepper
Sage, fresh or ground
Cider vinegar
Ground red pepper

If a pressure cooker is available, cook the ears and snouts together. The pig feet should be cooked by themselves and the fluid saved. If you do not have a pressure cooker, boil the ears and snouts together and throw away that liquid. The pork shoulder can be put into a pressure cooker or boiled. Discard this fluid also. Boil the pig feet by themselves and save the liquid. Drain the ears and snouts through a colander and put the meat in a large roaster. Do the same with the pork shoulder. Set the colander on top of a large pot and pour the feet and the fluid into the colander and save the fluid. Set the fluid aside until cool. The ears and snouts should be squeezed with the hands in the roaster. Cut the pork shoulder into small pieces and add it to the ears and snouts in the roaster. Then the feet will have to be squeezed with the hands and all bones, large and small, removed. Combine all the meat in the roaster. Take the fluid from the pig feet that has cooled and jellied and scoop off the top until just a solid white jelly is reached. You can warm it up on the stove so that it pours freely and add some of it to the meat in the roaster. Add salt, black pepper, sage and cider vinegar to taste. At this point, you can remove some of the meat from the roaster to another pan and add the ground red pepper. That way you will have two kinds of souse meat, hot and mild. It is suggested that the completed mixture be placed in meatloaf-sized aluminum pans and chilled in the refrigerator. Do not put in freezer. After the meat has become solid, it can be sliced and served. You can now remove the meat from the pans, wrap in a clear wrap and then in aluminum foil and put in the freezer for later use (Fred L. Williams).

YANKEE YAMS

2 yams
Salt and pepper to taste
A little shortening
¼ cup chopped peanuts

Boil yams until soft. Peel and mash them up. Add salt and pepper, oil and chopped nuts. Stir well, put in pan and bake for a few minutes with a little oil on top (Lydia Richardson).

REALLY BLACK-EYED PEAS

1 pound smoked neck bones
1 pound fresh green black-eyed peas
Garlic powder
½ teaspoon sugar
One dried red hot pepper
½ pound fresh okra

Clean the neck bones, removing bone fragments. Cook for about an hour on medium-low heat. Wash fresh peas several times. Drain peas and add to neck bones. Sprinkle with garlic powder and sugar and toss in red pepper. Let peas cook for about half an hour. Put fresh okra on top of peas and cook until tender but still firm (Beatrice Buck).

GETAWAY GUMBO

2 tablespoons butter
1 package Cajun gumbo vegetables
1½ cups chicken broth
2 cups tomato juice
1 stalk celery
1 medium onion

Polish sausage, chopped
Cooked shrimp, chopped
Cooked chicken, chopped
¼ teaspoon filé
¼ teaspoon Cajun seasoning
Salt and pepper to taste
Roux

Melt butter in heavy kettle. Add contents of vegetable package and chicken broth. Cover and cook for 15 minutes. Add tomato juice, celery, onion, sausage, shrimp, chicken, filé, Cajun seasonings, salt and pepper. Cook gently for 10 minutes.

ROUX

1 teaspoon butter
3 tablespoons flour

Brown butter and flour together and add to pot. Serve over rice (Shervonne Taylor and Anne Arrington).

ELEVEN

THE DANGER OF BEING DANGERFIELD

Ordinarily, a public hug from a whispered-about white woman might have ended a runaway slave's chances of remaining free. Ordinarily, pressuring the commissioner presiding over a runaway's trial might have killed a fugitive's bid for freedom. But there was nothing ordinary about the arrest and trial of fugitive slave Daniel Dangerfield.

Dangerfield grew up in the southern part of Loudoun County, Virginia, about ten miles from Aldie, a rural village sitting in the shadow of hills. During the Civil War, the area would become known as a base for one of the South's most feared and revered soldiers, Colonel John Singleton Mosby. The colonel and his free-wheeling rangers raided Union outposts and supply lines and then disappeared, earning Mosby the nickname the Gray Ghost. However, in the 1850s, Aldie was mostly known for a wheat- and corn-grinding mill powered by water wheels. By then, central Virginia had moved away from growing tobacco to producing grain, which required less labor than other cash crops. President James Monroe, who lived at nearby Oak Hill plantation, was a regular customer at the Aldie mill, but a black mill and farm hand named Daniel Dangerfield left his mark on the region, too.

As a hired-out slave who earned wages for his owners, French and Elizabeth Simpson, Daniel Dangerfield was a fixture at the mill. An observer at his 1859 trial in Pennsylvania would describe him as "a sturdy, sensible seeming man." It's not known if anyone in Virginia ever saw him that way, other than, perhaps, his family. The Simpsons owned thirteen black people in 1855, including Daniel's parents Betty and Cornelius Dangerfield. But though it was possible to own a slave's body, no owner ever could be sure he controlled an enslaved person's mind or will.

Dangerfield decided to run away in 1853 or 1855, the year of French Simpson's death. An owner's death changed a slave's life, and not always for the better. Dangerfield already had survived typhoid fever and a blow or injury that left him with a noticeable scar on his cheek. In the early 1850s, he apparently decided it was time to take control of his life.

He made it as far as Pennsylvania, a favorite refuge for fugitive slaves and free blacks from Loudoun, in part because members of the Society of Friends or Quakers in Loudoun County, Virginia, and in Pennsylvania were part of the secret slave-aiding network known as the Underground Railroad. In Harrisburg, Pennsylvania, the runaway began a new life as Daniel Webster. It was an ironic name choice, since some abolitionists considered U.S. secretary of state Daniel Webster a traitor for pushing the compromise that created the Fugitive Slave Act of 1850.

In Harrisburg, Dangerfield worked as a laborer, married and fathered two children. Early in 1859, the family of Daniel's deceased owner heard that he was in Harrisburg. Slave catchers often patrolled the rail line and road that ran between Carlisle and Harrisburg, but Dangerfield had eluded them while running from Aldie. This time, he was not so lucky. When G. H. Gulick, son-in-law of sixty-year-old Elizabeth Simpson, showed up in the vicinity in February, he quickly spotted Dangerfield. Gulick didn't try to snatch the tall, sturdy runaway immediately. Instead he shared the news in a letter to his brother-in-law and attorney, Sanford Rogers, who lived on the Simpson farm.

In April, the two men, along with slave catcher John W. Patton, met in Harrisburg. As Dangerfield was loading coal onto a railroad car, Gulick approached him and noted the identifying scar on his cheek. Assisted by law enforcement officials, the two men seized him. To discourage anyone from helping Dangerfield, Gulick shouted that the former slave was a thief. On the witness stand, Gulick would later admit, "I said a great many things to the people to stop any excitement; I said he was a burglar—at least I intimated as much."

Dangerfield's capture not only put his freedom at risk. It came at the worst possible time. Both of his children had just died, the second one's death coming just a week before his arrest.

On April 5, 1859, the Philadelphia trial began that would make Dangerfield one of America's best-known fugitives. Though his trial had been moved from Harrisburg, where people knew him, his black and white supporters jammed the courtroom. Famed Quaker abolitionist Lucretia Mott sat next to him throughout the trial. Outside swarmed nearly one thousand people of color and four hundred policemen. Meanwhile, U.S. commissioner J. Cooke Longstreth presided over the case, which was his first.

In the beginning, the proceedings seemed pretty predictable.

For Dangerfield, they also seemed pretty damaging.

"I am from Loudoun County, Virginia," testified Dr. Francis E. Luckett. "I reside in this city. I am no relative of Mrs. Simpson, only an acquaintance; have no interest in this suit . . . I know the negro man Daniel Dangerfield. I first saw him in Mansfield, Loudoun County, Virginia. I went with his owner, French Simpson, to see him as a physician. He was sick with typhoid fever. I found him at the house of Mr. Mount, by whom he had been hired. I saw him afterwards; I have seen him as many as 15 or 20 times; I have no doubt as to the prisoner being Daniel Dangerfield."

John W. Patton, another white man from Loudoun, gave even more pointed testimony. "I knew French Simpson well," he told the court. "I knew his negro man Daniel Dangerfield and he knows me; he is in this room; I first saw him in 1842, he was then a farm hand; from 1842 to 1849 I was a hand at labor; I worked for French Simpson; I worked at Mr. Simpson's threshing machine; in 1850 another man and I bought his machine, and threshed wheat for him; I saw the man then; saw him pass back and forwards; I saw him in July 1854 for the last time; I know him to be the man who belonged to Simpson's (but) was known as Daniel Dangerfield then."

Two other white Loudoun County men also testified that they had known Dangerfield since childhood.

Meanwhile, defense attorneys did their best to whip up antislavery sentiments. They knew their courtroom audience included people who not only considered slavery unconstitutional and inhumane but felt that anyone who resisted it should be freed. The defense team even insisted that one of the men who had seized Dangerfield fit the description of the murderous Simon Legree, the main villain in Harriet Beecher Stowe's famed antislavery novel, *Uncle Tom's Cabin.*

Then came the shift.

The petitioners claimed Dangerfield had been absent from Virginia for about six years, which would mean he might have escaped as early as 1853. A black man named Jones, age sixty-five, said he had seen Daniel in Harrisburg in 1853. James H. Smith, another black witness, testified that he had seen Daniel in Baltimore as early as 1848, working as a drayman, and then in Philadelphia in 1849 or 1850. He also said he'd seen him in Harrisburg in 1853, raising the possibility that Daniel was not the man some Virginians had identified.

Determined to avoid trouble when the verdict was rendered, Marshal Yost had sworn in fifty special marshals, "most of whom were men of nerve and prepared for any emergency," the *Democratic Mirror* noted. The *Mirror* also claimed that hundreds of blacks massed around the courthouse on the first day of the trial but had been cleared from the streets. Meanwhile, Yost offered to put up fifty or even one hundred dollars toward the thirteen-hundred-dollar purchase price for Dangerfield.

Throughout the trial, Lucretia Mott—minister of the Society of Friends in Philadelphia, women's rights activist, foe of strong drink and slavery and friend to "the poor of every race or condition," as the *Christian Recorder* put it—sat next to Dangerfield. At one point, she threw her arms around his neck. Coming from any other white woman, this public gesture might have seemed startling. But Mott was a plainspoken woman who had close friends with enslaved relatives, who had preached in black churches and who practiced integration as well as talked about it. After embracing Dangerfield, she then declared that she would rather "give one hundred dollars to rescue him" than any amount of money for his purchase. "An officer removed Mrs. Mott from beside the negro," the *Mirror* noted, "but she went back and took her old seat which she maintained."

The trial lumbered on for three days, one session lasting fourteen hours. That was possibly the longest court session ever held in Philadelphia. In some revival prayer meetings, "the preservation of Daniel was prayed for," according to Scottish abolitionist Eliza Wigham. Finally, the verdict came in. Dangerfield would go free because of the doubts that surrounded his identity. Even before the trial began, the commissioner had indicated he considered the evidence shaky and forced Dangerfield's captors to revise their paperwork.

Charlotte Forten, a free black antislavery poet, educator and civil rights advocate, was in the courtroom on the day of the verdict. During the Civil War, Forten would move to South Carolina to help prepare slaves for the future by teaching them reading, spelling and history. She claimed that some people in Philadelphia tended to believe that the commissioner had freed Daniel under "the pressure of public sentiment—which was, strange to say, almost universally on the right side." She also mentioned that others believed that the commissioner's own family, "even his wife, it is said, declared that they could discard him," if he returned Dangerfield to slavery.

Did Longstreth really collapse under pressure or did he believe that witnesses—possibly on both sides—either failed to correctly remember events or lied? In the end, it hardly seemed to matter. The *National Era* applauded the verdict, claiming that "no man should be consigned to Slavery or to the gallows, where a rational doubt can exist in his favor."

Rejoicing at the verdict, black and white abolitionists carried Daniel "down Fifth Street," placed him in a carriage and drove off. Hundreds of black men were said to have pulled the carriage through the streets.

"Daniel was taken by some of the officers and put into a cab," according to the *Philadelphia Press*. "The horses were taken out, a rope was tied to the carriage, and a crowd of colored people took hold and paraded him around the streets. . . . The enthusiasm was kept up into a late hour . . . general joy was manifested among his friends at the unexpected result."

It was a radical reversal of what had happened in August 1834 when race riots racked Philadelphia. That melee began when white men and boys attacked a group of blacks. The next night the mob wrecked a black church and vandalized a row of black homes. On the third night blacks gathered in self-defense when the mob returned to tear down another church. In all, thirty-one homes and two churches were destroyed.

But two days after the Daniel Dangerfield verdict, the former slave's coming-out party began losing its sizzle and steam. When Philadelphians held a celebratory antislavery meeting, a crowd of southerners attended, complaining about the verdict. Law enforcement officers arrested many hecklers and restored order. Forten called it an evening "long to be remembered." But many people probably wanted to forget what happened the next day. Warrants were issued for Dangerfield's rearrest. Forten noted that "there can be no rest for his weary feet nearer than the free soil of Canada."

Virginians certainly were not pleased that, as the *Mirror* put it, "The testimony of four citizens of the Commonwealth of Virginia is rejected . . . whilst that of negroes is admitted and approved in a

Pennsylvania Court. . . . If there be no legal remedy there must be power somewhere to provide one."

Colonel Mosby—Virginia's daring Gray Ghost—would have approved of Dangerfield's response to worrisome threats and warrants. The former slave vanished, fleeing to Canada. He later sent word to his friends that he was safe thanks to people willing to go to any lengths to give someone once considered property the right to be considered a man.

Fig. 14. Sondra Mose-Ursery contemplates a cornfield marking the possible site of a long-vanished runaway slave community near Vandalia, Michigan. (Photo by Larry O. Simmons)

———◆———

TWELVE

FAKE LAWYERS AND PHONY WASHING MACHINES

For the whole Law is fulfilled in one word: Thou shalt love thy
neighbor as thyself.

—Galatians 5:14, *The Holy Bible*

It seemed too late for love and almost too late for the law. The spy
had done his job so well it looked too late for anything except black
men and women trying to fight off their former masters with three-
legged stools. Runaway slave Perry Sanford managed to crawl onto a
roof and escape the raiders who were prepared to shoot their way
through three states to capture runaways from Kentucky. But a black
woman hiding in a cornfield surrendered so she could soothe the crying child she'd left behind.

This all happened not far from a southwestern Michigan village
now called Cassopolis, a place that had a jail before it had a court-

house and was known mostly for distilling whiskey and packaging pork. In the summer of 1847, the two sides in the war between slavery and freedom came together at the courthouse in Cassopolis and seemed ready to wrestle each other to the ground.

On one side stood several hundred free blacks, runaway slaves, humanitarian whites and members of the Society of Friends, a religious group known as Quakers who believed that God spoke directly to men's souls and guided them with an inner light. Most people in the freedom-supporting crowd carried clubs and farming tools. A few also came armed with the knowledge of a legal maneuver they hoped might be crafty enough to free the slaves who had just been captured.

On the other side stood a posse of slave raiders from Kentucky who had ridden into southwestern Michigan with the story that they were selling a new kind of washing machine. Armed with a map produced by one of their spies, which pinpointed the hiding places of runaway Kentucky slaves, they had managed to recapture nine or ten Kentucky fugitives. They carried carbines, pistols, pointed knives known as dirks and equally pointed bursts of anger.

The Quakers loved peace, hated war and had evolved into antislavery advocates. All the same, it might not have taken all that much to start a brawl between some not-so-peaceful members of the antislavery crowd and the slave raiders from Kentucky on an August day in Cass County, Michigan. Not when four former slaves were hatching a plan to ambush and shoot the invading slave catchers. Not when a Baptist minister and slave catcher from Kentucky had snatched a free-born baby and tried to claim it as a slave. Not when another slave raid in the area soon would break the heart of fugitive slave David Powell by seizing his wife, Lucy; and not when a fugitive named Aaron Roy would disappear completely from Cass County, leaving behind a note to his wife saying he expected to be killed.

BLACK PARADISE

But this story starts long before that summer day when it seemed that one more drawn gun, one more threat or one more skirmish might turn the standoff between rural Michigan slavery foes and Kentucky slave owners into a bloodbath. It starts with a unique experiment in racial harmony in Cass County, Michigan, in the vicinity of Cassopolis and nearby Vandalia, just across the state line from Indiana and about midway between Detroit and Chicago. Southwestern Michigan was an area that began accepting—and befriending—runaway slaves before Michigan became a state in 1837. One nineteenth-century editorial writer went so far as to call the village of Calvin in Cass County an "Ethiopians' Eden," or Negro paradise.

"Cassopolis (the seat of Cass County) was, in 1847, a community of white and black people, free born and escaped slaves, that was as integrated as the times allowed and somewhat more," agrees David Chardavoyne, who has written about the legal implications of the Kentucky raids.

That didn't mean the free state of Michigan as a whole was some paradise of pleasure filled, perhaps, with the famed West African "miracle fruit," which makes everything eaten immediately after it taste sweet. In most of the state, black settlers couldn't vote, were forbidden to have white spouses and, in some places, were forbidden by local customs from living in certain areas, eating in certain places, working on particular jobs or attending particular schools. However, in Cass County's Porter and Calvin townships, blacks could own land, demand a trial by jury, testify against white offenders, sue or be sued, exercise their right to an attorney, make bail, make use of the writ of habeas corpus and, in 1855, participate in school elections. Some blacks in those two communities, primarily mulattoes, could participate in presidential elections as well, a right that minorities in most of the country didn't have until after the Civil War.

"The Yahoos who think that colored people cannot manage affairs for themselves should pay this village a visit," urged an 1880 newspaper editorial about the Cass County village of Calvin.

But no Eden can survive if its enemies can stomp on its shrubbery, chop down its customs and scoop up its forbidden fruit. Black settlers tried to disappear inside their cabins and fields, hoping the outside world wouldn't catch the scent of freedom hovering over Cass County.

There is even some evidence that federal census marshals in 1840 and 1850 deliberately undercounted the black population to hide the size of local black communities. Even so, the census showed nearly four hundred blacks in the county by 1840, more than Chicago's black population at the time. Meanwhile, the area's policies drew more and more antislavery settlers, including Quakers, free blacks and runaway slaves.

By the late 1820s more than one hundred Quaker families had settled in Cass County on land that would eventually become Penn, Jefferson, Porter and Calvin townships. Some came from northern and central Indiana, others from Virginia and North Carolina. They were the kind of people who had left the South to avoid living in slave states and who refused to use such slave-produced goods as cotton, writing paper with rag content, molasses and sugar. All belonged to the Society of Friends, or Quakers, who called each other "thee," speaking as they believed Jesus spoke to his Apostles. Cass County Quakers who believed in actively fighting slavery considered good works one of the most telling signs of increased holiness; their good work was running the Underground Railroad's Quaker Line in Indiana and Michigan, every settlement on that line a station where runaways could rest, sleep or eat. But the thrifty, businesslike Cass County Quakers didn't help runaways only because they considered slavery this country's original sin.

According to some contemporary researchers, Quaker men would scour the Ohio River area during planting time, searching for potential runaways. The men then would make a deal with freedom-hungry slaves: Come to Michigan, work my land for five to ten years as an indentured servant and then become a landowner yourself. Some of the slaves who took the deal settled in parts of Vandalia and Cassopolis in Cass County. Each former slave received five acres of land, a cabin and the right to grow his own crops. The owners of escaped slaves or their owners would come through the county in search of their property, sometimes finding them and sometimes not. Eventually, some escaped slaves who stayed in the area began living in one of the small log-cabin settlements collectively known as Ramptown. The settlement was named for the wild, garlicky greens or ramps that sprouted in the woods in the spring and were considered cold remedies and tonics as well as food.

Blacks, though, had roots in the area that ran much deeper than the roots nourishing its wild ramps or leeks. Henry Way, a Quaker minister, brought the first fugitive slaves into the area in 1836. In the 1840s, the first group of free blacks migrated to Michigan from the Carolinas by way of Logan County, Ohio. They had been forced out by the severe punishments—including public whippings of slaves found on roads without permits—enacted following Nat Turner's bloody rebellion just across the state line in Southampton County, Virginia. The free blacks who left North Carolina were property owners and farmers, blacksmiths and coopers, people who had been free for over a century. In 1849, slaves freed by a wealthy Virginia planter named Sampson Saunders also established a colony in the fertile lands of southwestern Michigan. Besides freeing his slaves, Saunders left fifteen thousand dollars to establish the settlement; one hundred freed slaves settled in Cass County's Calvin township with money from Saunders's estate. Some of the money freed black settlers' wives, daughters and mothers as well.

Yet there was no way an "Ethiopians' Eden"—or several side-by-side Edens, in fact—could remain a secret from increasingly angry slave owners in Kentucky. As more and more Kentucky slaves crossed the Ohio River and wound up making new homes in Cass County and the surrounding area, the Kentuckians began plotting their revenge. By 1846, there were at least one hundred runaways in the county, mostly in Penn and Calvin townships. The Kentucky slave owners, in the words of one nineteenth-century newspaper, decided it was time they "scented out" the hiding places of some of their runaways.

THE SPY

When the Kentuckians declared war on southwestern Michigan's slave havens, they didn't immediately grab their guns and gallop north. They first sent a spy to Kalamazoo, Michigan, just northeast of Cass

County. In January 1847, a young man calling himself Carpenter showed up in Kalamazoo, Michigan, at the law offices of Charles E. Stuart, who would be elected to the U.S. House of Representatives later that year. Carpenter claimed he was a law student from Worcester County, Massachusetts, the home of many of the country's leading abolitionists, and that he strongly opposed slavery. After spending a short time allegedly studying law in Stuart's office, he learned the locations of the area's fugitive slave settlements. He then rode out to visit Cass County and neighboring Calhoun County. This time he claimed to represent an antislavery newspaper in the east, a story that got him into the homes of blacks, Quakers and other friends of the fugitives. He was able to collect firsthand information about the location of the runaways and the parts of Kentucky from which they had fled. He also may have passed on the news that fugitives were living with Cass County abolitionists and working their land, but it's possible he neglected to mention how close the bonds actually were between the fugitives and their hosts. He also may not have known—or thought to mention—that the antislavery Quakers and other white and black abolitionists in Cass County would fight in court or elsewhere for their friends and neighbors who had escaped from slavery.

After the spy who called himself Carpenter turned over his information to slave hunters in Kentucky, the Kentuckians struck back. They first showed up in January 1847 to capture the Adam and Sarah Crosswhite family in Calhoun County's Marshall, Michigan, just east of Kalamazoo. According to Sarah Crosswhite's later testimony, the slave-hunting party told the couple they'd leave them alone if the Crosswhites handed over their children. Did they really expect Adam and Sarah to trade their children's freedom for their own? If so, Sarah Crosswhite quickly made it clear that she had already given the best years of her life to slave masters and didn't intend to give up anything more. A signal shot fired at the Crosswhite house brought help, two hundred of the family's neighbors rushing to their aid. After Crosswhite charged the raiders with assault, battery and housebreaking, the raiders were arrested and the Crosswhites escaped to Canada.

But in August 1847, another Kentucky raiding party showed up in southwestern Michigan with a detailed map of the countryside prepared by the phony law student who had scouted the area. They were on the trail of a group of slaves who had run away in April from the same small, troubled patch of land in Kenton and nearby Boone County, Kentucky, fearing they were about to be sold to Deep South cotton planters. Perry Sanford, whose last master was Milton White Graves, claimed his master's son had told him he had been sold to Mississippians. After Sanford passed on that news to other slaves, they all decided to run, he said.

"One of our numbers got a pass, went to Covington [Kentucky] and made arrangements with a white man to take us over the river," Sanford told a reporter for Battle Creek's *Sunday Morning Call* in 1884. "We left on the night of Easter Monday. This was a holiday. On all holidays the slaves could either have their own time to do as they pleased or work."

The group left at about 10:00 P.M. but didn't arrive in Covington— some twelve miles away—until 4:00 A.M. the next day. They traveled across fields in order to avoid toll gates and groups of travelers, according to Sanford. The man who was supposed to wait for them in Covington gave up and went home. They started down the bank of the Ohio River and, luckily, found a boat.

THE WASHING MACHINE SCAM

Over the course of a month, escapees from Kenton and neighboring Boone County made their way to Michigan, many settling at Young's Prairie in Cass County's Calvin Township or in neighboring Calhoun County. They enjoyed several months of peace. Then, in August, a Kentucky raiding party showed up, claiming to represent a company selling a new kind of washing machine. Before the invention of electric washers and dryers, washing clothes meant making soap from ashes and fat, hauling and heating large buckets of water, cooking starch, scrubbing clothes on washboards, hauling and heating more

water for rinsing. Clothes then had to be dried and ironed. It was work
so time-consuming and tiresome that many women earned a living by
washing other people's laundry. In the mid-1800s several patents were
issued for washing machines in which the clothes were put in wooden
drums and rotated with hand-turned cranks. Presumably, these were
the kind of machines the raiders claimed to be selling. It's not known
if there was a demand for or even knowledge of such devices in rural
southwestern Michigan in 1847. If nothing else, though, the story gave
the raiders an excuse to knock on doors, step inside homes and pretend to sell their own low-rent version of paradise—a break from some
of the drudgery of washdays.

The slave-catching Kentucky posse's first stop was Battle Creek,
Michigan, which they expected to make their headquarters. Battle
Creek sits on the junction of two routes of the Underground Railroad
that came out of Indiana, running through Battle Creek eastward to
Detroit or northeast through Lansing and Flint to Port Huron, where
fugitives could cross the St. Clair River to Canada. There, the Kentucky raiders planned to divide into two groups, fan out and strike the
farms of Quakers who were conductors on the secret slave-aiding network known as the Underground Railroad. The plan seemed perfect
for rounding up escaped slaves, but it had some rather serious flaws.
The raiders had chosen the wrong city at the wrong time and then
managed to run into the wrong people.

Battle Creek was named for the site where, in 1824, two Indians
and two members of a surveying party fought it out on the banks of a
river. By 1849, it had a population of 993, many of them fighters, too.
Even before ex-slave and social reformer Sojourner Truth arrived there
in 1857, the town was hip-deep in the antislavery movement. It was
the home of men like Erastus Hussey, a newspaper editor, mayor, state
representative, state senator, Underground Railroad conductor, Quaker
and one of the founders of the Republican Party. Hussey, a man one
newspaper called "the first advocate of anti-slavery in Battle Creek,"
claimed he had fed and aided more than one thousand runaway slaves.
In fact, one observer described Battle Creek as a place where escaped

slaves "could have been escorted through the town to the accompaniment of a brass band and a hallelujah chorus without fear of arrest."

THE KENTUCKY RAID

But after the Adam and Sarah Crosswhite incident in nearby Marshall, Michigan, antislavery forces in Battle Creek were on their guard. So when a band of Kentucky raiders showed up in August 1847, residents immediately sensed trouble. It's not clear how many raiders there were. The number has been estimated at as low as thirteen and as high as sixty. However there were enough to stir up suspicion among the antislavery folks in Battle Creek. After spotting the Kentuckians drinking in a tavern, Hussey and the others accused them of slave hunting, told them there was no way they'd surrender any fugitives and warned them to leave Michigan.

The raiders left Battle Creek, but they didn't go far. They retreated across the border into Bristol, Indiana, just south of Cass County. Erastus Hussey quickly sent letters to Stephen Bogue and Zachariah Shugart, two white farmers who were part of Cass County's Underground Railroad. But Hussey's letters didn't reach them in time. On the evening of August 16, Sheriff John Leathers Graves led his heavily armed men into Cass County. They brought two-horse wagons with them for transporting women and children. They left their wagons about two miles down the road from where they stopped. They waited until dark about two miles south of Shavehead Lake, near the southeastern corner of Calvin Township, a place where freedmen and slaves had tilled the loamy soil before the Civil War.

Graves sent two groups to strike simultaneously at the farms of several Quakers and Underground Railroad conductors. They were then supposed to join a third group in attacking the farm of a third Quaker, Tennessee-born Josiah Osborn, son of a man who had publicly advocated immediate emancipation of the slaves and who had brought his family to Cass County when Calvin Township was almost unbroken wilderness with no schools in the neighborhood. After raiding the Osborn farm, the raiders planned to march the runaway slaves they captured to Odell's Mill, south of Vandalia, in Penn Township, and ride through Indiana to Kentucky.

As the Kentuckians descended on the farms of Stephen Bogue, Zachariah Shugart and Josiah Osborn, their plan seemed to be working: Five fugitives were staying and working at the Josiah Osborn farm. They included an old man, his wife, two sons and a daughter. The three males in this group, the first runaways captured by the raiders, were handcuffed in bed. The mother and daughter jumped from a window and hid. The manacled men marched out to the road. Osborn sent out messengers and a large group gathered at his house, including free blacks. The raiders at the Osborn farm moved northward with their captives, followed by a crowd of men and boys. A slave woman who had escaped the raiders at Shugart's farm aroused the family and then hid. At the Bogue farm, the raiders battered down the door of the cabin shielding a fugitive, overpowered the black man inside, knocking him down with a heavy riding whip. Shugart and Bogue both sent word to their neighbors that the fugitives among them were in danger. Bogue allegedly rode bareback to the county seat at Cassopolis.

Perry Sanford claimed some forty slave dealers swooped down on the fugitives, arriving with heavy tobacco wagons curved up at both ends like sleigh runners and hauled by six horses. The raiders planned to carry off the fugitives in these wagons, according to Sanford. Sanford and some other fugitives were asleep when they heard a knock on the door. It was Sheriff Graves, the brother of Sanford's master, Milton Graves, ordering Sanford to open the door. The slavers smashed in windows. Some slaves were captured, but Rube Stevens escaped. While Stephen Bogue rode off to Cassopolis, Bogue's wife hid Perry Sanford in their house's upstairs. Sanford pushed aside the wooden shingles or shakes on the roof, crawled onto the roof and then jumped to the ground. Three raiders struggled with fugitive slave William Casey, who had armed himself with a three-legged stool. Mrs. William Casey overpowered her young master. When Rube Stevens escaped, he headed for the home of William Holman Jones, another antislavery fighter. Jones headed off the raiding party, talking to them until forty men arrived from Cassopolis with Bogue.

Meanwhile, the other group of slave hunters had captured slaves in Penn Township and at the settlement in Calvin Township where William East and his sons, also Quakers, lived. The raiders captured three men, a woman and a child. One of the Kentuckians, the Reverend A. Stevens, a Baptist minister, claimed a two-year-old child found lying on a bed as his property, despite its birth on free soil. The mother had escaped, but Stevens grabbed the baby and made it cry as he started down the road. When the mother heard her baby's wails, she emerged from hiding and was captured, too.

News about the raids spread rapidly: Eden had been invaded, but there was still time, some residents decided, to rout the Kentuckians and reclaim their haven. The Kentucky raiders may not have been aware of the strong bonds that existed between blacks and whites who had lived together, worked together and planned futures together in Cass and nearby counties. They would soon experience the power of neighborly love. One group of white and black residents found the raiders' wagon and sank it in Birch Lake, while another group surprised and captured one of the raiding parties. Meanwhile, a party led by abolitionists Moses Brown and William Jones captured the group led by the Reverend Stevens, who was forced to surrender his horse to a black mother and carry the child he'd insisted he owned. As the rest of the raiders converged on Odell's Mill, just south of Vandalia, at dawn, they found themselves surrounded by between two hundred and three hundred armed residents, black and white, who had been alerted by Stephen Bogue. The Kentuckians carried pistols and bowie knives, and nearly every man among the abolitionists and free blacks wielded heavy hickory clubs, scythes and other farm implements.

The two opposing groups—slave traders and abolitionists—traded threats. In the August heat, resentments grew and tempers flamed.

THE TRICK

Trying to head off possible violence, the Quakers convinced the Kentuckians to go to Cassopolis, the county seat, surrender themselves and their captives to the court and wait for a legal decision. As the two groups journeyed to Cassopolis, William Jones, a white Kentucky-born abolitionist known as "Nigger Bill," walked beside Jonathan Hughbanks, one of the captives. He slipped his hands inside Hughbanks's chains so they could walk arm in arm. In 1848, Jones reportedly freed a young slave woman with an infant who had been captured on his land by a slave catcher. Later that week, he escorted that young woman and her child into Canada. On the trip to Cassopolis with the raiders, he is said to have smoothly disarmed a man who drew a pistol. He also forced Hubbard Buckner, one of the Kentuckians, to dismount so that one of the ill blacks taken at Osborn's place could ride. The Reverend Stevens was not only made to carry the baby he had captured; he was ridiculed as a child stealer.

Meanwhile, two abolitionist lawyers, E. S. Smith and James Sullivan, received a telegram alerting them about the raid and the planned hearing. In the absence of A. H. Redfield, Cass County's circuit court commissioner, the Berrien county commissioner—a New Englander named Ebenezer McIlvaine—was brought into the case. Unknown to the Kentucky raiders, McIlvaine was an agent for the Underground Railroad. An attorney named James Brown from Niles, Michigan, in Berrien County, was asked to assist Sullivan and Smith.

At about 9:00 A.M. on August 17, the motley procession of raiders, captives and Cass County residents straggled into Cassopolis, the county seat. It was no death march, but it was far from a joyous high-stepping parade. It included the Kentuckians, the shackled captives and at least three-hundred citizens, the crowd growing as other people met them on the road and joined them. In Cassopolis, more people crowded the public square, the majority of them supporting the fugitive slaves. The slaves were housed in Joshua Barnum's tavern and a guard stationed at the door. The raiders were served with a writ of habeas corpus and indicted for kidnapping, assault and battery.

According to Debian Marty, great-great-great-granddaughter of Ishmael and Mariam Lee—one of the Quaker families that fought the raiders—the Quakers both used the law and undermined it. They used the law to have the Kentuckians charged with attempted kidnapping and assault and battery. They also took advantage of the area's more liberal laws to have black people testify against whites. This allowed local authorities to remove the captives from the Kentuckians' custody. The Quakers also encouraged one of the captives, William Merriman, to file charges against the Kentuckians and one of the local black Underground Railroad participants, Henry Shepard, to do so as well. The Quakers also played a key role in helping captives and their families and friends escape.

"The interracial alliance that made community resistance possible during the Kentucky Raid . . . shows us not only what is possible, but what is required in response to injustice," says Marty.

On August 20 at the Cassopolis courthouse, local attorney George B. Turner, who had just been admitted to the bar in the previous year, argued that the raiders had acted lawfully and that local officials had a duty to help rather than hinder them. He was correct, but McIlvaine ruled against the raiders on a technicality. The raiders had failed, the commissioner noted, to present a certified copy of the Kentucky law on slavery. McIlvaine ordered the release of the fugitives.

"This decision, to the honor of the large assembly convened, was received with almost universal applause," one newspaper noted.

In the meantime, Zachariah Shugart ushered the captured runaway slaves and others—a group that would include as many as fifty people—on a journey that would end in Essex County in Ontario, Canada. But the raiders still hoped to be compensated for their lost slaves. A runaway slave one of them had claimed was serving a sentence in the county jail, unable to pay the fine for a petty crime of which he had been convicted. The Kentuckians believed they would be able to get him, but when they looked for him in the jail he was gone, someone having paid his fine. As they journeyed back to Kentucky, the raiders could have been shot by four armed blacks waiting in a cornfield for them to pass. Fortunately for them, Josiah Osborn had spotted the men a half hour earlier and persuaded them not to shoot.

Sheriff Graves and his men returned empty-handed to Kentucky, where newspapers cried foul and railed against "the Cassopolis outrage." Yet the raiders had not abandoned their plan to plunder paradise. In January 1849, nine white defendants from Cass County were sued for the value of the escaped fugitives and brought to trial. On December 18, 1850, the first trial of *Timberlake v. Osborn* began in Detroit. Slave owner and raider Thornton Timberlake sued Josiah Osborn and his sons, Jefferson and Ellison Osborn; David Thompson Nicholson, William Holman Jones, Ishmael Lee, Stephen Bogue, Zachariah Shugart and the Honorable Ebenezer McIlvaine.

The *Michigan Liberty Press* of Battle Creek was not pleased.

"Why not pass laws at once that shall give our neighbor states to understand that Michigan knows how to protect her citizens and that she will do so," the newspaper wrote.

THE PEOPLE WHO PAID FOR THE RAID

The defendants who risked losing their property and possibly their freedom for opposing the Kentuckians were not cookie-cutter abolitionists all shaped in the same mold. No one description could define them all except this: They all apparently believed that helping slaves escape and prosper represented what was often called "practical abolitionism." Quaker Stephen Bogue had moved to Cass County from Ohio, built one of the county's first gristmills and laid out the sites for the town of Vandalia. Nicholson was a Kentucky-born, Ohio-raised Baptist and a local organizer for the antislavery Liberty Party. Ishmael Lee, a Quaker, was married to Ruth Nicholson's niece. William Holman Jones had no known religious affiliations and was an orphan who had married an orphan. Zachariah Shugart, another Quaker, was one of the organizers of the Anti-Slavery Friends. Ebenezer McIlvaine, the judge who had presided over the case against the raiders, came from Vermont and had attended a university. At least three defendants were relatives of Charles Osborn, a pioneering Quaker who had lectured, preached and written about slavery. Josiah Osborn was Charles Osborn's son and Jefferson and Ellison were his grandchildren. Charles Osborn had been born in North Carolina and by 1814 he was in Tennessee, preaching about the need for immediately and unconditionally freeing the slaves. By 1816, he had been so persecuted for his views that he moved from Tennessee to Ohio and established a paper called the *Philanthropist,* which advocated emancipation. He then moved from Ohio to Indiana and finally, in 1842, to Michigan, where his boldness inspired his entire family.

It is estimated that there were one hundred runaway slaves in Cass County in 1846, the year before the raid. They, too, were distinct people, not just descriptions on wanted posters or dark faces passing through southwestern Michigan's cornfields on their way to somewhere else. It's not known whether people in Cass or Calhoun counties respectfully referred to their black neighbors by their last names, as did abolitionist John Brown. However, Jefferson Osborn, the grandson of Charles, of Cass County, was sharply criticized for allowing black people to vote in a local township election. Fortunately, that didn't stop the farmer and horticulturist from being elected county treasurer, county supervisor, township treasurer and justice of the peace. Shugart kept an account book in which he listed the shoes, fabrics and other goods that he provided to fugitives in exchange for scrubbing floors, laundering clothes and other chores. A number of black laborers were said to have boarded with Stephen Bogue as well. In fact, court documents claimed that Bogue, Josiah Osborn and others harbored runaways for months and even years.

Jacob Merritt Howard, an abolitionist and former member of Congress who would help found the Republican Party, represented the defendants at their trial. Timberlake asked for three thousand dollars for the loss of five slaves, Jonathon, Nancy, Mary, Robert and Gabriel. Jonathon was described as about forty-five, "inclined to be polite or plausible," Nancy was about thirty-five and reportedly "hysterical," and Mary was said to be "very black" and "sway backed." Robert was described as "sprightly" and Gabriel was said to be nineteen.

After the first trial ended in a hung jury, two defendants paid about thirteen hundred dollars in damages and court costs and settled the case. They had racked up heavy attorney fees during the first trial and faced similar fees during the second as well as the possibility of a judge's ruling against them. Faced with the prospect of a second trial and the possibility of being prosecuted under the newly passed Fugitive Slave Act of 1850, Thompson Nicholson decided to settle the lawsuit on his own. He then persuaded his relative Ishmael Lee to join him. When the other defendants became outraged, Nicholson published a letter to the editor of a local newspaper.

"Mr. Editor," he wrote, "I have been much abused and grossly misrepresented, because I thought it my interest to settle . . . I felt on the subject of Slavery as a majority of my fellow citizens felt, [and] made profession of deep hatred to Slavery—a hatred that has strangely and wonderfully died in these latter days."

Was this true? Or was Nicholson now trying to peddle his own brand of new and improved washing machines and avoid the most severe consequences of violating the Fugitive Slave Act? Not only did he renounce his former antislavery position, he criticized the other men for leaving him to face legal and financial burdens alone. He even praised the prosecuting attorney, saying Abner Pratt of Marshall, Michigan, had treated him better than some of the codefendants. However, history records that the defendants did reconcile and share the financial costs of the settlement.

Over the years, all of the Cass County defendants would pay a steep price for resisting the raids and spiriting away the Kentucky slaves. The heavy fines slapped on the Quakers in Cass County changed the lives of everyone involved. In June 1851, the Quakers involved in the Cass County case addressed an open letter to the community asking for donations. Some, like the Lees, lost their homes. Others, like the Osborns, spent years paying off the debt. It took Josiah Osborn ten years to meet his financial obligations. Ishmael Lee, William Jones and Thompson Nicholson sold their farms and moved west. Shortly before his death in 1860, Nicholson was working for the Republican Party in Illinois, suggesting he had not abandoned his antislavery principles after all. Osborn and Bogue helped maintain the antislavery refuge in Cass County. Ishmael Lee and William Holman Jones became active in the Underground Railroad in their new homes in Iowa and Kansas, respectively.

LUCY POWELL

Unfortunately, the August 1847 incident was not the last Kentucky raid. Once Eden had been uncovered and invaded, it was, perhaps, inevitable that other aggrieved slaveholders would attack it, too. David and Lucy Powell and their four sons had escaped from Boone County, Kentucky, into Indiana on October 9, 1847, and made their way to Cass County. Their owner, John Norris, discovered their whereabouts in 1849 and led a group to Michigan to capture them. On the morning of September 27, 1849, he found their home, held them at gunpoint, bound and gagged Lucy and three sons and placed them in a covered wagon. Her husband and one of the boys were away. An armed guard remained at the Powell home to keep the three other black men in their house from spreading warnings that evening. There is no record of David Powell's reaction when he discovered his wife and sons had been taken, but it is not difficult to imagine his anguish and anger.

Norris got as far as South Bend, Indiana, without attracting attention. However, Wright Maudlin, a white friend of the Powells, followed him. Joined by black and white friends of the Powells and the deputy sheriff, Maudlin pursued Norris to the outskirts of South Bend, Indiana. There the Norris group stopped to feed their horses. A rescue party gathered around the wagon as the deputy sheriff served a writ of habeas corpus for the captives. The Powells were jailed for their own safety until the trial. Norris never again had custody of them. After Judge Egbert ruled that Norris had failed to get the proper warrants, the Powells were released, returned to Cass County and then moved to Canada. After appealing the decision in Indiana federal courts, Norris eventually collected over five thousand dollars for one woman, one young man and two teenaged boys rescued from slavery by the combined interracial efforts of citizens of Cass County, Michigan, and South Bend, Indiana.

AARON ROY

However, it's not known what became of Aaron Roy, a captured fugitive from Cass County whose letter to his wife appeared in the *Lansing Republican* in 1857. The letter said he had been robbed, carried off to some unknown destination and locked inside a house but expected to be moved soon. While still in the house, he wrote a note to his wife, Mary Roy, of Newburg Township in Cass County. He dropped the note when his kidnappers moved him, urging whoever found it to forward it to his wife. Mary Roy received the letter but never saw her husband again. He was aware of his fate. "I have no doubt they will take my life soon," he wrote.

The various Kentucky raids and the lawsuits they spawned had many consequences. Some people believed these instances of slave resistance helped spur passage of a stricter Fugitive Slave Act of 1850. The persistence of Cass County's abolitionists certainly prodded Michigan to pass a Personal Liberty Law in 1855, which entitled accused escaped slaves in Michigan to the benefits of trial by jury, the right to appeal through county courts, the writ of habeas corpus and punishment for those who falsely accused someone of being a fugitive slave. Since this law contradicted the federal Fugitive Slave Act, strife over slavery continued.

Yet Cass County, with its 250 lakes and ponds, remained a haven, a destination point for liberty-loving blacks. Henry Wilson and his family arrived in the county in the late 1840s or early 1850s. The Wilsons sold pillows and mattresses stuffed with feathers and goose down from Canada geese. Ohio-born Zebedee Beverly, whose parents brought him to Cass County's La Grange Township in 1860, later attended a state agricultural college, taught school, ran a barber shop and was elected register of deeds for the country in 1892. George Peters, another pioneering black Cass County resident, extracted semen from the champion work horses he had purchased in Indiana. He sold both the semen and his skills in artificial insemination to those of his neighbors who wished to breed their work horses with his.

"Here is the richest and largest body of independent colored farmers I ever saw," declared a letter from William J. Anderson in an 1865 edition of the *Christian Recorder.*

Perhaps more important, memories of the struggles of the county's early black settlers continued to haunt it. A Harvard folklorist who in the early 1950s collected folktales from Cass County's Calvin Township—once a prime spot in the Ethiopians' Eden—heard stories about an old settler who bought the slave girl he loved and moved north. He also heard tales about an old pioneer who claimed he'd shot his master, crossed the Ohio River and received the applause of farmers on the other side for his act.

THE FORGOTTEN EDEN

The memory that seemed destined to slip away, though, was the story of a settlement once known as Ramptown, one hundred or so cabins housing runaway slaves and their families on the farm of a Cass County Quaker named James Bonine and elsewhere. It was named for the wild vegetables known as ramps—relatives of onions and garlic—that grew there. The long-legged garlicky ramps with their small white bulbs and green shoots grew only from April to May. They sustained settlers as food and medicine until other crops flourished. Ramptown was one of several areas in Penn and possibly Calvin townships where black freedmen and former slaves could build log cabins and grow crops on other men's land until they'd saved enough money to buy their own.

Today, the rural enclave, located near Vandalia, Michigan, which is believed to have housed hundreds of escaped slaves, is mostly cornfields. With just a little imagination, though, it is possible to stand amidst the corn and conjure up the strong, lingering smell of vitamin-

Fig. 15. Map of Michigans. (Drawing by Betty DeRamus)

rich ramps. *The Joy of Cooking,* a classic cookbook, does not recommend eating wild ramps, though its authors acknowledge that they "frequently see them praised by others." But they were, no doubt, a godsend to the intent, purpose-driven black families who picked them and stewed them. Yet by the twentieth century, the area had become folklore, a collection of half-buried legends, though there were always people such as Sondra Mose-Ursery, former mayor of Vandalia, who grew up believing in the place and its people.

Mose-Ursery was in high school when she first heard stories about Melissa Gibson Brown, one of the last people thought to have been born in Rampton. Eventually, she found Melissa Brown's death records, and found someone related to Brown who was still alive. Melissa Brown was born in 1858 to Hugh M. Gibson from North Carolina and Matilda Porter from Illinois. The eventual wife of Robert Brown, Melissa lived to be eighty-one years old, dying on September 20, 1939, in Calvin Center. In death, the evangelist, who preached in Cass and Berrien counties, became the symbol of a period with many important lessons for future generations about the power of solidarity and passion. For years, Mose-Ursery pushed for in-depth research on Rampton and the people who lived and died in its cabins. She finally succeeded.

In 2001, the Michigan Historical Center and the Vandalia Underground Railroad Foundation asked Dr. Michael Nassaney, Western Michigan University professor of anthropology, to locate its site to help highlight the Underground Railroad's role in Michigan history. In the spring of 2002, the project team surveyed seven hundred acres in southwestern Michigan and found fragments of a Mason jar, dishware, glass, a smoking pipe, ceramics, freshwater clam shells, nails, the bottom of an amethyst bottle, a button, animal bones, nails, pig mandibles, bricks and other items and concluded: "It is likely that individuals affiliated with Ramptown once occupied these sites." Their findings suggested that Ramptown would have included cabins and residences spread out over a wide area. The black families who established cabins on plots of land in Ramptown likely stayed from five to ten years, some moving eventually to Battle Creek, Michigan, or Canada. Many families got help from Connecticut-born George Redfield, who owned thousands of acres in various townships in southwestern Michigan and served as a senator. When blacks settled in Calvin Township, Redfield sold much of his land to them, in most cases allowing them to pay in installments.

"No poor man, either white or black, came to him for assistance and went away empty-handed," notes an 1893 collection of Cass and

Berrien county biographers. "For years a favorite quotation among the poor when they had no money to buy and went to him for their supply was, 'Going to Egypt for corn,' and they always got it."

The Kentucky raid of August 1847 has not been forgotten, either, nor has the strange but effective blend of duplicity and idealism, trickery and truth, that shaped its outcome. A bronze plaque detailing events related to the Kentucky raid has been permanently installed on the south side of the current courthouse in Cassopolis. It is close to the now-demolished original courthouse where the raiders and their captives appeared in 1847. The installation of the plaque in 2005 was part of the State Bar of Michigan's Michigan Legal Milestone Program, which recognizes significant legal cases in the state's history. The event was a creative solution to a dilemma faced by ordinary northern citizens who opposed slavery but wanted to honor the Constitution as well. Forced to choose between their consciences and the law, the people in Cassopolis and other nearby places risked everything to relieve their consciences, rescue their neighbors and obey at least the letter of the law. Back then, some people considered that enough to make the region an Eden, especially for blacks.

———◆◆◆———

THIRTEEN

HORSE HAIR
CAN BE HANDY

Daniel Hughes, who stood six feet eight inches tall and weighed around three hundred pounds, probably could have spooked or scared off most slave catchers with his size. But he didn't depend on his stature to prevail over the bounty hunters who showed up on his property near Williamsport, Pennsylvania, searching for hidden runaways. "I refer to him as a gentle giant," says his great-granddaughter, Mamie Sweeting Diggs.

Believed to be part Mohawk Indian and part African American, the river raftsman had an army of his own, sixteen children and a free black wife named Ann Rotch: All hid and transported runaway slaves. One of their favorite tricks involved horse hair, according to Diggs.

Horse hair? Why not? Hair from the manes or tails of horses has been used in everything from brushes and violin bows to padding for sofas and chairs, watchbands, wigs and rifle sighting. An amino acid found in horse hair also shows up in some nutritional supplements.

Fig. 16. Nothing could stop restless, determined and cunning slaves from crossing rivers, mountains and plains in search of freedom. (Photo by Timothy L. Hughes)

Daniel Hughes and his wife and children used it to help fleeing slaves gain their freedom.

The Hughes family sometimes stretched the coarse, long hair from one side of trails to the other in the woods behind their home in Lycoming County, Pennsylvania, hoping to unseat, disable or discourage horse-riding slave catchers. It's likely they succeeded, creating scenes of confusion and panic as men tumbled from their saddles. The family also hid slaves in the woods in "brush houses," quickly put-together temporary shelters made from simple wooden frames covered with branches, grass and leaves.

One of Daniel's sons, Robert, reminisced about carrying meals when he was a youngster to fugitives camped in bush houses. The Hughes family is believed to have hidden runaways in the limestone caves in back of their place as well. Hughes's land was just north of

Williamsport in an area once known as Nigger Hollow and later renamed Freedom Road.

Hughes transported lumber on the Susquehanna River between Williamsport and the Baltimore area and worked in lumber yards and drilled wells, according to Diggs. In the years preceding the Civil War, he smuggled escaped slaves from Maryland to Williamsport and hid them, the family usually operating on moonless nights.

Some of the slaves he picked up remained in the Williamsport area. Hughes or his sons took others to the next Underground Railroad station in Trout Run. From there, runaways aided by other conductors might reach Elmira, Binghamton, Olean or other parts of New York or journey to Canada. Slave catchers sometimes came to the Hughes's home looking for runaways but none were ever caught, according to Diggs. "He got 1,000 slaves through here and never lost one of them," she said. "His wife and children helped."

Though Pennsylvania was a free state with an antislavery society, that does not mean the Hughes clan had nothing to fear. The so-called Muncy Abolition Riot of 1842 was proof of that. Williamsport is about twenty miles west of Muncy, a town founded in 1797 and named for the Munsee Indians. It was the home of several Underground Railroad conductors, including two black residents, John Warner and Henry Harris. A riot broke out there after a Quaker man named Enos Hawley invited a lecturer to speak against slavery in a local schoolhouse in April 1842. Eighteen men threw rocks and other missiles at the school, injuring Hawley and others. The men then followed Hawley to his house and attacked it until midnight. Thirteen of the eighteen assailants were found guilty as charged at the October trial, largely because of the urgings of abolitionist Abraham Updegraff, one of several abolitionists in Williamsport. But Governor David R. Porter pardoned the rioters.

Daniel Hughes died in 1880 from what his death records called "gravel" and "para," most likely references to kidney stones and a paralyzing stroke. The limestone caves on his property have been sealed, and his house burned in 1975.

Still, Hughes has his memorial.

He donated a portion of the land along Freedom Road for use as an African American cemetery. Nine African American veterans of the Civil War still rest in that cemetery, their graves marked by flags and their grounds haunted by memories of the caves and horse hair that the Hughes family turned into agents of freedom.

———◆•◆———

FOURTEEN

AND THE OSCAR
GOES TO . . .

Let's pretend the Academy of Motion Pictures was around in the eighteenth and nineteenth centuries, handing out shiny trophies to people on both sides of the antislavery movement for superb acting and for producing compelling illusions. Just think of the prizes that might have been awarded back then to spies and soldiers, runaways and slave catchers, juries and judges.

Best Actor would have been an especially crowded field. Besides Nelson Gant, John Bowley, Frank Wanzer and other heroes already described, the nominees also would include the following people.

James Williams escaped slavery in Elkton, Maryland, at age thirteen. One day while he was still on the run, he walked into a restaurant in Trenton, New Jersey, too hungry to worry about caution or slave catchers. The future Underground Railroad conductor ate a "couple of pies, a few doughnuts, drank part of a bottle of spruce beer, put a few cakes into my pocket" and then asked for his bill. He, of course, knew full well he had no money. After receiving his bill, he told the

Fig. 17. Best Actor Oscar should go to Civil War spies, counterspies and other creative participants in the freedom struggle. (Photo by Dale Rich)

clerk to charge the forty cents to "Mr. Barnburner." The clerk wrote down the phony name in his book of debtors and invited Williams to come again.

William Parker was just as self-possessed and quick-thinking. At one point in his flight from Christiana, Pennsylvania, Parker, who had a price on his head, had to travel on a real train, not the network known as the Underground Railroad. Once he boarded the train, he was surrounded by passengers reading newspaper accounts of the shoot-out at his cabin between a posse trying to recapture some fugitives and Parker and his armed neighbors. He remained calm, questioning the other passengers about the story they were reading about him and asking them for their opinions. He even sat down and ate with one of the white passengers. He eventually made it to safety in Chatham, Ontario.

John Scobel did more than rise to the challenge of war: He turned it into an art form, becoming perhaps the most famous black Civil

War spy. In another time and place he might have become a classical actor, someone whose voice filled a room as he denounced traitors, pursued princesses and loudly challenged his enemies to duels. Instead he became a Civil War spy, an even more demanding role for a black man in the nineteenth century. The best known of the undercover military agents supervised by detective Allan Pinkerton, Scobel was recruited in the fall of 1861.

The former Mississippi slave had been well educated by the Scottish owner who freed him. He could pass for a cook, laborer, food seller or musician. He often worked with other Pinkerton agents, pretending to be their servants while in the South. He would seek out black leaders and collect information on fortifications and the location and state of rebel troops. He also belonged to the Legal League, a secret black southern group supporting freedom for slaves. Some members would sometimes carry Scobel's information to Union lines. He played a simple, always-happy darky, crooning plantation melodies and other songs in a sweet, powerful voice. Working as a cook and laborer, Scobel sang and toiled his way across Virginia. He also noted Confederate military preparations and passed on the information to the Yankees.

It might have been even tougher, though, playing the many roles attempted by James Armistead during the Revolutionary War. The enslaved man became a double agent, pretending to spy for the British while actually collecting information for the Americans. The British general Cornwallis actually believed James Armistead was a spy for him. He was convinced that all the slaves would go against their masters instead of gambling that the Americans might win and be generous. Cornwallis was not completely misinformed. According to historian Cassandra Pybus, thousands of slaves did defect to the British, some following them back to England or later migrating to British settlements in Nova Scotia and Sierra Leone. Yet Armistead was spying for Lafayette the whole time he was with Cornwallis.

Robert Smalls, born a slave in 1839 in Beaufort, South Carolina, was destined to become one of the Civil War's most ingenious heroes and a master actor as well. In Charleston, Smalls worked as a rigger, hack driver and hotel waiter before the Confederates forced him to become a deckhand on a southern gunboat called the *Planter*. After mastering the channels and currents of Charleston Harbor, he was promoted to pilot but clung to the hope of freedom. One night after his boat's crew and captain had left, Smalls and a dozen other blacks on the boat smuggled their families aboard the ship. They armed themselves with the weapons on board and sailed away. One man even put on a rebel uniform to help them pass any Confederate checkpoints. In the dark, Smalls pretended to be the captain and was able to provide all the right countersigns and responses. A Union ship came close to firing upon them, but Smalls's crew managed to run up the white flag of surrender and turn the gunboat over to the Union Navy. Smalls eventually became captain of the *Planter* for the Union.

Al Wood would have been a strong contender, too, especially on that night in 1864 when he saved his regiment by infiltrating an enemy camp. He would have been shot if he spooked his enemies' horses and shot if a rebel guard spotted him. He would have been shot if he tripped over a dead Confederate soldier and shot if he bumped into a living one. So Alfred moved carefully through the dense pine-smelling Mississippi night. Inch by cautious inch, he crawled past the first line of rebel guards and crept into the Confederate camp. On the way, he stopped to strip the uniform from a lifeless soldier. Without making a sound, he donned the uniform and grabbed the dead soldier's weapon and gear. Then he snaked through the ditches and valleys gouged out by heavy rains until he reached the horses stabled in the rear of the camp. Mounting a horse, he rode off, avoiding the rebel watchmen as he journeyed to a Union Army stronghold at Vicksburg, Mississippi.

The scout and sometime spy reached a Union cavalry unit and told them where to find his comrades, who had been pinned down during a raid and surrounded by a far larger enemy force. When day broke, Union soldiers rode to the rescue and saved the embattled Third U.S. Colored Cavalry.

Most of the nominees in the Best Actress category deserve special praise for living right under the noses of the people they deceived.

Former slave Mary Elizabeth Bowser voluntarily returned to being a house servant so she could report on what she saw and heard inside the household of Confederate president Jefferson Davis. Pretending to be slow-witted, Bowser dusted and served and paid attention, using her memory to record documents and overheard conversations. She also used common household items to pass on information to master spies. An empty eggshell might be filled with military plans, and a serving tray might have a false bottom.

Mary Touvestre, a freed slave, worked as a housekeeper for an engineer who was involved in the refitting and transformation of the USS *Merrimac* into the *Virginia*, the first Confederate ironclad warship. Overhearing her employer stress the importance of the project, she stole a set of plans for the ship and fled North. After she arrived in Washington, she arranged a meeting with Department of the Navy officials. The stolen plans and Touvestre's report convinced officials of the need to speed up construction of the Union's own ironclad ship, the *Monitor*. The *Virginia* was able to destroy two Union frigates and run another to ground before the Union's ironclad arrival. The *Virginia* would have had several more weeks to destroy Union ships if it hadn't been for Touvestre's information.

Other slavery-era women eligible for best acting Oscar nominations might have included Civil War nurses such as Susie King Taylor and Margaret Wood. Taylor followed the regiment in which her husband was a sergeant, laundering clothes, nursing the wounded and teaching black soldiers to read. Margaret Wood was not only an Army cook who actually knew how to prepare food; she tended the sick and wounded, too. That means she would have had to hold on to her composure and compassion while seeing and smelling the casualties of a war in which diseases killed more soldiers than repeating rifles or mortar bombs. Wood and Taylor would have encountered typhoid fever and typhus, transmitted by lice in unwashed clothing. They would have tended men with dysentery from water contaminated by sewage. They might have tried to soothe men after watching surgeons saw off their limbs and seal wounds with red-hot irons. Most likely, they had pressed cool water to thirsty lips or, possibly, fed custards made with turtle eggs to men who couldn't stomach solid food or whose shattered legs had been amputated above the knee two or three times. Wood and Taylor might even have met soldiers suffering from the unexplained night blindness that reportedly afflicted soldiers of the Army of Northern Virginia during the occupation of Fredericksburg.

The nominees for Best Supporting Actor would include three white men named John Morgan, John Shaw and Zachariah Shaw, who were arrested in 1854 in Frederick County, Maryland, for a slave-stealing scheme. They first would send someone among the slaves to encourage them to escape. After the slaves ran off, this trio would then capture them and collect a reward for returning them to their masters. However, in some cases, they would kidnap the slaves and sell them to slave traders. Supporting Actor awards might also go to rebel soldiers who blackened their faces with mud to fool Yankees into thinking they were black, and Yankee soldiers who wore Confederate uniforms to fool the rebels into thinking they were rebels.

Then there was a slave named Kitt, who ran away from North Carolina and in 1863 joined the military under the names Kitt Pond and Willie Hodges. He also used the name Powell, trying to avoid the nagging threat of recapture by his master.

"Kitt was an asset to anyone who was hiding him because he was a carpenter by trade," according to his descendant, Ernestine Bull.

And let's not forget the early congregations at St. John's–St. Luke Evangelical Church in downtown Detroit. According to stories passed from one generation to the next, the church's original German-speaking congregation sometimes staged fake funerals to aid escaping slaves. Runaways either hid in a leather casket or walked behind it with other make-believe mourners from the church. The casket would roll along on its horse-drawn cart until the procession reached the Detroit River. The fugitive in their midst would then jump into a waiting boat and cross the river to Canada.

The Best Costume Design award would have to go to an enslaved woman named Annie Weaver for hiding her husband, Henry, under her huge skirt during the enslaved couple's escape to Chatham, Ontario. However, other nominees for this award would be the runaway slaves who showed up at Union Army camps wearing beaver hats and fine muslin cloaks, rotting shirts or sleeveless coats or their masters' undergarments.

Thousands of African Americans might qualify for Best Set Decoration awards. Slaves and freedmen were cobblers and tailors, carpenters and blacksmiths, weavers and tanners. They created the graceful wrought-iron balconies in New Orleans as well as the decorative fences and gates of Charleston, South Carolina. Between 1790 and 1863, slave artisans and craftsmen worked on the nation's Capitol building, too, hauling stone and lumber, digging trenches and placing cut stone on the walls of the building.

We don't know how many of them had to swallow dreams or conceal wider ambitions. We do know that during the slavery era, Edmonia Lewis, a free black woman determined to become a sculptor, wound up living and selling her pieces in Rome. We know that Grafton T. Brown moved from Pennsylvania to California, where he produced paintings of snow-topped mountains and shiny lakes. We know that a black man named Joseph Proctor varnished and painted designs on furniture in New York and then painted more artistic pieces to please himself. We know that Henry Boyd, a former Kentucky slave, made furniture in Cincinnati, specializing in building beds in which the pieces fit together without nails. After he was burned out three times, he finally shut down. We also know that former slave William Kunze made chairs in St. Charles, Missouri.

Best Makeup is an easier category. The award should go to Underground Railroad conductor John Fairfield, who sometimes disguised light-skinned slaves with makeup and horse-hair wigs so they could escape slavery by passing for white.

The Best Song winner would be anything performed by a blind, black child known as Blind Tom. Tom was described as "an idiot in everything but music, language and imitation and perhaps memory" by author Lew Powell. One of Tom's feats included performing three pieces of music at once, playing one song with one hand, another song with the other and singing a third song.

The award for Best Picture? How about rewarding the best idea for a movie instead. One pair of candidates is a black couple known only as Mr. and Mrs. Dabney, who used blankets and shirts to send signals to the Union Army during the Civil War. Mrs. Dabney became a laundress for the rebel forces, which allowed her to eavesdrop on officers and learn in advance about troop movements. By moving clothes and blankets around on her clotheslines or taking down certain items, she sent coded messages to her husband, a Union cook and groom camped across the Rappahannock River at Fredericksburg, Virginia, with General Joseph Hooker in 1863. Shirts of different colors represented different generals. Blankets with pins at the bottom indicated phony Confederate troop movement designed to trick the Yankees.

Meanwhile, a movie based on Octave Johnson's life would rival *Raiders of the Lost Ark*. Angry when a new overseer forced him to work by the clock rather than by task, Johnson escaped to the Louisiana swamps in 1861. He became the leader of a colony of runaways in St. James Parish. Johnson and the other runaways were about four miles behind the plantation of Johnson's owner. They learned to navigate the swamps, memorizing the location of small tracts of firm ground. Sometimes they roped cattle or hogs and dragged them to their hiding places. They managed to get whatever they needed from plantation slaves, trading meat for meal and other goods. They also managed to elude tracking dogs. They slept on logs and burned cypress leaves to make a smoke that would keep away mosquitoes. At one point Johnson and other members of his group killed eight dogs pursuing them. They then jumped into the alligator-filled Bayou Faupron. In 1863, after a year and a half in the swamps, Johnson made his way to Camp Parapet and joined the Corps d'Afrique of the U.S. Colored Troops. After what he'd struggled with and slogged through, Army drills and even battles might have seemed like light duty.

BOOK III

———◆◆◆———

THAT COLD
BLACK MAGIC

Fig. 18. Mary Ellen Pleasant, mother of civil rights in California,
humanitarian, millionaire and alleged voodoo queen. (Photo courtesy
of the San Francisco History Center, San Francisco Public Library)

————◆◆◆————

FIFTEEN

DON'T CALL
HER MAMMY

Oh, the stories they whispered about her and the tales they tossed around.

The lawsuits she'd filed against trolley companies for refusing to accept black riders at all times made some people call her the Mother of Civil Rights in California. Yet some California newspapers also implied she'd used voodoo spells to enchant a wealthy white man. Others insisted she'd sold illegitimate babies to women trying to fool husbands and boyfriends into believing they were daddies. Though never charged with any crimes, she was even rumored to have committed two murders. So people must have stared when the most gossiped-about black woman in San Francisco glided into a courtroom in the early 1880s.

That tall, spare, seventy-year-old woman was Mary Ellen Pleasant. She was a witness in two San Francisco divorce trials that included testimony about socks soaked in whiskey, voodoo charms and a woman who said she hid behind a congressman's dresser to watch him make love to her friend. But the trials weren't only about a wealthy Nevada senator and the alleged hooker who claimed to be his wife and wanted alimony. Mary Ellen Pleasant, who paid the young woman's legal fees, was being judged, too. But her main "crime" might have been controlling whites and refusing to lead the scrub-dust-and-fold life expected of nineteenth-century women, especially those who were black.

At various times, people called Pleasant a witch, a voodoo queen, the daughter of a voodoo queen, a mammy, a blackmailer, a millionaire, an organizer of wild parties and a madam. She was said to be pale enough to pass for white, so dark-skinned she could only have been black, having one brown eye and one blue one and constantly rewriting and revising the details of her life. To some, she was the woman who had hidden a fugitive slave to keep him from being shipped back to Mississippi and who claimed to have helped fund John Brown's raid on the arsenal at Harper's Ferry. Others called her the black city hall, one of the pioneers of San Francisco, a protector of young black and white women in trouble, a matchmaker and a woman who became a freedom fighter in part to fulfill her beloved first husband's dying request. She also was described as a brilliant stock market speculator, a woman who served tea laced with gin to judges and future governors and a black woman canny enough to pretend to be the servant of the white man who actually was her business partner. Historical researcher J. Lloyd Conrich even labeled her a "female version of Robin Hood."

There was a bit of truth in many of the lies about Mary Pleasant and exaggerations in some of the truth, making it difficult to tell where the legend stopped and the actual woman began.

Journalist Lerone Bennett, Jr., argued that nineteenth-century San Franciscans were so baffled by the genius of a black woman who managed to own eight homes and a ranch during the slavery and postslavery era that they searched for all kinds of explanations, including voodoo, blackmail and prostitution. Yet she couldn't really be understood, Bennett noted, "without bitter struggle."

Her autobiographies and statements only added red pepper to an already steaming stew of contradictions. "Mary tailored different

memoirs at different times to counteract the gossip and criticism lev-
eled against her in the press," according to contemporary historian
Susheel Bibbs. So she did.

Pleasant claimed she was born free in Philadelphia, and she sometimes claimed to be the illegitimate child of a Virginia governor's son
and an enslaved voodoo priestess. At other times, she claimed her father was a free Hawaiian. She told Sam Davis, editor of the *San Francisco Pandex of the Press,* that she was born in Philadelphia on August 9,
1814, at 9 Barley Street and that her father was a native of the Sandwich Islands and her mother a full-blooded black woman from Louisiana. The federal censuses of 1870 and 1880 also identify her as
Philadelphia-born, suggesting it was a story she preferred and often
repeated. However, another equally persistent story is that she was
born a slave near Augusta, Georgia, around 1817. After witnessing the
torture and death of her mother at the hands of a plantation overseer,
she allegedly had to make her way on her own. In one of her memoirs,
she claimed that she was bought out of slavery at age nine by a sympathetic but unnamed planter, a story that may or may not be true. Sub-
sequently, she worked as a free servant for a Cincinnati merchant, Louis
Alexander Williams, expecting to receive an education eventually.

In this version of her story, Williams never educated Mary and in
the 1820s or 1830s placed her in a nine-year indenture or service contract in Nantucket, Massachusetts, with a Quaker merchant possibly
named Mary Hussey. A large island off the coast of Massachusetts,
Nantucket was not only surrounded by water: It was surrounded by
the glassy glare of silver-shingled cottages, the smell of codfish and
onion casseroles, the squawks of seagulls and the lure of a life at sea.
Many of its men spent more time in water than on land, trying to
catch the massive sperm whales whose blubber and oil produced can-
dles, soap and cosmetics. Nantucket's whalers, white and black, pursued the whales, sometimes traveling as far as China and spending as
long as five years away from home. Meanwhile, Nantucket's women
took charge of their lives. The Quaker religion these women practiced
played a key role in the nation's struggle against slavery, but their reli-

gion also valued competence and thrift and making do. As a result, in the early and middle part of the nineteenth century, the sharp-witted and shrewd women merchants of Nantucket ran thriving shops, selling everything from coal to fish hooks. Working for Hussey, Mary Ellen learned not only how to sell merchandise, but how to sell herself to Hussey's customers. "Few people ever got by that shop without buying something of me," she claimed in her dictated memoirs.

Young Mary also would have seen that blacks lived in segregated communities on Nantucket but breathed the same salt air as whites and were just as much a part of the island's culture. Between 1740 and 1850, Nantucket blacks worked as ship cooks, deck hands, whalers, sail makers and menders, ship carpenters, boarding house keepers, shepherds, shopkeepers, barbers, domestics, shoemakers, laborers and seamstresses. By 1840, 578 black men and women lived on Nantucket, some African Americans and some Cape Verdeans, the Afro-Portuguese who voluntarily came to the United States and were free seamen.

"Pleasant's successes as a capitalist and her antislavery and civil rights activism were nurtured and inspired by her growing up years on Nantucket," say historians Robert C. Hayden and Karen E. Hayden.

But Nantucket provided only the calm first act of a life that would churn with court battles, silver mines, sex scandals, steamy secrets, millions of dollars and an alleged journey to meet famed antislavery fighter John Brown.

When Mary's term as an indentured servant ended around 1841, the Hussey and Gardner families helped the twenty-something-year-old woman become a tailor's assistant in Boston, where she soon met and married her first husband, James W. Smith, a big man with olive-tinged skin. He was a mulatto who passed for a Cuban and spied for William Lloyd Garrison's antislavery newspaper, the *Liberator.* He also worked for the Underground Railroad, that trackless network of activists who helped slaves find freedom on various routes, leading as far north as Nova Scotia and as far south as Mexico. As a slave rescuer, James Smith helped run slaves from Virginia to Nova Scotia. His white father had left him a plantation in Virginia, and James staffed it with freed slaves, many of whom he had purchased out of slavery. Mary joined him in helping to free slaves.

"It was all for the cause," she would later say.

Yet she fell in love with the man as well as his mission. Then, sometime between 1844 and 1848, Smith died, leaving Mary with land and a fortune: She was said to have inherited from thirty thousand dollars to fifty thousand dollars from the sale of Cuban bonds, an immense sum in the nineteenth century. He also left her a legacy, urging her to do some great work. On Smith's deathbed, he made her promise to use the money for the liberation of enslaved blacks—or so the Mary Pleasant legend goes.

JOHN PLEASANTS

Around 1850, with slave catchers on her trail, Mary returned to Nantucket to live with the granddaughter of Mary or "Grandma" Hussey, Phebe Gardner, and her husband, Captain Edward W. Gardner. Phebe was a leading figure in Nantucket's antislavery society. There Mary must have encountered her second husband, John James Pleasants or Pleasance, a Virginia-born man who was working as a waiter in New Bedford, Massachusetts, in 1850. "She (first) met him in Virginia where he was the foreman of her first husband's plantation," says historian Susheel Bibbs. Like Nantucket, New Bedford was a whaling center and a place defined by the sea. The village of New Bedford also was Frederick Douglass's first free home and an Underground Railroad station: It had some seven hundred runaway slave residents during the 1850s.

Soon after marrying John Pleasants, however, Mary Ellen abandoned New England and is believed to have moved to New Orleans to avoid prosecution for aiding slaves. There, she hid out with relatives of her second husband, a ship's cook who was often away at sea. The belief in San Francisco that Pleasant practiced voodoo probably stems from her time in New Orleans, a city where the sweet thick air could induce summer trances. Because of its location on the Mississippi River and its reputation as a sugar capital, Louisiana was a major player in the slave trade. It also was the scene of a culture that blended French government, liberal slave-freeing laws and a tradition of racial mixing that gave a special flavor to New Orleans–style slavery. The largest city in the Old South, New Orleans was a place of narrow streets and semitropical weather, level deltas and swamps, food steeped in seductive spices and dragonflies almost large enough to ride. Genteel people of color walked an often very thin line between black and white. Quadroon balls where families presented their lightly colored daughters to white suitors for long-term relationships were part of New Orleans culture, too. So were duels and pastel-colored cottages. Slaves did indeed labor in Louisiana cotton fields and sugar cane plantations, but some light-skinned blacks owned slaves. New Orleans was a hodge-podge of rhythmic dances and slave screams, suffering and celebrations, special privilege and pain, and, above all, voodoo or voudou.

Forget all the movies you've seen about the walking and murderous dead. A New World faith that combined African traditions with other religions, especially Catholicism, voodoo was a religion in which believers called on spirits or divine beings for protection, retaliation and healing. Its followers looked on religion as something you could feel and something you could use. Priests and priestesses were the middlemen between this world and the next, the pleaders whose chants, dances and sacred objects allowed spirits to possess them. A more down-to-earth, results-oriented cousin of voodoo—known as hoodoo—also flourished on slave plantations and even entranced some whites who came to conjurers and obeahs for love potions and charms. Belief in conjurers helped unite Africans from different cultures and sometimes sparked uprisings, rousing plantation rebels with the belief that they couldn't fail.

MARIE LAVEAU

Mary Pleasant's teacher in the art of summoning the gods was said to have been the legendary Marie Laveau, the city's reigning voodoo queen and one of two voodoo practitioners with the same name—the other was her daughter, also named Marie. The elder Marie had the air of someone "born to command," according to an observer who remembered her in an 1886 article in the *St. Louis Globe-Democrat.* Religion, however, wasn't the only thing Marie Laveau could have taught a student as apt as Mary Pleasant. By all accounts, Laveau understood power and how to get it. As a hairdresser, she entered the homes of New Orleans' elite families. Society woman shared their secrets with her, and she profited from this knowledge in all kinds of ways. She would charge desperate wives a fee to free their faithless husbands from someone else's charms. Then she would let the husbands know she had cooled their wives' anger. Supposedly, they, too, would pay her. A Catholic, she organized public voodoo ceremonies in Congo Square and at Bayou St. John and thousands of people attended, swaying to melodies played on bamboo flutes. In large and small ways, the free black woman defied the slave system, helping slaves escape, arranging for a priest to marry and baptize interracial couples and using her knowledge of powerful people's secrets to gain the leverage to help her people.

Sometime between 1849 and 1852, Mary Ellen Pleasant's second husband, who was living in California, sent for her. "He went ahead of her to scout the area as a safer place for them," says Bibbs. She was in her thirties when she moved to California and became part of both the Gold Rush era and American history. Black women were scarce then in the West: California, in 1850, contained only 90 black females out of a total population of 962 blacks. The rush to California actually had begun in 1849, a year after gold was found there. By late 1849, in the public mind, California had become an earthly paradise where men could scoop up gold nuggets from the ground. People afflicted with gold fever flocked there from every corner of the globe, arriving on horses, wagons and crutches, deserting army posts to go there. However, travelers to California sometimes passed broken wagons and the graves of cholera victims or struck it rich and discovered onions sold for the unheard of-price of one dollar apiece and baked potatoes for seventy-five cents each.

THE WEST REALLY WAS WILD

Overnight, San Francisco, the city that would make Mary Ellen Pleasant famous, rich, beloved and scorned, stopped being the village of Yerba Buena and became the financial and cultural center of the West. It became a place where people changed the physical landscape by filling in ground and moving hills. It was transformed as well by the arrival of miners, merchants, seamen and lone men with enough cash to patronize saloons, gambling houses, houses of prostitution and hotels. A dancer and actress known as Lola Montez, the former mistress of King Ludwig I of Bavaria, kept a monkey and grizzly bear as pets. Singing, dancing and banjo-strumming Lotta Crabtree toured mining camps and piled up so much money that she was worth $4 million when she died. Elanor [*sic*] Dumont raised eyebrows when she began dealing blackjack and running a gambling parlor, but became affectionately known as Madame Mustache due to a faintly hairy upper lip. After losing both her man and her money, Dumont committed suicide. Meanwhile, domestic servants and boarding house stewards such as Mary Ellen Pleasant, earned ten times as much as in New York. General William Tecumseh Sherman describes winter in San Francisco's Gold Rush era as a time of heavy rains, mules and horses getting their legs entangled in the mud, drivers being thrown and drowned. He also described the inflated prices that accompanied the gold boom.

"Any room twenty by sixty feet would rent for a thousand dollars a month," he wrote. ". . . Captains and crews deserted for the gold mines," noted General Sherman. "Our servants also left us and nothing less than three hundred dollars a month would hire a man in California."

Not all whites and certainly not all blacks managed to find caches of gold in California, a state where even the foliage could be treacherous: As prospectors panned for gold, the topsoil washed away and poison oak grew bigger, stronger and more potent, infecting scores of miners with its maddening itch. Placerville, which was midway between Sacramento and Lake Tahoe and about ten miles from Sutter's Mill, was known at first as Old Dry Diggings and then Hang Town because of all the suspected murderers and thieves who'd been hung there from an old oak. Still, some black pioneers endured and prospered beyond their dreams.

Reuben Ruby, a black man from Portland, Maine, arrived in California early in 1849 and by April had earned $600 from four weeks of digging on the Stanislaus River. Richard Barber was another prosperous San Francisco black. He worked as a porter and accumulated $71,800. All but $1,800 of this he invested in real estate. Mose Rodgers, a former slave, had bought a number of California mines and become the first person to successfully drill for gas in Stockton. In Sonora, California, William and Mary Sugg built a small private hotel. Meanwhile, William Alexander Leidesdorff became the first black millionaire when gold was found on his property just before the thirty-eight-year-old man's death from meningitis. Robert Anthony, a black miner, owned the first quartz mill in the state. He had come to Sacramento from St. Louis, Missouri, traveling by ox team with his owner and working for two years in the mines to pay for his freedom.

But Mary Pleasant—who had more in common with home furnishings magnate Martha Stewart and civil rights pioneer Rosa Parks than with Lola Montez or Lotta Crabtree—created the most enduring legend.

A FREE STATE WITH SLAVES

For several years she worked as a household supervisor for a series of wealthy men and became famed as a cook. Some sources believe she led two lives in those days, sometimes passing for white and sometimes letting it be known that she was black. But others insist she wasn't light enough to pass. She did a good job, though, of passing for well-to-do. Working through commission bankers she knew, she began loaning money at 10 percent interest and sending gold to Panama and exchanging it for silver. She not only had a natural genius for financial speculation, but picked up stock and investment tips from the magnates whose dinners she supervised and from the overheard conversations other servants shared with her. By 1855, she owned a string of laundries. Unlike her first husband, John Pleasants seems to have been a shadowy figure, often away, but that didn't stop Mary Ellen from using her talents for money-making. She also soon became deeply involved in fighting slavery in the supposedly free state of California, a place where the witness to a black barber's pistol-whipping and fatal shooting couldn't testify because the shooter was white and the witness was one-sixteenth black, according to the two doctors who examined his hair.

California had entered the Union as part of the Compromise of 1850, but its antislavery constitution left the status of slaves who arrived before and after 1850 fuzzy and ill-defined. To make matters even vaguer, the constitution contained no language stating how long blacks could be held in bondage in California. These issues were left for the first state legislature to decide. In December of 1850, the first state assembly passed a bill that would have banned all blacks from living in the state, but it was defeated in the state senate. The California constitution did include language saying "no black or mulatto person, or Indian, shall be permitted to give evidence in any action to which a white person is a party, in any Court of this State." A mulatto was defined as anyone with "one eighth part or more of Negro blood." In the case of *People v. W. H. Potter*, this meant that Sarah J. Carroll, a nineteen-year-old free black woman who owned properties in both Sacramento and San Francisco in the 1850s, was out of luck when she filed a complaint against a white man named W. H. Potter for stealing seven hundred dollars of her gold coin and other valuables. The case was dismissed the same day it was filed solely because Potter was white and Carroll, under the law, couldn't testify against him.

As early as 1852, the California legislature also passed its own fugitive slave law; it allowed the arrest of any escaped slave found in the state and his return to slavery if he were taken out of California. It also permitted slave owners and their slaves to stay for an indefinite time in the free state of California. The 1852 bill was allowed to expire in 1855, but in the three years of its existence, many blacks were carried from California back into slavery.

Thanks to Mary Ellen Pleasant and others, George Mitchell wasn't among them. Mitchell was a young black man who was brought to California as a slave in 1849. His former owner arrested him and a trial over his status took place in San Jose in 1855. Three local lawyers defended him and were successful in delaying a decision until the California Fugitive Slave Act expired in April 1855. Pleasant supposedly hid him while the case stalled. Mitchell became a first-floor bellman at the Palace Hotel in San Francisco. From his wages and tips he had acquired a fortune of thirty thousand to forty thousand dollars by the time he died. Mary Ellen also fed, clothed and helped other newly arrived fugitives and freedmen and found them jobs or helped them start small businesses.

The Archy Lee case gave Mary Ellen Pleasant another chance to play a leading role in the freedom struggle in a supposedly free state. Lee was a Mississippi slave whose young master, Charles Stovall, had brought him to California in 1857 as a body servant. He allegedly slipped away from his master, though he denied this. By January 1858 he was hiding in a Sacramento resort owned by a black man. Arrested as a fugitive, he told the court he didn't wish to return to Mississippi. His case wound its way through courts in Sacramento, San Francisco and Stockton as well as the California Supreme Court. The supreme court finally ruled that Lee should be returned to his master because Stovall never would have brought a slave to a free state if he hadn't been hopelessly naïve.

Eventually, though, Archy Lee won his freedom, but only because free blacks, including Pleasant, raised the money for his continued legal fight. Mary Ellen is said to have hidden him in her home or the house of one of her wealthy friends until the Executive Committee of the Colored Committee could arrange his passage to Canada.

At the time, "San Francisco was on the verge of a riot," according to California historian Delilah Beasley.

BLACKS WHO LEFT CALIFORNIA

In 1858, hundreds of African Americans, including Archy Lee, Mary Ellen Pleasant and Pleasant's husband, all left California. Just as the Archy Lee case was drawing to a close, California lawmakers introduced a bill to prevent blacks from immigrating to or living in California, a piece of legislation that, Beasley claimed "sent terror to the hearts of the colored people living throughout the state." It would have required blacks already in the state to register and then carry around papers proving where they lived. Blacks who defied this law and entered the state would have to enter into a kind of slavery to pay for the expense of kicking them out. This bill never passed, but it was enough to convince scores of black Californians that it was time to leave.

If the bill wasn't enough, there was also the lure of another gold rush, this time on the Fraser River in British Columbia, Canada. Meanwhile, a special envoy from labor-short British Columbia invited black residents of San Francisco to move there and become full-fledged British citizens. Mifflin Gibbs and Peter Lester, partners in a San Francisco shoe and boot store, decided to move to Victoria, British Columbia, and open a similar store. Neither man had ever recovered from the day when a white man beat Lester for sport: The free-born Gibbs had watched helplessly, unable to intervene or press charges. Willis Bond, born enslaved in California and a servant during the Gold Rush, bought his freedom, moved to British Columbia for the Fraser River gold rush and lived in Yale beginning in July 1858. He and a Yorkshire man operated a system for delivering water for washing gold from soil. He returned to Victoria in 1861 and worked as a general contractor.

John Wilson, a black bootmaker in Sacramento, moved to Jamaica. John P. Williams, a New Jersey–born black man who worked as a barber, emigrated with his wife to Haiti in 1861 but returned to the United States after his wife's death. James Williams, who had escaped at thirteen from Maryland, spent time in Boston, Philadelphia, New

York, Trenton, New Bedford, Mexico and Panama. He emigrated from California to Vancouver Island to "breathe purer air," but later returned to the United States after deciding Canadian air was "somewhat tainted," too. Other former Californians wound up on Salt Spring Island, off the coast of Vancouver, British Columbia, where their closest neighbors were cougars, bears and foxes. There, on an island where mountain ridges separated communities and families stood alone, they would find out whether they could pay freedom's sometimes steep price.

JOHN BROWN

Mary Ellen Pleasant and her husband had embarked on a different sort of journey in 1858, but British Columbia wasn't their destination and escaping the restrictions of California wasn't their only goal. Mary Ellen allegedly went to Canada to meet John Brown, the antislavery warrior who wanted to set up a provisional government in Chatham, Ontario, a Canadian enclave that was then about one-third black. Mary Ellen reportedly brought with her a large sum of money, which she gave to Brown, according to Beasley. Brown was staying at the home of James Madison Bell, a free black man from Ohio.

"She maintained . . . until her dying day that [the story about her gift to Brown] was true," wrote Lerone Bennett, Jr.

Though there is no actual proof of Pleasant's contributions to Brown, the Pleasants were members of the fourteen-member Chatham Vigilance Committee that rescued a black man named Sylvanus Demerest from a train as a New Yorker named W. R. Merwin was trying to kidnap him. In September 1858, the Pleasants also owned four lots in Ontario's Harwich township. Mary Ellen Pleasant claimed she later spread news of Brown's upcoming Harpers Ferry raid, traveling through Virginia disguised as a jockey and accompanied by a white abolitionist who pretended to be her owner. Whether or not this part of her story was true, there was without question some kind of connection between Pleasant and Brown.

However, by the 1860s, Mary Ellen Pleasant was back in California, which became the perfect setting for the woman she would become. Pleasant worked for a series of wealthy merchants, including commission merchants. She also opened several laundries and boarding houses, one possibly an Underground Railroad safe house, according to historian Lynn Hudson. She made more mining investments and financed other people's investments. There's no hard evidence that her boarding houses were bordellos or whorehouses, as is frequently claimed; yet in San Francisco's rough and rowdy years, that would not have been unusual. What was unusual was that by the 1860s, city directories listed Pleasant for the first time as a boarding house keeper rather than a domestic.

In the mid- to late 1860s, Mary Ellen Pleasant also became a leader in the struggle for black rights, especially the right to ride streetcars consistently. Blacks could ride the trolleys, but conductors sometimes put them off at random or refused to pick them up. Pleasant and other black San Franciscans filed several lawsuits against trolley companies, helping set precedents that would spur the California legislature to ban racial discrimination in public accommodations in 1893.

In 1869, she moved to 920 Washington Street, her most elaborate boarding house. In keeping with the times, Pleasant's houses featured fine food, wines, private dining and bedroom combinations, balm tea laced with gin, artwork and draperies elegant enough to pass as works of art. The 1870 boarders at her house on Washington included William B. Hughes, U.S. quartermaster; Newton Booth, future governor of California; Charles Marshall, clerk in the U.S. Revenue Office, Thomas Wright, wealthy master mariner, and George Wright, a businessman who owned twenty thousand dollars in personal property and thirty thousand dollars in real estate. Her house on Washington Street was not quite as elegant as Chicago's Everleigh Club, which boasted a perfume-spouting fountain, eighteen-karat-gold spittoons and bedrooms with such amenities as a full-sized effigy of Cleopatra or a station for setting off firecrackers. But she fit right into the gaudy late nineteenth and early twentieth centuries. John Pleasants, who had dropped the final "s" from his name in California, died in 1877. That didn't slow down his widow.

THOMAS BELL

By the 1870s, Pleasant owned at least thirty thousand dollars' worth of declared real estate. That didn't make her the wealthiest African American in San Francisco, though. A porter named Richard Barber owned real estate worth seventy thousand dollars. In the 1870s, Pleasant moved into a mansion on Octavia and Bush streets. By then, her fortune had become linked to that of Scottish banker Thomas Bell, vice president of the Bank of California and her secret business partner. Bell lived in the hundred-thousand-dollar Octavia mansion, a two-story structure with bay windows, but it was built and furnished by Pleasant, who did the hiring and firing and, for all practical purposes, ran the household.

She and Bell were involved in all kinds of money-making ventures, and all kinds of stories still circulated about them. They included the claim that Pleasant held Bell prisoner, fed him dog food and was his mistress. She, in turn, called herself Bell's servant. Rumors also spread that she'd gained influence by learning the secrets of wealthy families from their servants, a charge that echoed the stories about Marie Laveau. Pleasant was never charged with a crime, but some detractors suggested that she had somehow hastened the death of her first husband. Bell married Teresa Clingan in 1879 one of the young women who became Pleasant's protégées, which didn't squash the rumors, only changed them.

"She exerted a mysterious influence over Bell and was able to extract from him, without security, any amount of money she desired," insisted writer William Savage. He claimed that Pleasant once sent Teresa Bell to a small town in California and then told Bell his wife was in New York. She then supposedly asked Bell for more money to replace what Teresa had supposedly lost, Savage wrote.

Pleasant lived more than twenty years with Thomas, Teresa and the Bell children.

Then came the 1884 and 1885 trials.

SARAH ALTHEA HILL

The two trials pitting Senator William Sharon against a young white woman named Sarah Althea Hill were bare-fisted brawls between a millionaire who couldn't keep his pants zipped and an alleged five-hundred-dollar-a-month hooker who claimed she was the senator's secret bride and deserved both money and a divorce. Mary Ellen Pleasant never climbed into the ring with Sharon and Hill, trading punches under hot lights, but, in many ways, the trial was as much about her as them.

Over the years, she became known as Mammy Pleasant, a name that reflected her supposed status as the Bell family's servant and a name that conjured up comforting images of black servants who loved their white families above all. But the name riled Pleasant.

"I don't like to be called mammy to everybody," she told reporter Isabel Fraser. "I'm not mammy to everybody in California."

Pleasant used her money to help Sarah Hill challenge Senator Sharon of Nevada, a man whose résumé was nearly as lengthy as Pleasant's. He was described as a merchant, an attorney, a realtor, a banker, a miner and owner of the Palace and Grand hotels in San Francisco. He had been a United States senator from Nevada between 1875 and 1881, living in San Francisco after 1872. As the owner of the Palace, then known as the largest hotel in the world, he was at the center of San Francisco's social circle. The Grand Hotel was supposedly the stage for this case, in which Sarah Althea Hill claimed she had secretly wed Sharon, who kept her in a hotel suite and then kicked her out after she allegedly took some of his papers and revealed his business secrets. She was seeking a divorce on grounds of adultery and a share of Sharon's wealth. Hill claimed he'd married her in secret and then abandoned her. The widower senator, who was worth around

$10 million, claimed he had paid Hill five hundred dollars a month for sex but never married her.

Susheel Bibbs, however, believes that the public respected Sarah Hill. "She was considered a lady and much admired by the public despite her liason with Sharon," she says. "She was also from a prominent family." Pleasant testified to the authenticity of the marriage between Sharon and Hill, portraying herself as the white woman's confidante. Pleasant also paid Sarah Hill's legal bills. In fact many people believed there would have been no trial without Pleasant pulling the strings.

Pleasant had a circle of young, single females, black and white, whom she allegedly groomed, transformed and then married off to rising clerks and magnates. In a memoir written two years before her death, she declared, "I have given all I had to others, and when I attached myself to any one as a friend, I have remained to the end." Yet some observers found it scandalous that a young white woman such as Sarah Hill held Pleasant in such high regard that she had confided in her.

"In my judgment, this case, and the forgeries and perjuries committed in its support, have their origin largely in the brain of this scheming, trafficking, crafty old woman," a judge insisted during one of the Sharon trials.

"Mrs. Pleasance [*sic*] occupies a very peculiar relation to the respondent in this case, one utterly inexplicable upon ordinary principle or upon any reasonable ground," agreed attorney William Barnes. "Her intimacy with Miss Hill, as now related, was one that ought not to have existed. . . . They were together daily according to the present story."

The opinion in the second trial noted, "Mary E. Pleasant, better known as Mammic [*sic*] Pleasant, is a conspicuous and important figure in this affair, without whom it would probably never have been brought before the public."

SOCKS DIPPED IN WHISKEY

This was America's so-called Gilded Age, an era defined by new tech-
nologies, new fortunes, new frontiers, growing cities, new, more ag-
gressive newspapers, grand buildings, huge hoaxes and lurid trials. It
was a time in which the *New York Sun* would run an article about the
sighting of winged people on the moon and a time in which showman
P. T. Barnum had exhibitions that sometimes included a tree trunk
under which Jesus' disciples supposedly sat. The William Sharon—
Althea Hill trials fit right in. They included testimony about Sarah
Hill's belief in fortune-telling and witnesses such as Laura Scott, a
black woman who claimed Sarah Hill had brought her a pair of socks
to turn into a love charm to bind Senator Sharon.

"So I took the two socks and tied the toes into a very hard knot,
and gave them to her with instructions to go home and dip the toes in
whiskey and wear them around her left knee," Scott testified.

Mary Ellen survived the original Sharon trial and the countersuit
filed by Sharon, but in time it opened her up to ridicule. The proceedings drew attention to her wealth and status; the defense team portrayed her as the evil mastermind behind the case, the woman who
had encouraged Hill to go after the wealthy senator. Reporters dwelled
on her property.

"Mrs. Mary Pleasant has an income from eight houses in San
Francisco, a ranch near San Mateo, and $100,000 in government
bonds," the *Observer and Gazette* noted in 1887. Her carefully crafted
façade of being Thomas Bell's servant rather than his business partner and co—mortgage holder fell apart. There had been talk during
the trials of stolen underwear, adultery, a secret marriage, voodoo
spells, wealth and property. Hill was ridiculed for having confided
in not just one black woman but several. Pleasant was described as
someone who profited from selling illegitimate babies. She also was
said to have advised Hill to put some kind of love potion in Sharon's
food.

Still, their lives rolled on.

Senator Sharon's only son, Fred, married a woman named Lucy Breckinridge in August 1884, but it was a quiet affair with only four or five "intimate friends" present. On December 24, 1884, the jury found Sharon guilty, but the senator's lawyer won an appeal of the verdict. Sarah Hill began her own set of appeals. Sharon died on November 13, 1885, at the age of sixty-four. In January 1886, Sarah Hill married her former attorney, Judge David Terry; he "dressed plainly" and Sarah wore "a dark woolen dress with a dark shawl." Sarah "had no female companion" at the wedding, the *Daily Evening Bulletin* noted. She was then thirty-two and Terry sixty-three. Their marriage swiftly disintegrated. In 1889, Judge Field's bodyguard shot and killed Terry in the dining room of a hotel depot after Terry slapped Judge Field. Field had denied Sarah's claim to be Sharon's wife. Sarah Hill Terry's alleged marriage contract burned in a fire, and she eventually lost her mind. Mary Ellen Pleasant took care of her for a time, but Sarah died in a state hospital in Stockton in 1937.

FRED BELL

The trials didn't destroy Mary Ellen Pleasant. She came away from them bruised but without any fatal wounds. In 1886, she and Thomas Bell were said to have provided a bond for a man in the county jail. In 1887, a North Carolina newspaper listed her in an article about "wealthy Negroes" worth "from half a million down." But the trials made her vulnerable to another legal battle after her longtime partner Thomas Bell tumbled, leaped or was pushed from stair railings and died in 1892. Teresa Bell and Pleasant would spar and wrangle over their mingled finances and living arrangements for years to come. In 1899 Fred Bell, Thomas's son, would accuse Pleasant of his father's murder. Nothing came of the claim. Fred also would accuse Pleasant of starving and beating the Bell children and of keeping Teresa from learning anything about business matters. Fred was seventeen when he began his suit. His widowed mother had turned against Pleasant for allegedly interfering with Teresa's romance with a con artist. She ousted Pleasant from the house Pleasant had built and designed. She also sued Pleasant for the property next to the mansion.

QUEEN OF THE VOODOOS

While Pleasant fought off creditors and tried to protect her investments, her enemies intensified their attacks. An 1899 article by James E. Brown, Jr., a former employee at Pleasant's house on Octavia Street, called Pleasant the Queen of the Voodoos and claimed she had an unnatural influence over both men and women. In the early twentieth century, a writer named Helen Holdredge would write a book calling Mary Ellen a "procuress" who staged "wild parties" attended by Thomas Bell. Holdredge's heavily fictionalized book also would refer to "the mad, evil passions of [Pleasant's] nature, inherited from her voodoo queen mother," using the tabloid and stereotype-rich style of other writers during America's segregated era.

Ultimately, Mary Ellen Pleasant would pay the same price as many other extraordinary women, black and white, who were too bold and accomplished for their times. Mary Ellen spent her final five years at a cottage on San Jose Road and in a house on Webster Street. She died in 1904 at the age of ninety in the home of friends, while one of those friends honored her last request by singing "Rock of Ages." The woman who once owned at least a million dollars' worth of property reportedly left an estate valued at only ten thousand dollars in 1910, the year her will was admitted to probate. Not everyone agrees with that estimate. "The insolvency papers I saw amounted to hundreds of thousands, and that assessment occurred after she had sold off many properties," says Bibbs. Yet Pleasant left behind far more than ten thousand or hundreds of thousands of dollars' worth of stories and questions.

Was Mary Ellen Pleasant the protector of young, defenseless females whom she sought to marry off or did she exploit them for financial gain? Was she a black female so ahead of her time and so unaccountably successful that people believed she must have some occult power?

Did she practice voodoo, study it or benefit from the fearsome image it gave her? Was she a San Francisco founding mother or merely another brassy slice of Gold Rush legend? Was she a madam or a mother hen, a brilliant investor or a schemer or, as the *Oakland Tribune* put it, "a wonderful woman, with a dominating mind . . . [who] bent everyone about her to her will"?

It may not ever be possible to fully answer such questions. However, in February 1965, the African American Historical and Cultural Society of San Francisco put a stone marker over her grave in Napa, California. Etched into it were the words Mary Ellen had chosen as her final ones: SHE WAS A FRIEND OF JOHN BROWN. Meanwhile, her trolley case was used in 1982 to win the first damages in a case of discrimination. Saint or sinner, schemer or genius, voodoo queen or entrepreneur or, perhaps, all of this and more, Mary Ellen Pleasant embraced life and left her mark on a city, a nation and an era.

So call her a capitalist and civil rights pioneer. Call her crafty, caring, bold, bewitching, super bright and super rich. Just don't call her mammy.

EPILOGUE

Nobody sits down and plans how to become larger than life. People become great thinkers, great social activists, great souls by meeting the greatest challenges of their times. The civil rights movements of the nineteenth and twentieth centuries produced more than their share of men and women—including Mary Ellen Pleasant—who woke up one morning determined not to suffer silently anymore. With each step along the road to progress, their vision grew and they found ways to do more. Mary Ellen Pleasant was known as the mother of the civil rights movement in California, but a score of other women could call themselves mothers of various phases and branches of that movement, too.

For many African Americans, the daily public humiliation of having to ride in a special section of a trolley or bus—or being refused a ride altogether—symbolized the whole Jim Crow system. That's why many early protests revolved around transportation. Elizabeth Jennings defied segregation on a horse-drawn streetcar in 1854. It started on a hot Sunday in July 1854 when the twenty-four-year-old schoolteacher and church organist boarded a horse-drawn streetcar. She was on her way to her church in Manhattan. Conductors could decide whether African Americans could ride. The conductor on Jennings's car decided she couldn't on that particular

Sunday. So he had her thrown off. Represented in court by Chester A. Arthur, who would later become president of the United States, she successfully sued the conductor, the driver and the Third Avenue Railway Company. In 1855, a Brooklyn circuit court judge ruled in her favor, ending racial segregation on public transportation in the city.

Ida B. Wells Barnett is credited with starting an antilynching crusade after whites lynched three black Memphis grocers in 1892. However, in 1884, when Wells was only twenty-two and teaching in Tennessee, she refused to sit in a segregated train car. She was thrown off the train but filed a successful lawsuit against the railroad company. The Tennessee Supreme Court later reversed the lower court's decision, but Wells had driven the first wedge into the system.

Born a slave in 1861, Callie House grew up in a poor family in central Tennessee. By 1898, she was a mother of five, earning about two dollars a week as a Nashville washerwoman. A talented organizer, she put together the first convention of the National Ex-Slave Mutual Relief, Bounty and Pension Association. It pushed state and federal governments for pensions for slaves who had received nothing for serving as teamsters, cooks, diggers, scouts, nurses, carpenters and day laborers for the Union Army. It was a forerunner of contemporary pushes for slave reparations.

In 1865, a trolley conductor refused to let antislavery activist Sojourner Truth board his horse-drawn car, dislocating her arm in the process. Truth launched a campaign that ended segregated public transportation in Washington, D.C. Charlotte Hawkins Brown was ejected from a Pullman berth on a train passing near Anniston, Alabama. She sued and won a small settlement but continued to express her discontent with the system. Founder of a black school that she kept alive through constant fund-raising in the North, Brown went out of her way to thwart segregation. Decades before the sit-ins of the 1960s, she demanded and was served coffee in North Carolina restaurants and would rent an entire movie theater for the day so her students could avoid sitting in the "colored" section. She was president of the North Carolina Federation of Women's Clubs from 1915 to 1936.

In 1944, Viola White was arrested on a bus in Montgomery for violating the segregation code and then beaten and jailed. She was released but when she died ten years later, her appeal had not yet been heard.

Also in 1944, twenty-seven-year-old Irene Morgan, who was recovering from a miscarriage, made history when she boarded a packed Greyhound bus in Gloucester, Virginia. She had left her son and daughter with her mother in Gloucester so she could return home to Baltimore for a checkup. She walked back to the fourth row from the rear and picked an aisle seat next to a young mother holding a baby. A few miles up the road, the driver ordered the two black women to stand and give their seats to a white couple. Morgan refused to move just as Rosa Parks, eleven years later, would refuse to stand along with three other black people so one white man could sit. Morgan not only kept her seat; she made the other black woman holding a baby stay put, too. When a sheriff's deputy tried to serve her with a warrant, she tore it up and threw it out the window. She was dragged off the bus, fighting all the way, and thrown in jail. She plead guilty to resisting arrest but not to violating Virginia's segregation laws. The NAACP appealed the case to the U.S. Supreme Court. On June 3, 1946, the high court struck down Virginia's segregation law on buses traveling from one state to another. This sparked the first freedom rides as black and white activists began riding interstate buses to test the ruling. In 1947, eight white and eight black activists from the newly formed Congress of Racial Equality set off on a two-week journey through four southern states to test the Morgan ruling. Twelve of them were arrested six times for sitting together. One of the riders arrested in Chapel Hill, North Carolina, was Bayard Rustin, who would later organize the 1963 March on Washington. He spent twenty-two days on a prison chain gang.

In 1953—two and half years before Rosa Parks's famous stand—Martha White heated up things in Baton Rouge. On a June morning, she boarded a crowded bus and sat down in the whites-only section. When told to move she did so, but when other blacks on the bus began to laugh and mock her, she sat back down. The driver called the police. Reverend T. J. Jemison stepped in then, and a radio announcement asked blacks to meet at McKinley High School. It did not take much to trigger a boycott in a city where black-owned buses had just been declared illegal and bus fares raised from ten to fifteen cents. The boycott lasted only eight days and failed to eliminate segregation. But it was the nation's first large-scale boycott protesting segregation.

In Montgomery, Alabama, where Rosa Parks took her stand, the movement also had a number of "mothers." One was Jo Ann Robinson. In 1949, a screaming bus driver humiliated Robinson when she absentmindedly sat in the white section of a nearly empty bus. She had accepted a position at Alabama State College, where she was a professor of English. Dr. Mary Fair Burks, head of the Alabama State College's English department, had founded the Women's Political Council in 1946 to push voter registration and activism by black women. Robinson joined the group in the fall of 1949. After her experience on a city bus, she focused on segregated transportation. In the early 1950s, she became president of the WPC. In May 1954, eighteen months before the arrest of Rosa Parks and several days after the U.S. Supreme Court's *Brown v. Board of Education* decision, Robinson wrote to Montgomery's mayor, gently threatening a boycott if abuses weren't corrected. They weren't.

In March 1955, nine months before Rosa Parks changed history, another black woman in Montgomery became an unlikely hero. A fifteen-year-old girl named Claudette Colvin refused to surrender her seat in the unreserved middle section of a Montgomery bus. Colvin was a junior at Booker T. Washington High School. She boarded the bus with three other students. When the driver asked them to move, three of the students complied, but Colvin said, "It's my constitutional right to sit here." That was one of the lessons she'd learned at NAACP youth council meeting led by Rosa Parks. When the bus stopped a few blocks later, two police officers boarded it. When Colvin refused to move, the officers grabbed her by her arms, took her off the bus and forced her to hold her handcuffed hands outside the window of their squad car. The officers claimed that Colvin, who weighed about 110 pounds, had clawed them. In later interviews, she said she didn't remember whether she had scratched the officers. On March 2, 1955, Colvin was jailed for two hours. She was sentenced to one year of probation for violating segregation laws and on other charges. Her arrest made bus seating an issue and black groups met with city commissioners and bus company officials. Rosa Parks was a member of the black delegation and mentor of the NAACP youth council of which Colvin was a member. A number of people refused to ride Montgomery buses for a few days after Colvin's conviction. However, civil rights leaders felt that Colvin, who by then was pregnant by a much older man—statutory rape, she later called it—wouldn't be the right spark to ignite a protest.

In April 1955, Aurelia Browder refused to surrender her seat to a white man on a Montgomery bus. On October 21, 1955, Mary Louise Smith, eighteen, did the same thing. Her employer had withheld a part of her pay and Smith was too angry to put up with discrimination. But once again, Montgomery's civil rights activists failed to turn a teenager's arrest into a cause. It would take Rosa Parks, a woman schooled in nonviolent resistance and a woman wrapped in dignity, to take the stand that would trigger change. However, the 1956 Supreme Court decision that banned segregated buses actually wasn't based on the Rosa Parks case. Parks had been charged only with disorderly conduct. The lawsuit against bus segregation was filed on behalf of four other Montgomery women—Aurelia Browder, Mary Louise Smith, Susie McDonald, a black woman in her seventies, and Claudette Colvin. The lawsuit resulted in the decision striking down Alabama's city and state bus segregation laws.

But, Mamie Till Mobley, mother of fourteen-year-old Emmett Till, who was lynched for allegedly wolf-whistling at a white woman, also helped usher in the age of modern protest. She smuggled the mutilated and almost unrecognizable body of her son out of Mississippi on a train. She then held his open-casket funeral in Chicago. Held in August 1955, that funeral stoked the flames of outrage around the country. Rosa Parks said that this case was in her head the day she refused to surrender her seat on a bus.

In 1958, yet another woman was described as the mother of civil rights. She was Clara Luper, an Oklahoma high school teacher. Luper had attended segregated schools stocked with discarded textbooks and microscopes without lenses. She and twelve members of the NAACP youth council made history after they ordered soft drinks in a downtown Oklahoma drugstore that refused to serve blacks. Their sit-in eventually desegregated the store and all of its branches. It also led to similar sit-ins in Oklahoma City and across the South. Luper would be jailed twenty-six times for nonviolent demonstrations against segregation. Like other women who bore the title mother of civil rights, she persevered and endured.

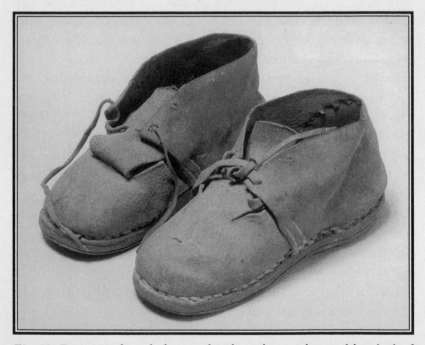

Fig. 19. Runaway slaves lucky enough to have shoes might travel hundreds of miles wearing rough slave-made shoes like these, replacing them as they wore out or, perhaps, creating makeshift shoes from cardboard soles and coat sleeves. (Photo courtesy of the North Carolina Museum of History)

SLAVES?

There used to be laws
against night-roaming Negroes,
against loose-jointed,
liberty-lusting people
who remembered a time
when Africans traded gold for salt and
perfumed their perspiration.
Yet no law could stop the Ibo and the Yoruba,
the Malinke or the Ashanti
from stalking freedom
or brewing pots of fiercely boiling,
Congo-smelling dreams.

No law could stop the Fulani
or the Wolof from leaping into the ocean
from nightmare ships
and drowning in chilly chains
while imagining they were eagles.
And no law could stop black men, women
and children from smearing raw onions
on their bleeding backs
and sprinkling red pepper
on swelling feet
to confound the hounds
on their trail.

They stirred poison
into porridge
and watched planters choke
on honey-sweetened rage.
They escaped on sleighs,
tramped through woods

on frost-bitten feet,
lashed themselves
to the undersides
of passenger trains
and floated across rivers
in molasses barrels.

They fled to the
Dismal Swamp
on the Virginia–North Carolina
border
wearing coats stuffed
with turkey feathers
to protect themselves
from bounty hunters
armed with bird shot.
They ran to Union Army lines
wearing silk cravats
and their masters' undergarments.

And, if recaptured,
some stood on auction blocks
and talked about
their ailments
and other truths
the men selling them
wanted to hide.
Their spirituals became
anthems of hope
and outrage
in which Jesus and Dambala
both held the keys
to deliverance.

Their attitudes were often poses,
their laughter artful lies.
Yet even yoked to plows
like mules
or imitating
the ragtime minstrels
who imitated them,
they were men
and women
not merely
slaves.

Fig. 20. This statue honors famed antislavery speaker, preacher and singer Sojourner Truth, who died in 1883 in Battle Creek, Michigan, where the statue stands. (Photo by Dale Rich)

MONUMENTS

I was a spy in the White House
of the rebel states,
a servant gliding like a whisper
through the home of Jefferson Davis.
I listened with my fingertips
and pores to war plots
struggling to be born,
then carried these infants,
squalling,
to the Union.

I flew an airplane when
women were just learning
how to cross their legs
In cars.
I looped the Loop and
glided,
etching victory signs in
the clouds above
Chicago.

I was Eva and Lucy
and Mamie and Bessie,
who sacrificed children
still wet from the womb
to the sun-soaked fields,
to the land's
hungry mouth.
why are there so few
monuments for me?

ACKNOWLEDGMENTS

I wish to thank my patient editor, Malaika Adero; my agent, Rita Rosenkranz; Virginia independent scholar and public historian Deborah Lee; the efficient and solicitous staff of the Thomas Balch Library in Leesburg, Va.; Katharine C. Dale, researcher, Iowa; Dale Rich, researcher, Detroit; Linda Showalter, librarian, Archives and Special Collections Room, Dawes Memorial Library, Marietta College, Marietta, Ohio; Ron Palmer, professor emeritus of the Practice of International Affairs, George Washington University, Washington, D.C.; the staff of the public library in Mobile, Alabama; Victoria Robinson, Alexandria, Va., descendant of Nelson T. Gant; Dr. Anita Jackson, Stephanie Kline and Wanda Bailey of the Nelson T. Gant Foundation, Zanesville, Ohio; the staff of the John McIntire Library, Zanesville, Ohio; Henry Burke, historian, Marietta, Ohio, and descendant of freedom fighter Rockingham John Curtis; Sondra Mose-Ursery, historical activist and former mayor of Vandalia, Mich.; Virginia Handy, log-cabin activist, Sodus, Mich.; Bryan Prince, historian, North Buxton, Ontario; officials at Woodlawn Cemetery, Zanesville, Ohio; the State Historical Society of Missouri; the Charleston County Public Library; the Saddlebred Horse Museum, Lexington, Kentucky; Guy Washington, Pacific West/Intermountain Program

Manager, National Park Service Pacific West Region; and the staff of the San Francisco Public Library History Room.

Also, Kate Clifford Larson, Department of History, Simmons College, Boston, and author of *Bound for the Promised Land*; John Creighton, copartner, Many Rivers Community History Project, Cambridge, Md.; William Jarmon, Old Field Church Creek Community Improvement Association, Cambridge, Md.; Gwen Robinson, historian, Heritage Room, W.I.S.H. Centre, Chatham, Ontario; Mark Patrick of the Burton Historical Collection, Detroit Public Library; Patricia Marshall and Eric Blivens of the North Carolina Museum of History, Raleigh, N.C.; Wanda Hunter, local and state history manager, Cumberland County Public Library & Information Center, Fayetteville, N.C.; Debian Marty, associate professor and chair, California State University, Monterey Bay, and descendant of Ishmael Lee of Cass County, Mich.; Al Miller and Randy Lee Hill, tour guides, Charleston, S.C.; South Carolina Department of Archives and History, Columbia, S.C.; Marianne Cawley, South Carolina Room, Charleston County Public Library; Lori Kimball, Virginia preservationist and researcher; Winona Nelson, great-great-granddaughter of freedom fighter Frank Wanzer; Allen Uzikee Nelson, great-great-grandson of Frank Wanzer; Nancy L. Thompson, Tri-County Genealogical Society, Nevada, Mo.; Veta Tucker, associate professor of English and affiliate professor of African American and Women and Gender Studies, Grand Valley State University, Allendale, Mich.; Michael S. Nassaney, Department of Anthropology, Western Michigan University; Karen Levenback, reference librarian, Kiplinger Research Library, Historical Society of Washington, D.C.; and Gabrielle Bradby Greene, descendant of James H. Cole.

SELECTED BIBLIOGRAPHY

CHAPTER I

African Americans, Voices of Triumph: Leadership. Alexandria, Va.: Time-Life Books, 1994, pp. 83–84.

African Americans, Voices of Triumph: Perseverance, Alexandria, Va.: Time-Life Books, 1993, pp. 62–65.

Ancestry.com. 1900 United States Federal Census (database on-line). Provo, Utah: The Generations Network, Inc., 2004. Original data: United States of America, Bureau of the Census, Twelfth Census of the United States, 1900, Washington, D.C.: National Archives and Records Administration, 1900. T623, 1854 rolls. This is census data for Mrs. Laura L. Bowley, wife of James Alfred Bowley, who was 49 in 1900 and living in Georgetown, South Carolina.

Arps, Walter E., compiler. *Before the Fire: Genealogical Gleanings from the Cambridge Chronicle, 1830–55.* Lutherville, Md.: Bettie Carothers.

"A Worthy Cause," *Christian Recorder,* July 25, 1901.

Bell, Madison Smartt, "Prophetic Dreams, James McBride's protagonist is a slave reminiscent of Harriet Tubman." *New York Times Book Review,* March 2, 2008, p. 14.

Blockson, Charles L. *African Americans in Pennsylvania, Above Ground and Underground: An Illustrated Guide.* Harrisburg, Pa.: RB Books, 2001.

Boritt, Gabor S. *Lincoln the War President: The Gettysburg Lectures.* New York: Oxford University Press, 1992.

Bowley, James Alfred. Letter to Harriet Tubman, 1868. The Kate Clifford Larson digital collection.

Bowman, John S., *The Civil War Day by Day.* Greenwich. Conn.: Dorset Press, 1990, p. 6.

Bradford, Sarah H. *Scenes in the Life of Harriet Tubman,* Dec. 1, 1868. Dorchester County Library, Cambridge, Md., online

Bureau of the Census, U.S. Federal Census, 1870, Dorchester County, Maryland. This documents John and Kessiah's return to Dorchester County. Though the exact date of their return is not known, their youngest son, John R. Bowley, was 2 years old in 1870 and listed as born in Maryland.

Cambridge Democrat, notice, Feb. 6, 1850, signed by Major Bowley, Richard Bowley, and John Bowley. The notice reads: "The subscribers respectfully inform their creditors that they will pay every cent they owe by the First of August next. We hope they will have compass(s)ion on us until that day, which will enable us to pay every cent we owe by that time. It has never been our wish to defraud those who have been kind enough to credit us." The date of signature is given as Jan. 23, 1850.

Canadian Census, Chatham, Ontario, 1861, p. 8. This records 45-year-old John Bowley living with 37-year-old Kessiah and 7 children, ranging in ages from 1 to 17. Five are described as Canadian born.

Carruth, Gorton. *The Encyclopedia of American Facts and Dates,* 9th ed. New York: Harper-Collins, 1993.

"The Celebration at Corinthian Hall," *Frederick Douglass's Paper,* July 9, 1852.

Chadwick, Bruce. *Traveling the Underground Railroad.* Secaucus, N.J.: Carol Publishing Group, 1999.

Chatham's Early Black Community, a project of the Chatham-Kent Black Historical Society, Chatham, Ontario.

Clayton, Ralph. *Cash for Blood: The Baltimore to New Orleans Domestic Slave Trade.* Bowie, Md.: Heritage Books, Inc., 2002.

———. *Black Baltimore, 1820–1870.* Bowie, Md.: Heritage Books, Inc., 1987.

———. *Slavery, Slaveholding, and the Free Black Population of Antebellum Baltimore.* Bowie, Md.: Heritage Books, Inc., 1993.

Cobb, James C. *The Most Southern Place on Earth.* New York: Oxford University Press, 1992, p. 312.

The Conductor, the official newsletter of the National Capital Region Network to Freedom Program, No. 22. Spring 2008, This mentions some blacks who escaped slavery by sea, including Anthony Burns, Thomas Sims, Henry Jarvis and John S. Jacobs.

Conrad, Earl. *Harriet Tubman.* Washington, D.C.: Associated Publishers, Inc., 1943. This includes Harkless Bowley's Aug. 15, 1939, letter to Conrad.

Copeland, Peter F. *The Story of the Underground Railroad.* Mineola, N.Y.: Dover Publications, Inc., 2000.

Creighton, John. "Following Tubman's Trail from North Dorchester High School to Harlem to the Dorchester County Courthouse," an unpublished paper, 1992.

———. Many Rivers Community History Project, copartner. Cambridge, Md.: Interview and tour of Dorchester County on June 27, 2008.

DeRamus, Betty. "Slaves met tricksters, spies on freedom's trail," *Detroit News,* Feb. 8, 2000.

Detroit Tribune, Sunday, Jan. 17, 1886, reminiscences of William Lambert, Detroit Underground Railroad conductor, about slave-stealing gangs and desperadoes.

Dorchester County Circuit Court Equity Papers, Chancery Case #394, State of Maryland v. Polish G. Mills and Bannamon Mills, admins of John Mills, Nov. 1858. Complaint of Eliza A. Brodess v. Polish Mills, testimony of Polish Mills, Oct. 26, 1859. Maryland State Archives.

Dyer, Frederick H. *A Compendium of the War of the Rebellion,* 3 vols. special contents of this edition, New York and London: Thomas Yoseloff, Sagamore Press, Inc., 1959.

Ely, Melvin Patrick. *Israel on the Appomattox: A Southern Experiment in Black Freedom from the 1790s Through the Civil War.* New York: Alfred A. Knopf, 2004.

Emery, Theo. "Watch Night Services Link Past and Future for Blacks," *New York Times,* Dec. 31, 2006.

Farmer's Almanac for the Year of Our Lord 1864, New York: M.T. Cozans, 122 Nassau Street.

"Finding a Way to Freedom: The Underground Railroad in Dorchester and Caroline Counties in the 1850s; a Driving Tour." This publication was made possible with support from the National Park Service, Chesapeake Bay Gateways Network, Dorchester County and Caroline County, Maryland, and financed in part by the Maryland Heritage Areas Authority, an instrument of the State of Maryland.

"First of May Celebration," *Christian Recorder,* May 18, 1867.

Franklin, John Hope, and Loren Schweninger. *Runaway Slaves: Rebels on the Plantation.* New York: Oxford University Press, 1999, pp. 111, 203.

Gladstone, William A. *United States Colored Troops, 1863–1867.* Gettysburg: Thomas Publications, 1990.

Grimes, William. "A Long Surrender: The Guerilla War After the Civil War," *New York Times,* Jan. 30, 2008, B1.

Guy, Anita Aidt. *Maryland's Persistent Pursuit to End Slavery, 1850–1864.* New York: Garland Publishing, Inc., 1997.

Hand, Bill. *A Walking Guide to North Carolina's Historic New Bern.* Charleston: History Press, 2007, pp. 136–39.

Heilprin, Angelo, and Louis Heilprin, eds. *Lippincott's New Gazetteer, a Complete Pronouncing Gazetteer of the World (containing the most recent and authentic information respecting the countries, cities, towns, resorts, islands, rivers, mountains, seas, lakes, etc. in every portion of the globe).* Philadelphia: J.B. Lippincott Co., 1910.

Huelle, Walter E. *Footnotes to Dorchester History.* Cambridge, Md.: Tidewater Publishers, 1969.

Jones, Elias. *Revised History of Dorchester County, Maryland.* Baltimore: The Read-Taylor Press, 1925, pp. 36, 37, 38, 39, 62, 63, 67, 68, 71, 189, 190, 203, 205.

Kimmel, Janice Martz. "Break Your Chains and Fly for Freedom," *Michigan History Magazine* Vol. 80, No. 1, Jan./Feb. 1996, p. 22.

Larson, Kate Clifford. *Bound for the Promised Land.* New York: One World Books, 2004, pp. 89, 90. This tells the story of John Bowley's rescue of his wife, Kessiah Jolley Bowley.

———. Correspondence with Larson, who teaches in the department of history, Simmons College, Boston, Mass. and is author of *Bound for the Promised Land,* a 2004 biography of Harriet Tubman, June 2008.

Lowry, Beverly. *Harriet Tubman: Imagining a Life.* New York: Doubleday, 2007.

Main, Edwin M. *The Story of the Marches, Battles and Incidents of the Third United States Colored Cavalry.* Louisville, Ky.: Globe Printing Company, 1908; reprint, New York: Negro Universities Press, 1970. This is the only nonfiction account of the war experiences of Alfred and Margaret Wood. Allen Ballard's novel, *Where I'm Bound,* is a fictionalized account of Wood's exploits.

Marshall, Nellie M., compiler. *Bible Records of Dorchester County, Maryland, 1612–1969 and*

Baptismal and Marriage Records, 1855–1866, Zion United Methodist Church. Cambridge, Md.: Dorchester County Historical Society, 1971.

Maryland: A Guide to the Old Line State. Compiled by workers of the Writers' Program of the Work Projects Administration in the State of Maryland. New York: Oxford University Press, 1940, pp. 49, 57.

McElvey, Kay Najiyyah. *Early Black Dorchester, 1776–1870: A History of the Struggle of African Americans in Dorchester County, Maryland, to Be Free to Make Their Own Choices.* Dissertation submitted to the faculty of the Graduate School of the University of Maryland in partial fulfillment of the requirements for the degree of Doctor of Education. University of Maryland, College Park, 1991.

McPherson, James M. *Marching Toward Freedom: Blacks in the Civil War, 1861–1865.* New York: Facts on File, Inc., 1991.

McRae, Bennie, military historian. Email about his search for information about Alfred and Margaret Wood, www.coax.net/people/lwf/wood.htm, Oct. 21, 2003.

Martin, David G. *The Vicksburg Campaign, April 1862–July 1863.* New York: Gallery Books, 1990.

Michener, James A. *Chesapeake.* New York: Fawcett Books, 1978.

Miller, Francis Trevelyan, editor in chief. *The Photographic History of The Civil War in Ten Volumes,* Vol. 8. Articles cited include "Boys Who Made Good Soldiers," by Charles King, pp. 189–94; "The Secret Service of the Federal Armies," by George H. Casamajor," p. 261; and "The Secret Service of the Confederacy," by John W. Headley, p. 285. Information and quotations about boys who fought in the war come from the article by Charles King, brigadier general, United States Volunteers. The quotation about boys under 18 being forbidden to carry muskets is King's as well. Frank Robinson, a drummer in Musician Company E of Michigan's 102nd U.S. Colored Infantry, was only 10 years old when the Civil War finally staggered and bled to a close.

Morris, Holly. "Landscape Artist: Robert Mcfarlane hikes, climbs and swims through the British Isles in search of parts unspoiled." *New York Times Book Review,* July 6, 2008, p. 5.

Moxey, Debra S. *Dorchester County Genealogical Magazine,* Vol. 14, No. 5, Jan. 1995, Madison, Md., Chattel Records 1827–1833.

"Negro for Sale." Advertisement in *Cambridge Democrat,* Sep. 5, 1849.

Oickle, Alvin F. *Jonathan Walker, the Man with the Branded Hand: An Historical Biography.* Everett, Mass.: Lorelli Slater Publisher, 1998.

Osborn, Albert. *John Fletcher Hurst: A Biography.* New York: Eaton & Mains, 1905.

Phillips, Christopher. *Freedom's Port: The African American Community of Baltimore, 1790–1860.* Chicago: University of Chicago, 1997, p. 106.

Polacsek, John, former curator of Dossin Great Lakes Museum. Interview about watermen. Detroit, Jan. 24, 2000.

Rambow, John D., ed. *Fodor's Virginia and Maryland: The Guide for All Budgets, Where to Stay, Eat and Explore On and Off the Beaten Path.* New York: Fodor's LLC, 2003.

Rehbein, Leslie, and Kate E. Peterson, eds. *Beyond the White Marble Steps: A Look at Baltimore Neighborhoods.* Baltimore: The Livelier Baltimore Committee of the Citizens Planning and Housing Association, Aug. 8, 1979.

Robinson, Gwendolyn, and John W. Robinson. *Seek the Truth: A Story of Chatham's Black Community.* Copyright 1989 by Gwendolyn Robinson and John W. Robinson and printed and bound in Canada.

Rogers, Barbara Radcliffe, and Stillman Rogers. *Adventure Guide to the Chesapeake Bay.* Edison, N.J.: Hunter Publishing, Inc., 2001.

Rukert, Norman G. *The Fells Point Story.* Baltimore: Bodine & Associates, Inc., 1976.

Schedule I, Inhabitants in town of Georgetown in the County of Georgetown, state of South Carolina, enumerated on the 7th day of June, 1870, p. 19. According to census data, James Alfred Bowley was 26 in 1870 and living in Georgetown, South Carolina, with Laura C. Bowley, 20.

Sernett, Milton C. *Harriet Tubman: Myth, Memory and History.* Durham, N.C.: Duke University Press, 2007.

Seton, Ernest Thompson. *The Nature Library: Animals.* Garden City, N.Y.: Doubleday, Doran & Co., Inc., orig. pub. 1909. Seton also wrote that the white-tailed deer "has actually accompanied the settler into the woods; that has followed affair into newly opened parts of New England and Canada; that has fitted its map to man's, and that can hold its own on the frontier. The white-tail is the American deer of the past and the American deer of the future."

Sharp, Saundra. *Black Women for Beginners.* New York: Writers and Readers Publishing, Inc., 1993.

Switala, William Jr. *Underground Railroad in Pennsylvania.* Mechanicsburg, Pa.: Stackpole Books, 2001.

Thompson, John. *The Life of John Thompson, a Fugitive Slave, Containing His History of 25 Years in Bondage, and His Providential Escape, Written by Himself.* Worcester, Mass.: J. Thompson, 1856.

Tilghman, Mary K. *Frommer's: Maryland and Delaware,* 7th ed. Hoboken, N.J.: Wiley Publishing, Inc., 2006.

Titus, Charles. *The Old Line State: Her Heritage.* Cambridge, Md.: Tidewater Publishers, 1971.

U.S. Federal Census Mortality Schedule, 1850–1880, for Daniel Hughes, ancestry.com. He is described as male, black, married and 63 years old and the cause of death as "Gravel & Para."

Washington, Booker T. *Up from Slavery: An Autobiography.* Grand Rapids, Mich.: Candace Press, 1996, p. 4.

Webster, W. W. *Traditions, Legends and History of Trappe, Star Democrat,* June 21, 1940, www.unicornbookshop.com/trappehistory/first_known_history.pdf. accessed on Feb. 22, 2008.

Wennersten, John R. *Journey in Time and Place.* Centreville, Md.: Tidewater Publishers, 1992.

Williams, T. J. C., and Folger McKinsey. *History of Frederick County Maryland from the Earliest Settlement to the Beginning of the War Between the States, Continued from the Beginning of the Year 1861 Down to the Present Time,* 2 vols., illustrated, Vol. 1, Hagerstown, Md.: The Mail Publishing Company, 1910, pp. 219, 220, 221.

"The Wrath of the Fearful," *National Era,* April 26, 1855.

Wright, Deborah L. "Being Harriet Tubman," bayweekly.com, The Chesapeake's Independent Newspaper Online, Vol. 12, Issue 6, February 5–11, 2004. www.bayweekly.com/year04/issueii06/leadxii06.html. Retrieved on June 14, 2008.

CHAPTER 2

Aptheker, Herbert, ed. *A Documentary History of the Negro People in the United States.* New York: The Citadel Press, 1951. See p. 263 for Frederick Douglass's letter about Ohio.

Beach, Arthur G. *A Pioneer College: the Story of Marietta.* Privately printed, 1935, pp. 56–58.

Biscoe, Alice M. "Underground Railroad," Manuscript Collection, Marietta College, 1899. This unpublished, typed manuscript has handwritten annotations. Alice Biscoe was the daughter of Marietta College professor Thomas Dwight Biscoe.

Black, Donald F. *History of Wood County, West Virginia,* Vol. 1. Marietta, Ohio: Donald F. Black, 1975.

Boss, L. R. "Tabb Family of Mason Co.," *Kentucky Families,* Vol. 6, No. 2, Oct. 1970.

Boyle, Kevin. "White Terrorists: How racists defrauded black voters in a Louisiana town in 1872, and then attacked and killed those who resisted." *New York Times Book Review,* May 18, 2008, p. 24.

Burke, Henry Robert, and Charles Hart Fogle. *Washington County Underground Railroad,* Images of America Series. Charleston, S.C.: Arcadia Publishing, 2004.

Burke, Henry Robert. Lecture aboard the steamer *Margaret,* July 26, 2007, near Parkersburg, West Virginia.

Burke, Henry, and Dick Croy. *The River Jordan, a True Story of the Underground Railroad.* Marietta, Ohio: Watershed Books, 2001.

Burke, Sandra Moats, of Wheeling, Ohio. Letter posted on Underground Railroad Research Forum, Underground Railroad is American History, Sep. 28, 2004, at 10:42 P.M., www.afrigeneas.com/forum-ugrr.

Burson, Roberta S. "Famous Old Landmark Soon to Give Way to Modern Progress," *Marietta Times (Ohio),* Oct. 2, 1953.

Burt, Alvah Walford. *Cushman Genealogy and General History, Including the Descendants of the Fayette County, Pennsylvania, and Monongalia County, Virginia, Families.* Cincinnati: Alvah H. Burt, 1942.

Carruth, Gorton. *The Encyclopedia of American Facts and Dates,* 9th ed. New York: HarperCollins, 1993.

Cayton, Robert Frank, ed. *The City of Marietta, Ohio, 1788–1987, a Bibliography.* Marietta, Ohio: Robert F. Cayton, 1987.

Curtis, Nancy C. *Black Heritage Sites: The North.* New York: New Press, 1996, p. 174. This contains a brief account of John Rankin's exploits.

"David Putnam Jr., Obituary," *Marietta Leader (Ohio),* Jan. 9, 1892.

DeRamus, Betty. "Slaves met tricksters, spies on freedom's trail," *Detroit News,* Feb. 8, 2001, p. D1.

———. "Strait of Detroit shaped our fate," *Detroit News,* May 29, 2001, p. D1.

Eldridge, Ann, and Henry Burke. *Passages to Freedom: An Ohio Underground Railroad Story,* videotape produced by Ann Eldgridge and Gary Baker Production and presented by Ohio University–Zanesville and the Ohio Humanities Council, in collaboration with the Muskingum County Community Foundation and the Putnam Underground Railroad Education Center, Zanesville, Ohio.

Hagedorn, Ann. *Beyond the River.* New York: Simon & Schuster, 2005.

Harris, Jessica B. "Juneteenth," *American Legacy,* Summer 2006, p. 16.

Horton, James Oliver, and Lois E. Horton. *Slavery and the Making of America.* New York: Oxford University Press, 2005.

"A Lawsuit in Slavery Times." Cutler Collection, June 25, 1849, unpublished, unsigned, handwritten manuscript, which appears to be in the handwriting of Julia P. Cutler, daughter of Ephraim Cutler and granddaughter of Manasseh Cutler.

Leahy, Ethel C., ed. *Who's Who on the Ohio River and Its Tributaries: The Ohio River from the Ice Age to the Future.* Cincinnati: E.C. Leahy Publishing Co., 1931.

Leavengood, Betty. *Wood County West Virginia,* Images of America Series. Charleston: Arcadia Publishing, 2003.

Letters (1) from Cesar Fairfax and (2) from Allen Fairfax to David Putnam in 1847 and 1848. The letters appear to be in the handwriting of Julia P. Cutler, daughter of Ephraim Cutler and granddaughter of Manasseh Cutler. Librarians at Marietta College believe they are Julia Cutler's handwritten copies of original documents about the David Putnam Jr. case.

Lutz, Ashton, and Susanna Ashton, eds. *These "Colored United States."* New Brunswick, N.J.: Rutgers University Press, 1996. Wendell P. Dabney's essay on Ohio appears on pp. 218–26.

Niven, John. *Salmon P. Chase: A Biography.* New York: Oxford University Press, 1995.

———. ed. *The Salmon P. Chase Papers,* Vol. 2, *Correspondence, 1823–1857.* Kent, Ohio: The Kent State University Press, 1994.

The Ohio Guide, compiled by workers of the Writers' Program of the Work Projects Administration in the state of Ohio. New York: Oxford University Press, 1940, pp. 436–37.

Parker, John P. *His Promised Land: The Autobiography of John P. Parker, Former Slave and Conductor on the Underground Railroad.* New York: W. W. Norton & Co., 1996.

Pender, Rick. "Opening the Door," *City Beat,* July 13–19, 2005. A piece on the staging of an opera about Margaret Garner in Cincinnati.

Rawick, George P., ed. *The American Slave: A Composite Autobiography,* Vol. 17, *Florida Narratives,* orig. pub. 1941; reprint, Westport, Conn.: Greenwood Publishing Co., 1974, pp. 146–54.

Rebok, Barbara, and Doug Rebok. *State of West Virginia, Wood & Wirt Counties, Compiled from Early Historical Writings.* Tucson, Ariz.: Aplusprint, 2000.

Runyon, Randolph Paul. *Delia Webster and the Underground Railroad.* Lexington, Ky.: University Press of Kentucky, 1996.

Siebert, Wilbur. *The Underground Railroad.* New York: Macmillan Co., 1898. Siebert names three Underground Railroad agents living in the West Virginia area, Joshua Steele, Dick Naler, a free black who operated in the Wheeling area, and Joseph Bryant, who helped fugitives in Brooke County. Siebert also speaks of an unidentified black man near Martin's Ferry, Ohio, who would cross the river and go through the Panhandle region of West Virginia, encouraging slaves to escape and telling them how to do it.

"A Station on the Old Underground Railroad," *Marietta Daily Register,* Vol. 1, No. 115, Marietta, Ohio, Oct. 19, 1891, p. 3, cols. 1 and 2.

Summers, William B. "Insuperable Barriers: A Case Study of the Henderson v. Putnam Fugitive Slave Case," *The Tallow Light,* Vol. 26, No. 3, Winter 1995. Magazine of the Washington County Historical Society, Marietta, Ohio. Summers tells the story of two brothers who ran away from George Washington Henderson, made it to Canada and then both wrote letters to Henderson. They apologized for running away and asked to return to his plantation. Henderson agreed to let them come back. Isaac ran away a second time on February 15, 1846, taking with him $150 of Henderson's property and stealing his wife, Fanny, and his daughter, June, two slaves belonging to Joseph Tomlinson, Jr. According to Summers, the brothers were named Simon and Isaac Harris. Ohio historian Henry Burke says one of the brothers was named Isaac Fairfax and that he may have returned from Canada expressly to rescue his family.

Swick, Ray, and Christina Little. *Blennerhassett Island.* Charleston: Arcadia Publishing, 2005.

"Two Slaves," *Marietta Intelligencer,* Feb. 11, 1847, p. 2, col. 6.

Walker, Alice, ed. *I Love Myself When I Am Laughing: A Zora Neale Hurston Reader.* Old Westbury, N.Y.: Feminist Press, 1979.

White, Larry Nash, Ph.D., and Emily Blankenship. *Marietta,* Images of America Series. Charleston, S.C.: Arcadia Publishing, 2004.

Willey, Larry. "John Rankin, Antislavery Prophet, and the Free Presbyterian Church," *American Presbyterian.* 72, No. 3 (Fall 1994).

Wright, Alice. *The Ohio River.* Marietta, Ohio: Hyde Brothers Printing Co.

Wright, Roberta Hughes, and Wilbur B. Hughes III. *Lay Down Body: Living History in African American Cemeteries.* Detroit: Visible Ink Press, 1996, p. 113.

www.teachingwithstories.com/teachers/stories.htm. This tells the story of Allen Watkins. It was accessed on March 27, 2008.

Zimmer, Louis. *More True Stories from Pioneer Valley.* Marietta, Ohio: Sugden Book Store, 1993.

CHAPTER 3

Advertisement for Nelson Gant's strawberries in the *Daily Zanesville Courier,* Vol. III, No. 127, whole no. 1637, June 2, 1854.

African Americans: Voices of Triumph. Alexandria, Va.: Time-Life Books, 1993, p. 93.

Alexander, Adele Logan. *Homelands and Waterways: The American Journey of the Bond Family, 1846–1926.* New York: Pantheon Books, 1999.

Alexandria Gazette and Weekly Advertiser, March 17, 1840, p. 3.

Alsberg, Henry G., ed. *The American Guide.* New York: Hastings House, 1949.

Appiah, Kwame Anthony. "A Slow Emancipation," *New York Times Magazine,* March 18, 2007.

Blight, David. *A Slave No More: Two Men Who Escaped to Freedom, Including Their Own Narratives of Emancipation.* Orlando: Harcourt, Inc., 2007.

Biographical and Historical Memoirs of Muskingum County, Ohio: Embracing an Authentic and Comprehensive Account of the Chief Events in the History of the County and a Record of the Lives of Many of the Most Worthy Families and Individuals. Illustrated. Chicago: Goodspeed Publishing Co., 1892, A Reproduction by Unigraphic, Inc., 1401 North Fares Avenue, Evansville, Ind., pp. 270, 462, 463.

"Black History Month events at Ohio University–Zanesville," Feb. 20, 2002. News release from Ohio University–Zanesville public relations coordinator.

Blassingame, John W., ed. *Slave Testimony: Two Centuries of Letters, Speeches, Interviews and Autobiographies.* Baton Rouge: Louisiana State University Press, 1977, p. 109, footnotes.

Blockson, Charles L. *The Underground Railroad.* New York: Prentice Hall Press, 1987, p. 151.

Boritt, Gabor S., ed. *Lincoln the War President: The Gettysburg Lectures.* New York: Oxford University Press, 1992.

Bowman, John S., ed. *The Civil War, Day by Day: An Illustrated Almanac of America's Bloodiest War.* Greenwich, Conn.: Dorset Press, 1989.

Brodie, Fawn M. "Thomas Jefferson's Unknown Grandchildren." *American Heritage* Vol. XXVII, No. 6 (Oct. 1976).

Catterall, Helen Tunnicliff, ed. *Judicial Cases Concerning American Slavery and the Negro,* Vol. I, *Cases from the Courts of England, Virginia, West Virginia and Kentucky.* New York: Octagon Books, Inc., 1968, pp. 120, 122.

Cave, Janet P., ed. *African Americans, Voices of Triumph,* Vol. I, *Perseverance.* Alexandria, Va.: Time Life Books, 1993.

Christian Recorder, Dec. 8, 1866.

Cleveland Gazette, Oct. 23, 1886, 1, 5, notes that Nelson Gant "began with laundry work and selling milk, is today worth $100,000."

Douglass, Margaret. *Educational Laws of Virginia: The Personal Narrative of Mrs. Margaret Douglass, a Southern Woman Who was Imprisoned for one Month in the Common Jail of Norfolk, Under the Laws of Virginia, for The Crime of Teaching Free Colored Children to Read.* Boston: Jewett, Proctor & Worthington, 1854. Reprinted by the Cornell University Library Digital Collections, www.library.cornell.edu.

Drew, Benjamin. *A North-side View of Slavery.* New York: Negro University Press, 1968, pp. 105–9. Contains the narrative of Charles Peyton Lucas, an enslaved Leesburg blacksmith who swam across the Potomac River to become free and then migrated to Canada where he eventually told his story.

Eldridge, Ann, and Henry Burke. *Passages to Freedom, an Ohio Underground Railroad Story,* videotape produced by Ann Eldridge and Gary Baker Production and presented by Ohio University–Zanesville and the Ohio Humanities Council, in collaboration with the Muskingum County Community Foundation and the Putnam Underground Railroad Education Center, Zanesville, Ohio.

Ely, Melvin Patrick. *Israel on the Appomattox: A Southern Experiment in Black Freedom from the 1790s Through the Civil War.* New York: Alfred A. Knopf, 2004. This recounts the tale of a black colony of slaves freed by Virginia aristocrat Richard Randolph in the 1790s. He granted them 400 acres of his land in an area that came to be known as Israel Hill.

The Essence of a People: Portraits of African Americans Who Made a Difference in Loudoun County, Virginia. Leesburg, Va.: Black History Committee of the Friends of the Thomas Balch Library, May 2001.

Farr, John, Ann M. Farr, his wife, and Thomas J. Stanhope. Affidavits, March 13, 1840, before John Gunnell, Fairfax County justice of the peace, filed with Petition for Pardon of Leonard Grimes, Virginia Executive Papers, Letters Received, Rejected Claims 1842 folder, in Jan.–March 1843 box, Library of Virginia.

Flanigan, Daniel J. "Criminal Procedure in Slave Trials in the Antebellum South." *Journal of Southern History* Vol. 40, No. 4 (Nov. 1974): pp. 537–64.

France, Grace. *Principle Farmers, Muskingum County 1877–1878.* Muskingum County Genealogical Society, Jan. 1998. The pamphlet documents that Gant was a major farmer in Muskingum County in the late 1800s.

Gant, Nelson Talbourt (sic), to Dr. Julius LeMoyne. Copy of handwritten letter dictated or written June 7, 1847. In the letter, Gant explains, "I have seen and felt much of the horrors of slavery . . . my wife was confined in Leesburg jail . . . days and threatened by one of her owners to be sold to the far South if she did not testify against me this she refused to do . . . my lawyers pleaded on the grounds that we were lawfully married and with the consent of our master and mistress and upon these grounds we were acquitted by the county court. The lawsuit and purchase of my wife amounts to upwards $775 with the assistance of my friends and borrowing about $225 from Thomas Nichols all is settled."

Gordon, Robert B. *The Natural Vegetation of Ohio in Pioneer Days.* Columbus, Ohio: Ohio State University, 1969.

Guild, June Purcell. *Black Laws of Virginia,* fourth printing. Lovettsville, Va.: Willow Bend Books, 1996. Orig. pub. 1936 by Whittet & Shepperson.

Hagedorn, Ann. *Beyond the River: The Untold Story of the Heroes of the Underground Railroad.* New York: Simon & Schuster, 2002, p. 99.

Hamilton, Kendra Y., ed. *The Essence of a People II: African Americans Who Made Their World Anew in Loudoun County, Virginia, and Beyond.* Leesburg, Va.: Friends of the Thomas Balch Library, 2002.

Head, James W. *History of Loudoun County Virginia.* Park View Press, copyright 1908 by James W. Head.

Hine, Darlene Clark, Elsa Barkley Brown, Rosalyn Terborg-Penn, eds. *Black Women in America: An Historical Encyclopedia,* Vol. 2, M-Z. Bloomington: Indiana University Press, 1993, pp. 766–67.

Huff, Rea, member, Muskingum County Genealogical Society. Interview, June 23, Zanesville, Ohio, about the characteristics of Dresden melons.

"An Interesting Case and an Important Decision," *National Era,* Vol. 1, No. 1, Jan. 7, 1847, p. 4.

Jackson, Dr. Anita, of the Nelson T. Gant Foundation. Interview, June 21, 2007, about plans to turn the old Gant homestead into a museum and cultural center in Zanesville, Ohio.

Jackson, L. P. "The Daniel Family of Virginia," *Negro History Bulletin,* Vol. 11, No. 3 (Dec. 1947): p. 51. This article documents that a number of free blacks bought members of their own families to keep them from being sold away. Maria Langston, the child of a mixed-race woman and a white planter, inherited land and slaves from her father, including her husband, Joseph Powell. Although she held Powell in bondage all of his life, he functioned as a free man and they had 21 children together. Maria and Joseph's daughter, Lucinda Powell, married an enslaved shoemaker named William Daniel, whom she owned. He, too, lived as a free man. In 1847, as a result of his wife's last will and testament, he became legally free.

Kaufman, Polly Welts, Bonnie Hurd Smith, Mary Howland Smoyer, and Susan Wilson. *Boston Women's Heritage Trail, Four Centuries of Boston Women,* Gloucester, Mass.: Curious Traveller Press, 1999.

Kehr, Dave. "Critic's Choice: New DVDs," *New York Times,* May 22, 2007. The article describes Gary Cooper as the "face of the American West" and the embodiment of all the flinty virtues of heroes depicted by people such as Zanesville-born author Zane Grey.

Kline, Stephanie, and Wanda Bailey, illustrator. *The Life and Times of Nelson T. Gant in Color.* Copyright 2003 by Stephanie Kline, Wanda Bailey and the Education Committee of the Nelson T. Gant Foundation, Zanesville, Ohio.

Knappman, Edward W. *Great American Trials.* Detroit: Gale Research, Inc., 1994, p. 173.

Lee, Deborah A. *African American Heritage Trail.* Leesburg, Va.: Loudoun Museum and the Black History Committee of the Friends of the Thomas Balch Library, 2001.

Lewis, Thomas W. *Zanesville and Muskingum County, Ohio: A History of the Indians Who Trod This Section Ere the White Man Came; of the Making of City and County by the Heroic Pioneers, and of the Growth of Local Civilization During Six Score Fruitful Years,* Vol. II. Chicago: S.J. Clarke Publishing Company, 1927, pp. 331, 530, 532.

Loudoun County Minute Book, Dec. 14, 1846, p. 209, records the decision in Nelson T. Gant's case which led to Gant being found "not guilty of the offense of which he stands charged."

Loudoun County's African American Communities: A Tour Map and Guide. Leesburg, Va.: Black History Committee of the Friends of the Thomas Balch Library, 2002.

Loudoun County, Virginia, Personal Property Tax Records, 1846, 1848, 1849, 1850.

Loudoun County, Virginia, Will Book, Administrations, 1846. The second proviso of John Nixon's will required that his 22 slaves be relocated to a free state when freed.

Lutz, Ashton, and Susanna Ashton, eds. *These Colored United States.* New Brunswick, N.J.: Rutgers University Press, 1996. Wendell P. Dabney's essay on Ohio, on pp. 218–26, mentions Nelson Gant and other successful black Ohioans.

Martin, Chuck, "Preserving Local History," *Zanesville Times Recorder,* Feb. 26, 2003, p. 1A.

"Meeting of the Colored Citizens in Muskingum County," *North Star* (Rochester, N.Y.), Dec. 5, 1850.

Middleton, Stephen. *The Black Laws, Race and the Legal Process in Early Ohio.* Athens, Ohio: Ohio University Press, 2005.

"Monument Dedication Honors 19th Century Freedom Fighter, Black Nationalist, Major Martin R. Delany," press release from the National Afro-American Museum and Cultural Center, Sep. 7, 2006, Wilberforce, Ohio.

"Mrs. E. H. Gee Dies Suddenly," *Zanesville Signal,* Oct. 16, 1905.

"Nelson T. Gant rose from slavery to become wealthy, respected," *Zanesville Times Recorder,* Feb. 10, 1996, p. 6A.

"Nelson T. Gant," *Newark Advocate,* July 17, 1905.

Notice of Public Sale at a public auction on Nov. 23, 1905, of goods and chattels of Nelson T. Gant, executed by C. T. Marshall and N. T. Gant, Jr., executors of the estate.

The Ohio Guide. Compiled by workers of the Writers' Program of the Work Projects Administration in the State of Ohio. New York: Oxford University Press, 1940.

Patterson, Daniel. "Curd Mentality: To make butter (and sweet buttermilk), first discard excess skepticism," *New York Times Sunday Magazine,* July 1, 2007, p. 63.

"Pioneer Colored Citizen N. T. Gant Dies Suddenly at West Pike Home Last Night," *Zanesville Times Recorder,* July 15, 1905.

Paige, Howard. *African-American Cookery.* Southfield, Mich.: Aspects Publishing Co., 1995. Paige relates the story of Alethia Tanner's successful garden on p. 94 and talks about William Leidesdorf, America's first black millionaire, on p. 101.

Palmer, Ronald, professor emeritus at George Washington University. Email concerning erection of an Underground Railroad memorial to Leonard Grimes at a minipark on the GWU campus at 22nd and H streets. The plaque reads: "Leonard A. Grimes (1815–1873) Leonard A. Grimes, A black man born free in Leesburg, Virginia, owned a residence on this corner from 1836 to 1846. In the 1830s, he owned a successful coach business transporting passengers in and around Washington. He also carried slaves seeking freedom in the North and was an early organizer of The Underground Railroad. From 1840 to 1842, he was imprisoned in Richmond for aiding an escape. In 1846, Grimes moved with his family (in) New Bedford, Massachusetts where he continued his anti-slavery activities. Seeking a larger scope for his work, in 1848 he moved to Boston where he distinguished himself as a cleric, abolitionist and statesman."

Pawlak, Debra Ann. *Farmington and Farmington Hills,* Making of America Series. Charleston, S.C.: Arcadia Publishing, 2003, pp. 8, 9, 21, 22, 24.

Payne, Daniel. "Biographical Sketch of Mrs. Anna Maria Gant," *Christian Recorder,* April 11, 1878. Payne claims that Maria bore 18 children in as many years.

Pelham, Benjamin B. *Family History,* an undated, handwritten manuscript among the Pelham Papers. Detroit: The Burton Historical Collection of the Detroit Public Library.

Powell, William S. *When the Past Refused to Die: A History of Caswell County, North Carolina, 1777–1977.* Yanceyville, N.C.: Caswell County Historical Association, Inc., 1994; orig. pub. Moore Publishing Co.: Durham. N.C., 1977. See p. 531 for an 1837 Caswell County, North Carolina, court case in which a slave who left his "wife" became angry when she took up with another man. After he killed his ex-wife's new "husband," the local court declared that she could testify against her former husband, Samuel. Samuel was convicted and his case appealed to the State Supreme Court where "the justices discovered that this was a question never before raised in North Carolina nor, as their investigation revealed, had it ever been raised in the adjacent states." The court ruled that the slave, named Mima, was a valid witness against Samuel, her former slave husband.

Quarles, Benjamin. *Black Abolitionists.* New York: Oxford University Press, 1969, pp. 82, 146, 206, 208, 209, 242.

Ramsdell, William S. "Woodlawn's sexton," *Chemung Historical Journal* 43, No. 1 (Sep. 1997).

Rawick, George P. *From Sundown to Sunup: The Making of the Black Community,* Westport, Conn.: Greenwood Publishing Company, 1972, pp. 88–91.

Register of Free Negroes, Loudoun County, Virginia. Certificate number 1406, Feb. 14, 1847.

Residence of N. T. Gant, photo from the *New Historical Atlas of Muskingum Co., Ohio,* L. H. Everts & Co., 1875. The photo includes the old Gant homestead, a barn and three outbuildings.

Robinson, Victoria III, great-granddaughter, Nelson and Maria Gant, living in Alexandria, Va. Interviews, April 9, 2007, and May 18, 2007, Leesburg, Virginia.

Robinson, Victoria J. "Registered in the Chancery of Heaven: The Marriage of Nelson Talbot Gant and Anna Maria Hughes," draft of a paper being revised by Robinson and originally presented at the AAAHRP 3rd Annual History Conference in 2006.

Rubin, Anne Sarah. Honorable Whig: The Life and Politics of John Janney of Virginia. A Thesis Presented to the Graduate Faculty of the University of Virginia in Candidacy for the Degree of Master of Arts. Department of History, University of Virginia, January 1993.

Saillant, John, ed. *Afro-Virginian History and Culture.* New York: Garland Publishing, Inc., 1999, p. 161. Gregg Kimball's essay, "Richmond's Place in the African American Diaspora," on p. 161, talks about how escaped slaves managed to communicate with those they'd left behind by sending letters to their friends in care of area churches.

Schneider, Norris F. *Y Bridge City: The Story of Zanesville and Muskingum County.* Cleveland:

World Publishing Co., copyright 1950 by Norris G. Schneider, copyright 1983, Muskingum County Chapter, OGS.

————. *Zanesville Stories, A Subject Index,* Vol. II, *1946–1951.* Zanesville, Ohio, 1965. On pp. 101–2 is an article by Schneider entitled, "Nelson T. Gant Remembered as Outstanding Herein 1847 from Louden County, Virginia: April 14, 1946."

Schwaegerle, Edward G., volunteer in research, Oberlin College Archives. Email to Stephanie Kline, Zanesville, Ohio, researcher on March 10, 2003, about members of the Gant family who attended Oberlin College.

Schwartz, Philip. *Migrants Against Slavery, Virginians and the Nation.* Charlottesville: University Press of Virginia, 2001, p. 33.

"A Scrap of History," *Zanesville Courier,* Thursday, August 16, 1888, p. 2.

Smith, Rev. David. *Biography of Rev. David Smith of the A.M.E. Church; Being a Complete History, Embracing over Sixty Years' labor in the Advancement of the Redeemer's Kingdom on Earth. Including "The History of the Origin and Development of Wilberforce University":* Electronic Edition, docsouth.unc.edu/neh/dsmith/dsmith.html.

Stevenson, Brenda E. *Life in Black and White: Family and Community in the Slave South.* New York: Oxford University Press, 1996.

Still, William. *The Underground Railroad.* Philadelphia: Porter & Coates, 1872. This tells the story of Joshua Pusey's escaped slave.

Sutor, J. Hope. *Past and Present of the City of Zanesville and Muskingum County.* Ohio, Chicago, 1905, p. 374. Wilbur H. Siebert Collection, Microfilm Edition Roll 12, frame 675.

Switala, William J. *Underground Railroad in Pennsylvania.* Mechanicsburg, Pa.: Stackpole Books, 2001, p. 70.

Virginia, A Guide to the Old Dominion. Compiled by Workers of the Writers' Program of the Work Projects Administration in the State of Virginia, Virginia State Library and Archives, in cooperation with the Virginia Center for the Book, Richmond, 1992; orig. pub., Oxford University Press, 1940.

Washington, Booker T. *Up from Slavery: An Autobiography.* Grand Rapids, Mich. Candace Press, 1996, p. 15.

Washington Newspaper, July 11, 1846. Thomas Balch Library, Leesburg, Va. This contains an advertisement for wood choppers, which Nelson Gant may have answered.

Wertz, Mary Alice, compiler. *Marriages of Loudoun County, Virginia, 1757–1853.* Baltimore: Genealogical Publishing Co., Inc., 1985.

Wierman, Lydia. Letter, *Pennsylvania Freeman,* Nov. 20, 1845, p. 1. A Quaker abolitionist in Pennsylvania, Wierman had visited John Nixon, Nelson Gant's owner, in Loudoun County. She published a letter in 1845 talking about her experiences with slave owners, including Nixon.

Williams, Stacy. "The Black Preacher and the Black Church." Lecture #2 on the Black Church, Council of Baptists Pastors, Pleasant Grove Baptist Church, Detroit, September 16, 1980.

Woodford, Arthur M, principal author. *Detroit: American Urban Renaissance.* Tulsa: Continental Heritage, Inc., 1979.

Wright, Roberta Hughes, and Wilbur B. Hughes III. *Lay Down Body: Living History in African American Cemeteries.* Detroit: Visible Ink Press, 1996.

www.nps.gov/archive/fone/classroom/nr4teacher.htm. This National Park Service website is a guide for teachers instructing students about the National Road.

Zanesville Signal, June 1, 1921. Obituary for Sarah Speed.

CHAPTER 4

African American Voices of Triumph: Perseverance, by the editors of Time-Life Books. Alexandria, Va.: Time-Life Books, 1993, pp. 38, 48, 54.

African Americans Voices of Triumph: Leadership, by the editors of Time-Life Books. Alexandria, Va.: Time-Life Books, 1993, pp. 20, 90–91, 127.

Alexander, Adele Logan. *Homelands and Waterways: The American Journey of the Bond Family, 1846–1926.* New York: Pantheon Books, 1999. This is an account of the life and times of John Robert Bond, a young mulatto man who grew up in Liverpool, England.

Aptheker, Herbert. "South Carolina Poll Tax, 1737–1895," *Journal of Negro History* 31, No. 2 (April 1946): pp. 131–39.

Bennett, John. *The Doctor to the Dead: Grotesque Legends and Folk Tales of Old Charleston.* Columbia, S.C.: University of South Carolina Press, 1955; orig. pub. New York: Rinehart, 1946.

Bleser, Carol, ed. *Secret and Sacred: The Diaries of James Henry Hammond, a Southern Slaveholder.* New York: Oxford University Press, 1988.

Bleser, Carol, ed. *The Hammonds of Redcliffe.* New York: Oxford University Press, 1981.

British & Foreign Anti-Slavery Reporter, Sep. 18, 1844, p. 183.

British & Foreign Anti-Slavery Reporter, Nov. 14, 1842, pp. 202–3. Results of emancipation in Jamaica.

"Capital Punishment in South Carolina," *New York Herald,* Jan. 10, 1844.

"Capital Punishment in South Carolina," *North American and Daily Advertiser,* Jan. 23, 1844.

"Capital Punishment in South Carolina," *Cleveland Herald,* Jan. 11, 1844.

"Capital Punishment in South Carolina," *Raleigh Register and North-Carolina Gazette,* Feb. 2, 1844.

"The case of John Brown, who was sentenced to be hung, in South Carolina, for aiding a female slave to escape, has caused a great sensation in Great Britain," *New-Hampshire Statesman and State Journal,* May 17, 1844, No. 3, col. B.

Caterall, Helen Tunnicliff, ed. *Judicial Cases Concerning American Slavery and the Negro,* Vol. II, *Cases from the Courts of North Carolina, South Carolina and Tennessee.* New York: Octagon Books, Inc., 1968, pp. 267, 268, 275.

Charleston County Public Library, South Carolina Room, Sep. 2, 2007. Email identifying John L. Brown of South Carolina as "a black abolitionist."

Columbia Telescope, July 21, 1838, issue 30. In an advertisement, W. E. Richardson, sheriff of South Carolina's Sumter District, offers a $100 reward for the capture of Mina McCoy.

Curtis, Nancy C., Ph.D. *Black Heritage Sites: The South.* New York: New Press, 1996.

Davis, Kenneth C. *Don't Know Much About History.* New York: Crown Publishers, Inc., 1990, pp. 125–26.

DeBow, J. D. B., compiler. *Statistical View of the United States . . . Being a Compendium of the Seventh Census, 1850.* Washington, D.C.: Census Office, 1854, pp. 94, 178. The superintendent of the 1850 census estimated that 2.5 million slaves were agricultural workers, including 125,000 who worked with rice.

Dixon, Chris. "36 Hours, Charleston, S.C.," *New York Times,* March 11, 2007, p. 14, Travel.

Douglass, Frederick. "British Influence on the Abolition Movement in America: An Address

Delivered in Paisley, Scotland, on April 17, 1846," *Renfrewshire Advertiser,* April 25, 1846. Reprinted in John Blassingame et al., eds., *The Frederick Douglass Papers, Series One—Speeches, Debates and Interviews.* New Haven: Yale University Press, 1979, Vol. 1, p. 215.

Drescher, Seymour. "Servile Insurrection and John Brown's Body in Europe," *Journal of American History* 80, No. 2 (Sep. 1993): pp. 518–19.

Edgar, Walter, ed. *The South Carolina Encyclopedia.* Refers to the "fertile cotton regions such as Sumter District."

Encyclopedia of South Carolina, 2nd ed., Vol. I, St. Clair Shores, Mich.: Somerset Publishers, Inc., 2000.

Faust, Drew Gilpin. *James Henry Hammond and the Old South: A Design for Mastery.* Baton Rouge: Louisiana State University Press, 1982.

Flanigan, Daniel J. "Criminal Procedure in Slave Trials in the Antebellum South," *Journal of Southern History* 40, No. 4 (Nov. 1974): pp. 537–64.

Fox, William Price. *South Carolina, Off the Beaten Path: A Guide to Unique Places.* Guilford, Conn.: The Globe Pequot Press, 2003.

"From Our European Correspondent," *Daily National Intelligencer,* April 26, 1844.

Geraty, Virginia Mixson. *Gullah Fuh Oonuh (Gullah for You), A Guide to the Gullah Language.* Orangeburg, S.C.: Sandlapper Publishing Co., Inc., 1997, p. 98.

Goodheart, Adam. "The Outsiders: Fictional portraits of real-life black Britons," *New York Times,* Dec. 23, 2007, Book Review section, p. 6.

Gottlieb, Gabriele. "Theater of Death: Capital Punishment in Early America, 1750–1800." Submitted to the Graduate Faculty of the University of Pittsburgh in partial fulfillment of the requirements for the degree of Doctor of Philosophy, University of Pittsburgh, 2005.

Gutman, Herbert G. *The Black Family in Slavery and Freedom, 1750–1925.* New York: Vintage Books, 1977, p. 237. This contains information about wealthy planter Nathaniel Heyward and about slaves who had surnames they didn't share with their masters.

Horton, James Oliver. Interview on National Public Radio about the role of black and white sailors and other watermen in the struggle against slavery, Jan. 2, 2008.

Horton, James Oliver, and Lois E. Horton *Slavery and the Making of America.* New York: Oxford University Press, 2005, pp. 32, 33.

"The Independent vs. The Divine Law," *Charleston Mercury,* April 1, 1857.

"An Interesting Case and an Important Decision," *National Era,* Jan. 7, 1848, Vol. I, No. 1, p. 4.

Jack, Ian. "Britannia Bites, A social history told through the medium of food," *New York Times Sunday Magazine,* Dec. 9, 2007, p. 16.

"John L. Brown Pardoned," *Cleveland Herald,* March 25, 1844.

"John L. Brown Pardoned," *Cleveland Plain Dealer,* March 27, 1844.

LaBrew, Arthur R. *The Detroit History That Nobody Knew (or Bothered to Remember), 1800–1900.* Detroit: privately printed, 2001. See pp. 59–60.

Liberator, March 1, 1844, p. 34.

Liberator, March 29, 1844, p. 51. This article mentions that John L. Brown came from Bathe, Maine, and that his case ought to set that town on fire.

Liberator, April 19, 1844, p. 62.

Liberator, April 26, 1844, p. 67.

McCrea, Scott, "Tragedian of Colour," *American Legacy: The Magazine of African-American History & Culture,* Spring 2005, pp. 56–64.

Merritt, Elizabeth. *James Henry Hammond, 1807–1864.* Baltimore: Johns Hopkins Press, 1923.

North American and Daily Advertiser, Dec. 4, 1844. An advertisement announces a reward of $500 offered by South Carolina governor James H. Hammond for Mina McCoy, who had escaped from jail before his scheduled hanging in November 1844.

Olwell, Robert. *Masters, Slaves & Subjects: The Culture of Power in the South Carolina Low Country, 1740–1790.* Ithaca, N.Y.: Cornell University Press, 1998.

O'Neall, Judge. Letter, Case of John I. Brown, The Late Meeting in Glasgow, Scotland, Springfield, Newberry District, South Carolina, May 1, 1844. *Greenville Mountaineer,* Greenville, S.C., Friday, Aug. 16, 1844, issue 14, col. A. This is a letter from O'Neall to Bailie Hastie, Chairman of the Anti-Slavery Meeting, Glasgow, Scotland.

"Petitions Presented by John Quincy Adams to the House of Representatives of the United States at the 28th Congress, 1st Session, with the disposal of them by the House, Continued from the National Intelligencer of Saturday, Feb. 10, 1844," *Daily National Intelligencer,* Feb. 29, 1844.

Pillsbury, Rev. Parker. *Acts of the Anti-Slavery Apostles.* Concord, N.H., 1883, pp. 58–60.

Pollitzer, William S. *The Gullah People and Their African Heritage.* Athens and London: University of Georgia Press, 1999; paperback edition, 2005.

Pratt, Rita Henderson. *The Bahamas and South Carolina, USA Gullah/Geechee African Americans Share the Same African Roots Inspired Doll-Making Craft History.* Nassau, Bahamas: Rita Henderson Pratt, 2007.

"Proclamation from Pierce M. Butler, governor of South Carolina," *Columbia (SC) Southern Times & State Gazette,* March 2, 1838, issue 8. This proclamation from Butler spells out the alleged crimes of Mina McCoy and offers a reward of $300 for his capture and delivery to jail.

Rawick, George P., ed. *The American Slave: A Composite Autobiography,* Vol. 2, *South Carolina Narratives, Parts 1 and 2.* Orig. pub., 1941; reprint, Westport, Conn.: Greenwood Publishing Co., 1972.

Reader, John, "The Fungus That Conquered Europe," *New York Times,* March 17, 2008, p. A23.

Roller, David C., and Robert W. Twyman, eds. *The Encyclopedia of Southern History.* Baton Rouge: Louisiana State University Press, 1979, p. 1140.

Rowe, David L. *Thunder and Trumpets, Millerites and Dissenting Religion in Upstate New York, 1800–1850.* Chico, Calif.: Scholars Press, 1985.

Rucker, Walter. "Conjure, Magic, and Power: The Influence of Afro-Atlantic Religious Practices on Slave Resistance and Rebellion," *Journal of Black Studies* 32, No. 1 (Sep. 2001): pp. 84–100.

"The Schirmer Diary," *South Carolina Historical Magazine,* Vol. 72, 1978, p. 177. This mentions the 1843 comet.

A Sense of History: The Best Writing from the Pages of American Heritage. New York: American Heritage Press, Inc., 1985, p. 337.

Sirmans, M. Eugene, "The Legal Status of the Slave in South Carolina, 1670–1740," *Journal of Southern History,* Vol. 28, No. 4 (Nov. 1962): pp. 462–73.

South Carolina: Smiling Faces, Beautiful Places. A booklet produced by South Carolina Division of Tourism, Columbia, S.C., 1993. The story of Fairfield County's Town Clock appears on p. 65.

South Carolina, The WPA Guide to the Palmetto State, with a new introduction by Walter B. Edgar, compiled by workers of the Writers' Program of the Works Projects Administration in the state of South Carolina. Columbia, S.C.: University of South Carolina Press, 1988. Copyright 1941 by Burnet R. Maybank, governor of South Carolina. See pp. 92, 316 and 356 for references to Winnsboro.

Spears, R. H. *Reports of Cases at Law, Argued and Determined in the Court of Appeals and Court of Errors at South Carolina . . . from November 1842 to May 1844 . . . Both Inclusive.* Columbia, S.C.: A.S. Johnston, 1843–44, pp. 132–37.

The State vs. John L. Brown, Fairfield District, Court of General Sessions, Indictments Nov. Term 1843 #88, L20144 Box 2, South Carolina Department of Archives and History, Columbia, S.C.

Stauffer, John. *The Black Hearts of Men, Radical Abolitionists and the Transformation of Race.* Cambridge, Mass.: Harvard University Press, 2002. William Miller's predictions that the world would end with the second coming of Christ, first predicted in 1843 and again in 1844, spread through America's cities. The New York State Lunatic Asylum at Utica even blamed the mental problems of about one-third of its patients in 1843–44 on "Millerism." See discussions of William Miller's apocalyptic teachings on pp. 105, 106, 109–10, 116, 129–30.

Swift, Lindsay. *William Lloyd Garrison.* Philadelphia: George W. Jacobs & Company, 1911, p. 261.

Tappan, Lewis. "Correspondence of Lewis Tappan and Others with the British and Foreign Anti-Slavery Society, Part 6," *Journal of Negro History,* Vol. 12, No. 2 (April 1927): pp. 305–29.

"Threatened Dissolution of the Union—Very Exciting News from South Carolina—Where Will It End?" *Weekly Herald,* Dec. 14, 1844, issue 50, p. 398. This is an item about the controversy surrounding a South Carolina law under which free black seamen from other states were imprisoned in South Carolina until their vessels were ready to leave South Carolina's waters.

Tour of Charleston conducted by tour guide Randy Lee Hill, Jan. 16, 2008.

Tour of Charleston conducted by tour guide Al Miller, Jan. 17, 2008.

Tucker, Robert Cinnamond. James Henry Hammond, South Carolinian. A thesis submitted to the faculty of the University of North Carolina in partial fulfillment of the requirements for the degree of Doctor of Philosophy in the Department of History, Chapel Hill, 1958. See p. 241 for Hammond's views on slavery. See p. 285 for a description of the 1837 incident in which Hammond struck a European servant who tried to keep him from leaving an inn without paying his full bill. See p. 431 for his comparison of Britain's laboring "wage slaves" and America's black slaves. On pp. 424–25 is a description of Hammond's alleged seduction of the daughter of one of his wife's in-laws.

U.K., Hansard Parliamentary Debates, 3d series, Vol. 73, 1844, cols. 491–92, 1156–60.

Vermont Chronicle, May 1, 1844, p. 71, issue 18. The article notes that the Brown case "has set all England in commotion."

Vermont Chronicle, Dec. 25, 1844. Article about Samuel Hoar, Massachusetts agent for black seamen from Massachusetts temporarily jailed in South Carolina.

Visvanathan, T. R. *Earthquakes of South Carolina.* Geology Survey, 1980.

Wigham, Eliza. *The Anti-Slavery Cause in America and Its Martyrs.* London: A. W. Bennett, 1863, p. 61.

Williams, Jack Kenny. Crime and Punishment in South Carolina, 1790–1860. A dissertation submitted to the faculty of the Graduate School of Emory University in partial fulfillment of the requirements for the degree of Doctor of Philosophy, Emory University, 1953.

Wood, Peter H. *Black Majority: Negroes in Colonial South Carolina, From 1670 Through the Stono Rebellion.* New York: Alfred A. Knopf, 1974.

Woodson, Carter Godwin. *The Negro in Our History,* Washington, D.C.: Associated Publishers, Inc., 1922.

Yanak, Ted, and Pam Cornelison. *The Great American History Fact-Finder.* Boston: Houghton Mifflin Company, 1993.

CHAPTER 5

Adams Express Company Journal, 1855–1863, Special Collections, University of Kentucky: Lexington, Ky.

African Americans: Voices of Triumph, Alexandria, Va.: Time-Life Books, 1993, pp. 48, 52, 93.

Allen, M. *North Carolina Sketch.* Self-published, 1946, p. 12.

Ancestry.com. 1860 United States Federal Census (database online). Provo, Utah, USA: The Generations Network, Inc., 2004. Original data: United States of America, Bureau of the Census. Eighth Census of the United States, 1860. Washington, D.C.: National Archives and Records Administration, 1860. M653, 1,438 rolls. Isaac Williams was 51 in the 1860 census and married to 40-year-old Harriet.

Ancestry.com. Alabama Deaths, 1908–59 (database online). Provo, Utah, USA; The Generations Network, Inc., 2000. Original data: State of Alabama. Index of Vital Records for Alabama: Deaths, 1908–59. Montgomery, Ala., USA: State of Alabama Center for Health Statistics, Record Services Division. According to this data, Georgiana Williams, Isaac's second wife, died on Dec. 18, 1917, in Mobile.

Ancestry.com and the Church of Jesus Christ of Latter-Day Saints. 1880 United States Federal Census (database online). Provo, Utah, USA: The Generations Network, Inc., 2005. 1880 U.S. Census Index provided by the Church of Jesus Christ of Latter-Day Saints, copyright 1999 Intellectual Reserve, Inc. All rights reserved. All use is subject to the limited-use license and other terms and conditions applicable to this site. Original data: United States of America, Bureau of the Census. Tenth Census of the United States, 1880. Washington, D.C.: National Archives and Records Administration, 1880. T9, 1,454 rolls. This is the 1880 United States Federal Census record for Isaac M. Williams, "Minister of Gospel," then living in Nashville, Tennessee.

Anonymous. *Aunt Sally: or, The Cross the Way of freedom; a narrative of the slave-life and purchase of the mother of Rev. Isaac Williams of Detroit, Michigan.* Cincinnati: The American Reform Tract and Book Society, 1862. Orig. pub. 1858.

"Another Trunk Mystery, A Ghastly Find in the Adams Express Office in Baltimore," *Marion (Ohio) Daily Star,* Jan. 27, 1887.

Arango, Jorge. "Thomas Day: Master Craftsman," *Essence,* Vol. 32, issue 10, Feb. 2002, p. 120.

"Ask a Librarian," Nashville Public Library, June 10, 2004, email. This email states: "The Nashville Room does have the city directories, and I checked them for Rev. Isaac Williams. He appears only once, in the 1880 edition. His home was 182 N. Vine St. He does not appear after that year. There are death certificates for that time, and I did check, but did not find an entry."

Athearn, Robert G. *American Heritage Illustrated History of the United States,* Vol. II, *The Gilded Age.* New York: Choice Publishing, Inc. Created in association with the editors of American Heritage and for the updated edition, Media Projects Incorporated, 1988, pp. 915–16.

Baldwin, Lewis V. *Invisible Strands in African Methodism: A History of the African Union Methodist Protestant and Union American Methodist Episcopal Churches, 1805–1980.* Metuchen, N.J., and London: American Theological Library Association and the Scarecrow Press, Inc., 1983.

Baltimore County Maryland Federal Census, 1790, pp. 203–31, http://ftp.rootsweb.com/pub/usgenweb/md/baltimore/census/1790/page203.txt.

Barfield, Rodney D., and Patricia M. Marshall. *Thomas Day: African American Furniture Maker.* Raleigh: North Carolina Office of Archives and History, 2005.

Bates-Rudd, Rhonda. "4 Women Who Left a Mark," *Detroit News,* March 30, 1995.

Bearden, Romare, and Harry Henderson. *A History of African American Artists from 1792 to the Present.* New York: Pantheon Books, 1993.

Beltaire, Mark. "The Town Crier." *Detroit Free Press,* May 3, 1975, p. B-1.

"Bethel AME and the Underground Railroad," a press release issued by U.S. Rep. Joe Pitts, 16th District of Pennsylvania, March 20, 2000.

Black Historic Sites in Detroit, written by the Black Historic Sites Committee, Detroit Historical Department, 1989.

Blanchan, Neltje. *The Nature Library: Birds.* Oyster Bay, N.Y.: Doubleday, Doran & Co., 1917, pp. 130–31. This describes the appearance and behavior of bobolinks.

Blanton, Wyndham B. *Medicine in Virginia in the Nineteenth Century.* Richmond: Garrett & Massie, Inc., 1933, pp. 241, 264, 297.

Blassingame, John W. "Using the Testimony of Ex-Slaves: Approaches and Problems," *Journal of Southern History,* Vol. 14, No. 4 (Nov. 1975): pp. 473–92.

Blight, David W. *A Slave No More: Two Men Who Escaped to Freedom, Including Their Own Narratives of Emancipation.* Orlando: Harcourt, Inc., 2007.

Boyd, William K. *History of North Carolina,* Vol. II, *The Federal Period, 1783–1860.* Chicago: Lewis Publishing Company, 1919.

Boykin, James H. *The Negro in North Carolina Prior to 1861: An Historical Monograph.* New York: Pageant Press, Inc., 1958.

Catlin, George. "The Story of Detroit," *Detroit News,* 1926.

Chapman, Carol Sue, reference librarian, Central Library, Indianapolis, Marion County Public Library. Email of Dec. 14, 2003, about Rev. Isaac M. Williams's residences in Indianapolis.

Christian Recorder, Nov. 17, 1866, electronic edition. Remarks from Bishop Paul William Quinn about the growth of the AME Church.

"A Church and School for Mobile," *New York Age,* issue 38, June 29, 1889, p. 1, Col. E.

Coggan, Blanche B. "The Underground Railroad . . . and Black-White Cooperation," *Michigan Challenge,* Lansing, Mich.: Michigan State Chamber of Commerce, June 1968, pp. 12–13, 50–51.

Cohen, Irwin. *Echoes of Detroit: A 300-Year History.* Haslett, Mich.: City Vision Publishing, 2000.

Conant, Roger, and Joseph T. Collins. *Peterson Field Guides: Reptiles and Amphibians.* New York: Houghton Mifflin Company, 1991.

Connor, R. D. W. *North Carolina: Rebuilding an Ancient Commonwealth, 1584–1925.* Vol. II, Chicago and New York: American Historical Society, Inc., 1929.

Connor, R. D. W., W. W. Pierson, and C. P. Higby, eds. *The James Sprunt Historical Publications,* published under the direction of the Department of History and Government. Vol. 18, Nos. 1–2. Chapel Hill: University of North Carolina Press, 1926. See "Slaveholding in North Carolina: An Economic View," by Rosser Howard Taylor, pp. 31–96.

Cook, Harry, and Joyce Walker-Tyson. "Politics and the Pulpit: A Tradition," from *Blacks in Detroit.* Detroit: The Detroit Free Press, 1980.

Crow, Jeffrey J. *The Black Experience in Revolutionary North Carolina.* Raleigh: North Carolina Department of Cultural Resources, 1977.

Darlington, Jane, compiler. Marion County, Indiana, Mortality Record: Sep. 1, 1872, to Dec. 31, 1881.

DeBow, J. D. B., compiler. *Statistical View of the United States . . . Being a Compendium of the Seventh Census, 1850.* Washington, D.C.: Census Office, 1854, pp. 94, 178. The superintendent of the 1850 census estimated that 2.5 million slaves were agricultural workers, including 125,000 working with rice.

DeRamus, Betty, "A testament to freedom: Memorial represents all who fled along Underground Railroad," *Detroit News,* Oct. 18, 2001.

Detroit Daily Advertiser, Feb. 12, 1846. This piece praises portrait painter Robert S. Duncanson for his portrait of young William Berthelet, a member of one of Detroit's wealthiest families. The article notes that Duncanson, who spent one year in Detroit, "executed with great skill" his assignment.

Doss, Harriet E. Amos. "Commerce, nationalism and unionism: Mobilians' observances of the death of U.S. Grant," *Alabama Review,* Vol. 55, No. 2 (April 2002): p. 122.

Douglass, Frederick. *Narrative of the Life of Frederick Douglass, An American Slave, Written by Himself.* New York: Penguin Books, USA, Inc., 1968.

DuBois, W. E. B. *The Souls of Black Folk.* New York: New American Library, Inc., 1969.

Durham, Michael S. "I Am Going to Be Thomas Day," *American Legacy* (Winter 1998): pp. 49–53. This publication and others make the point that white support for Thomas Day was based, in part, on the belief that as a fellow slave owner, he would uphold the system. When the passage of the 1826 law prohibiting free blacks from entering the state made it likely Thomas Day would leave, 61 whites sent a petition to the General Assembly of the state describing Thomas Day's bride, Aquilla Wilson, as a "woman of color of good family and character." They also asked lawmakers to pass a bill giving Aquilla "the privilege of migrating to the state free from fines and penalties." Cinching the deal, the state's attorney general, Romulus Saunders, attached a letter to the petition. It called Day a "free man of color of very fair character, an excellent mechanic, industrious, honest and sober." Saunders added that the cabinetmaker was a slave owner himself and, therefore, had a vested interest in the system. If any disturbance broke out among the blacks, Saunders said, "I should rely with confidence upon a disclosure from him, as he is the owner of slaves as well as real estate." Thomas Day owned 14 slaves (according to James Sprunt historical publications), but there is no record of how he treated them or what his relationship to them might have been. Had he freed his slaves after 1831, he would have needed legal approval, and his freed slaves also would have had to leave North Carolina after 1826.

Dusinberre, William. *Them Dark Days: Slavery in the American Rice Swamps.* New York: Oxford University Press, 1996, pp. 410–16, 682–97, 7–13.

Elliott, Stuart. "Uncle Ben, Board Chairman: A Madison Ave. Makeover Gives a Racially Charges Symbol a Title but Still No Last Name," *New York Times,* March 30, 2007.

"Express Dead Babies," *Sheboygan (WI), Press.* June 6, 1913, p. 1.

Federal Census, Schedule 1, Free Inhabitants in 7th Ward, Detroit City in the County of Wayne on 7th day of June 1860, p. 9. In Detroit's 1860 census, James Robinson is identified as a 107-year-old black man from Maryland; Isaac Williams as a 51-year-old male, black preacher of the Wesleyan Church who was born in North Carolina; Sally Williams as a 72-year-old black female from North Carolina and Harriet Williams as a 40-year-old black female from Tennessee. They lived in Ward 7 in Detroit.

Fitch, James Marston, "When Housekeeping Became a Science," *American Heritage,* Vol. XII, No. 5 (August 1961): p. 34.

Fradin, Dennis Brindell. *My Family Shall Be Free: The Life of Peter Still.* New York: Harper-Collins, 2001. See pp. 113–14 for discussion of Alabama law on emancipated slaves.

Franck, Michael S. *Elmwood Endures: History of a Detroit Cemetery.* Detroit: Wayne State University Press, 1996, pp. 50, 162. This book identifies James Robinson, the Williams family's neighbor and possibly boarder in Detroit, as the oldest person in Elmwood Cemetery. Robinson died in 1868 at the age of 115.

Funkhouser, Darlene. *Civil War Cookin', Stories, 'n Such: One Hundred Twenty-nine Recipes Used by the Troops in the Field.* Weaver, Iowa: Quixote Press, 2000. This book talks about the high death toll that diseases took on Civil War soldiers.

Gavrilovich, Peter, and Bill McGraw, eds. *The Detroit Almanac: 300 Years of Life in the Motor City.* Detroit: Detroit Free Press, 2000, p. 190.

Glazer, Sidney. *Detroit: A Study in Urban Development.* New York: Bookman Associates, Inc., 1965.

———, ed. *Negroes in Michigan During the Civil War.* Lansing, Mich.: Michigan Civil War Centennial Observance Commission, 1966. The names of many Michigan UGRR agents appear on p. 12.

Goings, Kenneth W. *Mammy and Uncle Mose, Black Collectibles and American Stereotyping.* Bloomington and Indianapolis: Indiana University Press, 1994.

Green, John M. *Negroes in Michigan History.* Detroit: John M. Green, 1985. A reprint of Michigan Manual of Freedmen's Progress, compiled by Francis H. Warren, secretary of Freedmen's Progress Commission, Detroit, 1915.

Gregg, Howard D. *History of the African Methodist Episcopal Church (The Black Church in Action).* Atlantic City: African Methodist Episcopal Church Sunday School Union, 1980.

Grimm, Joe, ed. *Michigan Voices: Our State's History in the Words of the People Who Lived It.* Detroit: Detroit Free Press and Wayne State University Press, 1987, p. 54.

Gutman, Herbert G. *The Black Family in Slavery and Freedom, 1750–1925.* New York: Vintage Books, 1977, p. 349. This tells the story of a black couple who committed suicide to avoid separation, as reported in 1746 in the *Boston Evening Post.*

Hairr, John. *North Carolina Rivers: Facts, Legends and Lore.* Charleston: History Press, 2007.

"A Half Century's Growth: An Interesting Anniversary of a Famous Express Company," *New York Times,* May 5, 1890, p. 8 (1 pp.).

Hamilton, J. G. de Roulhac, Henry McGilbert Wagstaff, and William Whatley Pierson Jr., eds. *The James Sprunt Historical Publications,* published under the direction of the North Carolina Historical Society, Vol. 17, No. 1. Chapel Hill: University of North Carolina Press, 1920. See "The Free Negro in North Carolina," by R. H. Taylor, p. 20.

Hand, Bill. *A Walking Guide to North Carolina's Historic New Bern.* Charleston, S.C.: History Press, 2007. This book talks about the achievements of free blacks in New Bern. See pp. 64–65 for a story that resembles the Aunt Sally narrative.

Hine, Darlene Clark. *Hine Sight: Black Women and the Re-Construction of American History.* Bloomington and Indianapolis: Indiana University Press, 1994.

Hine, Darlene Clark, Elsa Barkley Brown, and Rosalyn Terborg-Penn, eds. *Black Women in America: An Historical Encyclopedia,* Vol. I, A–L. Bloomington: Indiana University Press, 1993. Elleanor Eldridge information is on pp. 389–90.

Historical Negro Biographies. Detroit: Burton Historical Collection.

Hogg, Gordon E., special collections library director, University of Kentucky, Lexington, Ky. Email of Jan. 30, 2007, about the Adams Express Company's shipment of two black women to their owners.

"Horrid Atrocities," *Liberator,* May 24, 1839, issue 21, col. C. This contains the narrative of Mr. Nehemiah Caulkins of New London County, Conn., as well as testimonials from various individuals vouching for Caulkins's good character.

Hunter, Wanda, local and state history manager, Cumberland County Public Library and Information Center. Email about Aunt Sally Williams on March 1, 2008. Hunter points out that rice wasn't grown in Fayetteville but that Sally could have lived in one of Cumberland County's neighboring counties.

Independent (N.Y.), "Devoted to the Consideration of Politics, Social and Economic Tendencies, History, Literature and the Arts," July 4, 1889, 41, 2118, p. 12. This newspaper identifies the author of the Aunt Sally narrative as New England writer Edna Dean Proctor. Proctor had written many poems and a book based on the speeches of Henry Ward Beecher, the minister Aunt Sally heard preach in Brooklyn.

Johnston's *Detroit City Directory and Business Advertiser,* 1857/58, 1859, and 1860/61. James Robinson, colored, is listed as living at 251 Fort E., as being 109 years old and having fought under Gen. Jackson at New Orleans and under Gen. Washington at Yorktown and generally through the Revolutionary War, for seven years with Col. De Shiel, his master. He lives with "Aunt Sally."

Katz, William Loren. *The Black West.* Seattle: Open Hand Publishing, Inc., 1987. Orig. pub., Doubleday & Co., 1971.

Katzman, David M. "Early Settlers in Michigan," *Michigan Challenge,* Lansing, Mich.: Michigan State Chamber of Commerce, June 1968, p. 11.

LaBrew, Arthur R. *The Afro-American Music Legacy in Michigan.* Detroit: Michigan Music Research Center, Inc. 1987, p. 95. Note about musician Alexander D. Moore, who played in a string band, owned a barbershop and had a dancing school.

———. *The Detroit History That Nobody Knew (Or Bothered to Remember, 1800–1900),* Part I. Privately printed by LaBrew, Detroit, 2001.

LaRoche, Cheryl Janifer. On the Edge of Freedom: Free Black Communities, Archaeology, and the Underground Railroad. Ph.D. dissertation, University of Maryland, 2004, pp. 258–61.

Larson, Kate Clifford. *Bound for the Promised Land.* New York: One World Books, 2004.

Lewis, Ferris E. *Michigan Yesterday and Today.* Hillsdale, Mich.: Hillsdale Educational Publishers, Inc., 1956.

Lustig, Lillie S., S. Claire Sondheim, and Sarah Rensel, compilers and editors. *The Southern Cook Book of Fine Old Recipes.* Reading, Pa.: Culinary Arts Press, 1939.

Lyons, Mary F. *Master of Mahogany: Tom Day, Free Black Cabinetmaker.* New York: Charles Scribner's Sons, 1994.

McGehee, Scott, and Susan Watson. *Blacks in Detroit.* Detroit: Detroit Free Press, 1980, pp. 4–6.

McRae, Norman. Blacks in Detroit, 1736–1833: The Search for Freedom and Community and Its Implications for Educators. A dissertation submitted in partial fulfillment of the requirements for the degree of Doctor of Philosophy (Education), University of Michigan, 1982.

Mebane, Mary E. *Mary: An Autobiography.* Chapel Hill, N.C.: University of North Carolina Press, 1981, p. 5.

———. *Mary, Wayfarer: An Autobiography.* New York: The Viking Press, 1983. Mebane talks about the psychological as well as physical differences between growing corn and growing tobacco.

Michigan Anti-Slavery Society notices, *Liberator,* Sep. 19, 1856, p. 1.

The Narrative of James Roberts, a Soldier under Gen. Washington in the Revolutionary War, and Under Gen. Jackson at the Battle of New Orleans, in the War of 1812: "a Battle which Cost Me a Limb, Some Blood, and Almost My Life." Chicago, printed for the author, 1858, available online in the electronic edition, copyright 2004 by the University Library, University of North Carolina at Chapel Hill, http:docsouth.unc.edu/neh/Roberts/Roberts.html.

Niven, John, ed. *The Salmon P. Chase Papers,* Vol. 2, *Correspondence, 1823–1857.* Kent, Ohio: The Kent State University Press, 1994. On p. 53, Chase describes an 1832 cholera epidemic in Cincinnati, noting that "the streets were deserted at night: and in the day few ventured forth: and then they stole along cautiously, muffled in cloaks, as if fearful of encountering the pestilence at every turn."

North Carolina: A Guide to the Old North State, compiled and written by the Federal Writers Project of the Federal Works Agency Works Projects Administration for the state of North Carolina. Chapel Hill, N.C.: University of North Carolina Press, 1939, pp. 9, 16, 17, 52, 307, and 308. The statement about the coral snake's tenacious hold is on p. 16.

"A Northern Republic," *Liberator,* Sep. 19, 1856, p. 1. A speech given in Detroit on Sep. 2, 1856, by a speaker identified only as Henry.

O'Neill, Molly. "A 19th-Century Ghost Awakens to Redefine 'Soul,'" *New York Times,* Nov. 21, 2007, Dining and Wine Section, pp. 1 and 8. This article talks about a free black woman named Malinda Russell's 1866 cookbook, the earliest known cookbook by an African American woman. Facsimiles are available from the William L. Clements Library, University of Michigan.

Paige, Howard. *African American Family Cookery.* Southfield, Mich.: Aspects Publishing Co., 1995, p. 94.

Palmer, Ronald, professor emeritus of the Practice of International Affairs, George Washington University. "DeBaptiste, Underground Railroad Leader," a speech delivered on Aug. 30, 2002, at the U.S./Canadian History and Genealogy Conference, North Buxton, Ontario.

Palmer, Ronald D., and Cheryl J. LaRoche. "William Paul Quinn, Senior Bishop of the

AME Church, 1849–1872," a paper presented at the AAHGS Annual Meeting, Little Rock, Ark., Oct. 2004.

"People and Things," *Inter Ocean (Chicago),* Jan. 8, 1876, p. 4, issue 248, col E. This is a brief obituary for Sally Williams.

Personal and General Notes (News), *(New Orleans) Daily Picayune,* Oct. 18, 1887, p. 4.

Petersen, Wayne R. *National Audubon Society Pocket Guide: Songbirds and Familiar Backyard Birds, East.* New York: Alfred A. Knopf, 1994, p. 160.

Pickard, Kate E. R. *The Kidnapped and the Ransomed, Being the Personal Recollection of Peter Still and his Wife "Vina," after Forty Years of Slavery.* Syracuse: William T. Hamilton, 1856.

Poremba, David Lee. *Detroit 1860–1899,* Images of America Series. Charleston, S.C.: Arcadia Publishing, 1998.

Powell, William S. *When the Past Refused to Die: A History of Caswell County North Carolina, 1777–1977.* Yanceyville, N.C.: Caswell County Historical Association, Inc., 1994. Orig. pub. Moore Publishing Co: Durham. N.C., 1977.

Quarles, Benjamin. *Black Abolitionists.* New York: Da Capo Press, Inc., 1991. Contains information about the activities of the Colored Vigilance Committee of Detroit.

Rambeau, David, ed. *Conant Gardens: A Black Urban Community, 1925 to 1950.* Detroit: Conant Gardeners, 2001. This Conant Gardens neighborhood in southeastern Detroit was built on the estate of abolitionist Shubael Conant, who died in 1877.

Rawick, George P, ed. *The American Slave: A Composite Autobiography,* Vol. 14, *North Carolina Narratives, Part 1,* orig. pub. 1941; reprint, Westport, Conn.: Greenwood Publishing Co., 1974. See also Vol. 7, *Oklahoma,* p. 66.

———, ed. *The American Slave: A Composite Autobiography,* Vol. 19, *God Struck Me Dead,* orig. pub. 1941; reprint, Westport, Conn.: Greenwood Publishing Group, Inc., 1974.

"Review: A Strange Trip to Freedom," *Journal of Blacks in Higher Education,* No. 37 (Autumn 2002): pp. 136–37.

Rich, Motoko. "A Family Tree of Literary Fakers," *New York Times,* March 8, 2008, p. A17.

Ripley, Peter C., ed. *The Black Abolitionist Papers,* Vol. II, *Canada, 1830–1865.* Chapel Hill and London: University of North Carolina Press, 1986, p. 484.

Robinson, Wilhelmena S. *International Library of Negro Life and History: Historical Negro Biographies.* New York: Association for the Study of Negro Life and History, 1967, p. 71.

"The Sabine Family," *Detroit Society for Genealogical Research Magazine,* Vol. 67, No. 3, Spring 2004, p. 99. Reprinted from the *Sunday News Tribune,* January 31, 1897.

Sharp, Saundra. *Black Women for Beginners.* New York: Writers and Readers Publishing, Incorporated, 1993.

Sherman, Rev. David, D. D. *History of the Wesleyan Academy at Wilbraham, Mass., 1817–1890.* Boston: McDonald 7 Gill Company, 1893.

Simon, Seymour. *Crocodiles & Alligators.* New York: HarperCollins, 1999.

Singleton, George A. *The Romance of African Methodism.* New York: Exposition Press, 1952.

Smith, Jessie Carney, ed. *Notable Black American Women.* Detroit: Gale Research, 1992, pp. 234, 733.

Soodalter, Ron. *Hanging Captain Gordon: The Life and Trial of an American Slave Trader.* New York: Atria Books, 2006.

Southwestern Christian Advocate (New Orleans), "The Right Way: A Colored Man's Views on the Race Problem of the Day," letter to the editor, March 5, 1885, p. 2, issue 10, col E.

Southwestern Christian Advocate, "The Canton Indignation Meeting," March 15, 1883, issue 11, col. A.

Southwestern Christian Advocate, "Editorial Perambulations," Dec. 31, 1885, p. 4, issue 52. This article notes that "the venerable and well known Isaac M. Williams is rector of the Episcopalian Church" in Mobile.

Steckel, Richard H. "Slave Mortality: Analysis of Evidence from Plantation Records," *Social Sciences Hisory,* Vol. 3, No. 3, 4 (1979): pp. 86–114.

Tise, Larry E., editor in chief. *The North Carolina Historical Review,* Vol. LV, No. 3, July 1978, North Carolina Division of Archives ad History, pp. 347, 370. This book includes a review of a book that asserts that North Carolina slaves managed to sustain "themselves culturally against fierce odds" through things such as carnival rituals.

Tucker, Veta, Grand Valley State University, Allen Park, Mich. Email of March 4, 2008, about the coping skills Sally Williams and her son, Isaac, display in Aunt Sally's narrative.

Turner, Patricia A. *Ceramic Uncles & Celluloid Mammies: Black Images and Their Influence on Culture.* New York: Anchor Books, 1994.

Tyree, Marion Cabell. *Housekeeping in Old Virginia.* Louisville: John P. Morton and Company, 1879, p. 19.

Virgin, Rev. E. W. "Lydia Spear Memorial," *Zion's Herald,* July 15, 1908.

"War Tax in Supreme Court: Chief Tribunal Hears Arguments as to Whether Express Companies or Patrons Must Bear the Burden," *New York Times,* Nov. 9, 1899, p. 4.

Washington, Booker T. *Up from Slavery: An Autobiography.* Grand Rapids, Mich.: Candace Press, 1996. See p. 1 for Washington's remark about his place of birth and p. 5 for his remarks about the information-spreading slave grapevine.

Wheeler, John Hill. *Historical Sketches of North Carolina from 1584 to 1851, 2 Volumes in 1.* Baltimore: Genealogical Publishing Co., Inc., 2000. Orig. published Philadelphia, 1851; reprinted New York, 1964.

Wilford, John Noble. "Plague: How Cholera Helped Shape New York." *New York Times,* April 15, 2008, p. D4.

Willey, Larry G. "John Rankin, Antislavery Prophet, and the Free Presbyterian Church," *American Presbyterian* 72, No. 3 (Fall 1994): p. 168.

Woodford, Frank B., and Arthur M. Woodford. *All Our Yesterdays.* Detroit: Wayne State University Press, 1969.

Williams, Isaac M. "The Right Way: A Colored Man's Views on the Race Problem of the Day," *Southwestern Christian Advocate (New Orleans),* March 5, 1885, p. 2, issue 10, col. E.

Williams, John A. "A Dissenting Look at American History: Race, War and Politics," *Negro Digest,* Vol. XVI, No. 10 (Aug. 1967): pp. 4–9.

Wright, Roberta Hughes, and Wilbur B. Hughes III. *Lay Down Body: Living History in African American Cemeteries.* Detroit: Visible Ink Press, 1996. The book notes that blacks buried in Elmwood Cemetery with Underground Railroad connections include William Lambert, George DeBaptiste, Dr. Joseph Ferguson, William Webb, John D. Richards, who helped organize the 102nd U.S. Colored infantry, and James Robinson, the oldest person buried in Elmwood.

Yancey, Barlett Jr. Letter to Thomas Henderson, editor of *(Raleigh, N.C.) Star,* Aug. 11, 1810. Original in the Thomas Henderson Papers private collection (PC 19.1) at the NC Archives, Raleigh, N.C.

CHAPTER 6

Abels, Jules. *Man on Fire: John Brown and the Cause of Liberty.* New York: Macmillan, 1971. On p. 216, he describes Albert Hazlett, one of the men suspected of killing David Cruise. On p. 223, he claims that a pregnant woman on the trip bore a girl named Captain John Brown.

Appendix to Message 1, Documents Related to Harpers Ferry Invasion, Richmond: William F. Ritchie, 1859, p. 138. The quotation from John Kagi about how war would benefit slaves is on p. 141. Perkins Library, Duke University.

"The Battle of the Spurs," *Freedom's Champion (Atchison, Kans.),* Feb. 5, 1859, issue 47.

Blackmar, Frank W., ed. *A Cyclopedia of State History, Embracing Events, Institutions, Industries, Counties, Cities, Towns, Prominent Persons, Etc.,* in two volumes, Vol. I, illustrated. Chicago: Standard Publishing Company, 1912.

————, ed. *A Cyclopedia of State History, Embracing Events, Institutions, Industries, Counties, Cities, Towns, Prominent Persons, Etc.,* in two volumes, Vol. II, illustrated. Chicago: Standard Publishing Company, 1912, pp. 730–31.

Blanton, Wyndham B. *Medicine in Virginia in the Nineteenth Century.* Richmond: Garrett & Massie, Inc., 1933. See p. 158 for diseases afflicting pregnant nineteenth-century women.

"A Bloodthirsty Letter," *National Era,* Dec. 8, 1859.

The Border Ruffian Code. New York: Tribune Office, 1856. Excerpt from The Border Ruffian Code enacted in Kansas in 1856: sect. 4. "If any person shall entice, decoy or carry away out of this Territory any slave belonging to another, with intent to deprive the owner thereof of the services of such slave, or with intent to effect or procure the freedom of such slave, he shall be adjudged guilty of grand larceny and, on conviction thereof, shall suffer death or be imprisoned at hard labor for not less than ten years."

Boykin, Ulysses W. *A Hand Book on the Detroit Negro.* Detroit: Minority Study Associates, 1943, p. 23.

Brophy, Patrick. "100 Years Ago Today Pro-Union Militia Burned Nevada." *Nevada Herald,* May 26, 1963.

————. "Bushwacker Musings, Historical Notes from Vernon County Historical Society." *Bushwacker Weekly Magazine (Nevada, Mo.),* Vol. 1, No. 44, Dec. 10, 1980, Nevada, Mo., pp. 4–5 A.

Centennial Observance, John Brown Raid, Harpers Ferry, West Virginia. Historical booklet, Charleston, West Virginia.

Christian, Nichole M. "Recalling Timbuctoo, A Slice of Black History." *New York Times,* Feb. 19, 2002, p. B1.

Connor, James. "The Antislavery Movement in Iowa," *Annals of Iowa,* 3rd series, 40, No. 6 (Fall 1970): pp. 450–79.

Dedmon, Emmett. *Fabulous Chicago.* New York: Random House, 1953, p. 50. This book talks about Allan Pinkerton.

DeVillers, David. *The John Brown Slavery Revolt Trial.* Berkeley Heights, N.J.: Enslow Publishers, Inc., 2000, p. 25.

DuBois, W. E. B. *John Brown.* New York: Modern Library, 2001.

Featherstonhaugh, Thomas. "The Final Burial of the Followers of John Brown," *New England Magazine,* Vol. XXIV, No. 2, April 1901, pp. 128–34.

————. "John Brown's men; The lives of those killed at Harpers Ferry, with a supplementary bibliography of John Brown," *Publications of the Southern History Association*, Vol. 3, 1899. Washington, D.C.: Southern History Association.

Fisher, Ian. "Rome at Night," *New York Times*, April 20, 2008, Travel Section, p. 8.

Fried, Albert. *John Brown's Journey, Notes & Reflections on His America and Mine.* Garden City, N.Y.: Anchor Press/Doubleday, 1978.

Gue, B.F. "John Brown and His Iowa Friends," *Midland Monthly*, March 1897, issue VII, pp. 273–74.

Hamilton, James Cleland. "John Brown in Canada," *Canadian Magazine of Politics, Science, Art and Literature*, ed. J. Gordon Mowat, Vol. IV. Toronto: The Ontario Publishing Co. Ltd., 1895, pp. 120–35.

Harding, Vincent. *There Is a River: The Black Struggle for Freedom in America.* New York: Harcourt Brace Jovanovich, pp. 211–15.

Harnack, Curt, "The Iowa Underground Railroad" *Iowan* 4 (June/July 1956): pp. 20–23, 44, 47.

Harrison, Wendell Phillips. *The Preludes of Harper's Ferry*, 1891.

Head, James W. *History and Comprehensive Description of Loudoun County, Virginia*, 1908, p. 185. Head claims that enslaved black women were more sullen and less good-natured than their men and that their only ambitions were to wear fine clothes.

Hinton, Richard J. *John Brown and His Men.* New York: Arno Press and *New York Times*, 1968, pp. 218–28. See p. 223 for quotation about Dr. Blunt.

History of Vernon County, Missouri, written and compiled from the most authentic official and private sources, including a history of its Townships, Towns and Villages, together with Condensed History of Missouri; a reliable and detailed history of Vernon County—its pioneer record, resources, biographical sketches of prominent citizens; general and local statistics of great value; incidents and reminiscences. St. Louis: Brown & Co., 1887, pp. 158, 204, 224–36, and 410–13. The letter from Rufus Cruise giving his version of the incidents leading to his father's slaying and Jane's escape appears on pp. 411–12.

Jackson, Harvey C. "The Response of Blacks in Canada," from a broadside issued in Simcoe, Ontario, and dated five days after Brown's hanging.

Johnson, W. A. *The History of Anderson County, Kansas, From Its First Settlement to the Fourth of July, 1876.* Kauffman & Iler, Garnett Plaindealer, 1877.

Johnston, Rev. N. R. *Looking Back from the Sunset Land.* Oakland, Calif.: 1898. The Ohio-born author was an abolitionist and a Reform Presbyterian minister.

LaBrew, Arthur. *The Afro-American Music Legacy in Michigan.* Detroit: Michigan Music Research Center, Inc., 1987.

"Lecture on Kansas," *New York Herald*, May 19, 1860, p. 7. This describes Dr. John Doy's speech about the conflicts in Kansas and his rescue from jail. During the lecture he "exhibited a pair of manacles which he claimed were taken from the wrists of a boy whom he saw sold into slavery by his own father, a preacher of fifteen years standing," according to the newspaper report.

Lerner, Eric. *Pinkerton's Secret.* New York: Henry Holt and Company, 2008.

"Letter from Kansas," *Newark (Ohio) Advocate*, Oct. 15, 1856, issues 11 and 9.

Libby, Jean, ed. and compiler. *John Brown Mysteries.* Missoula, Mont.: Pictorial Histories Publishing Company, 1999, pp. 1–19.

———, ed. *The Californians, After Harper's Ferry: California Refuge for John Brown's Family.* Palo Alto, Calif.: WaltsPress.com, 2006.

Liberator (Boston), June 1, 1860, p. 87, issue 22, col. D. Obituary for Judge E. Graham.

Mabee, Carlton. *Black Freedom, The Nonviolent Abolitionists from 1830 Through the Civil War.* New York: Macmillan Company, 1970, p. 320.

McRae, Norman. Black Participation in the Civil War: The Underground Railroad in Michigan. Draft of a proposed middle school curriculum for Detroit Public Schools.

Missouri: A Guide to the Show Me State, compiled by Workers of the Writers' Program of the Work Projects Administration in the state of Missouri, American Guide Series, copyrighted 1941, the Missouri State Highway Department, pp. 50–51.

Missouri History: Vernon County. Chicago: Cooper & Co., 1911, pp. 228–37.

Morris, Charles. *Famous Men and Great Events of the Nineteenth Century.* Washington, D.C.: W. E. Scull, 1899, pp. 432, 433.

Newhall, J. B. *A Glimpse of Iowa in 1846; or, the Emigrant's Guide and State Directory; with a description of the New Purchase; Embracing Much practical advice and useful information to Intending emigrants. Also, the New State Constitution,* 2nd ed. Burlington, Iowa: W. D. Skillman, 1846, pp. 13–14.

Oates, Stephen B. *God's Angry Man,* Mt. Morris, Ill.: American History Illustrated, pp. 15–16.

———. *To Purge This Land with Blood: A Biography of John Brown.* New York: Harper & Row, 1970, pp. 261–65.

Ontario, Canada, Census Index, 1871 (database online) Provo, Utah: The Generations Network, Inc., 2006. Original data: Ontario, Canada, 1871, Canada Census, Ottawa, Canada. This lists Samuel Harper as born in 1838 or 1839 in the United States and residing in 1871 in Windsor Town, Ontario. In the 1901 Census of Canada, Jane Harper appears with her spouse, Samuel. Jane is said to have been born in 1824. Her 1901 residence is Essex County, Ontario.

Pittsburgh Courier, April 30, 1932. Editorial commenting on the annual pilgrimage to John Brown's gravesite at North Elba, New York, begun by the John Brown Memorial Association in 1922.

Prince, Bryan. *I Came As a Stranger.* Toronto: Tundra Books, 2004.

Quarles, Benjamin, ed. *Blacks on John Brown.* Urbana, Ill.: University of Illinois Press, 1972. The introduction describes Brown as being uncommonly egalitarian in his treatment of blacks, calling them by their last names and seating them at his table.

Rawick, George P., ed. *The American Slave: A Composite Autobiography,* Vol. 16, *Kansas, Kentucky, Maryland, Ohio, Virginia and Tennessee Narratives.* Westport, Conn.: Greenwood Publishing Company, 1972, pp. 8–13.

Rivarola, Mayra. "Tour visits sites from Underground Railroad," *Kansas State Collegian,* Sep. 17, 2007. This is an interview with Richard Pitts, author of *A Self-Guided Tour of the Underground Railroad in Kansas,* and executive producer of the documentary *The Kansas Underground Railroad.*

Santway, Alfred W. *A Brief Sketch of the Life of John Brown, The Martyr-Emancipator.* Watertown, N.Y.: Alfred W. Santway, 1934.

Siebert, Wilbur H. *The Underground Railroad from Slavery to Freedom.* New York: Arno Press, Inc., and the *New York Times,* 1968, pp. 162–64. Reprint. The book includes an introduction on page viii by Albert Bushnell Hart that makes abolition work sound like a purgative: "He [the abolitionist] was taking risks, defying the laws and making himself liable to punishment and yet could glow with the healthful pleasure of duty done."

"Stevens, the Companion of Brown," *Weekly Raleigh Register,* Nov. 9, 1859, issue 45.

Van Ek, Jacob. "Underground Railroad in Iowa," *Palimpsest* (a publication of the State Historical Society of Iowa), Vol. II, No. 5 (May 1921).

www.andersoncountyks.net. This site has a photograph of the Gerth cabin and information about Valentin Gerth.

www.territorialkansasonline.org. accessed Sep. 19, 2007. Letter, Mary Brown to Dear Brother Willie Brown, Lawrence, Jan. 30, 1859, written by Mary Brown from Lawrence and addressed to her brother, William, who was studying at Phillip Exeter Academy. Territorial Kansas Online—Transcripts.

"Yesterday's Headlines," March 1960, published by the Detroit Historical Society and reprinted from the *Detroit Advertiser,* March 15, 1859.

CHAPTER 7

"Achievers in Washtenaw County," *Ann Arbor News,* Feb. 26, 1986.

Ancestry.com. The index to the 1871 Ontario, Canada, Census, data from Library and Archives, Canada, Ontario, Census Index 1871 (database online). Provo, Utah: The Generations Network Inc., 2006. Original data: Ontario, Canada, 1871, Canada Census, Ottawa Canada, Library and Archives. Division 4, Microfilm Roll: C-9967 p. 92. This is census data for Francis Wanzer, born around 1830 or 1831 in the United States.

Ancestry.com, Ontario, Canada, Census Index, 1871. This index to the 1871 Ontario, Canada, Census was created by volunteers from the Ontario Genealogical Society from data supplied by Library and Archives, Canada, Ontario, Canada, Census Index, 1871 (database online). Provo, Utah: The Generations Network, Inc., 2006. It describes Francis Wanzer as a male born in the USA around 1831 and living in York West or Toronto and as an African of the Wesleyan Methodist faith. According to family records he actually was born Feb. 1, 1830.

Ancestry.com. Ontario, Canada, Deaths, 1869–1934 (database online). Provo, Utah: The Generations Network, Inc., 2007.

Ancestry.com. 1860 United States Federal Census (database online). Provo, Utah: The Generations Network, Inc. This is census data for Luther Sullivan, born around 1815 and living in Washington, D.C., in 1860.

Ancestry.com. 1900 United States Federal Census (database online). Provo, Utah: The Generations Network, Inc., 2004. Original data: United States of America, Bureau of the Census, Twelfth Census of the United States, 1900; Washington, D.C., National Archives and Records Administration, 1900, T623, 1854 rolls. Census data for Millie McCoy in 1900.

Bagwell, Orlando. *Frederick Douglass: When the Lion Wrote History.* Washington, D.C.: WETA, 1994.

Beltaire, Mark. "The Town Crier," *Detroit Free Press,* May 3, 1975, p. B-1.

Bibb, Henry, ed. and proprietor, *Voice of the Fugitive,* Jan. 1, 1851, Vol. I, No. I, Sandwich, Canada West.

———. *Voice of the Fugitive,* March 11, 1852, Vol. 2, No. 6, Sandwich, Canada West.

Black Historic Sites in Detroit, by the Black Historic Sites Committee, the Detroit Historical Department, 1989.

Blockson, Charles L. "Escape from Slavery, The Underground Railroad," *National Geographic,* July 1984, Vol. 166, 1, pp. 9, 30, 31.

Brown, Misty. "Legacy of Underground Railroad Freedom Fighter Frank Wanzer." *Washington Informer,* June 30, 2005.

Bruce, Dwight H., ed. *Memorial History of Syracuse, New York.* Syracuse: H. P. Smith & Co., 1891, pp. 172–73.

Carpenter, Frank G. "Our Colored Citizen, Facts and Figures Showing His Rapid Advance," *Atchison (Kans.) Daily Globe,* March 13, 1888, issue 3,202, p. 1, col A.

Carter, Lawrence T. "The Real McCoy," *Detroit News,* Feb. 1981.

"The Celebration at Corinthian Hall," *Frederick Douglass's Paper,* July 9, 1852.

Chargot, Patricia. "Ypsilanti's Tracks on the Underground Railroad," *Detroit Free Press,* Feb. 6, 2007, p. 4-G.

Christian Recorder, "Personal Items," March 16, 1876. This roundup of news items includes an obituary for William Whipper.

Connor, R. D. W., W. W. Pierson and C. P. Higby, eds. *The James Sprunt Historical Publications,* published under the direction of the Department of History and Government, Vol. 18, Nos. 1–2. Chapel Hill: University of North Carolina Press, 1926. See "Slaveholding in North Carolina: An Economic View," by Rosser Howard Taylor, p. 90, for a discussion of slaves who received Christmas gifts.

Dorris, Mary C. *Preservation of the Hermitage, 1889–1915:* Annals, History and Stories, 1915.

Douglass, Frederick. *Narrative of Life of Frederick Douglass, An American Slave, Written by Himself.* Boston: Anti-Slavery Office, 1845, pp. 83–84.

Drew, Benjamin. *A North-Side View of Slavery: The Refugee; Or the Narratives of Fugitive Slaves in Canada. Related by Themselves, with an account of the History and Conditions of the Colored Population of Upper Canada.* Boston: John P. Jewett and Company, 1856, pp. 302–5. This book describes Harry Thomas's 14 attempts to escape slavery.

Duncan, Patricia B. *Loudoun County, Virginia Birth Register 1853–1879.* Westminster, Md.: Willow Bend Books, 1998.

Duncan, Patricia B., and Elizabeth R. Frain. *Loudoun County, Virginia, Marriages After 1850,* Vol. 2. Westminster, Md.: Willow Bend Books, 2000.

Frain, Elizabeth R., and Marty Hiatt. *Loudoun County, Virginia Death Register 1853–1896.* Westminster, Md.: Willow Bend Books, 1998.

Franklin, John Hope, and Loren Schweninger. *Runaway Slaves, Rebels on the Plantation.* New York: Oxford University Press, 1999.

"Fresh Arrival of Fugitives," *Provincial Freeman,* Feb. 2, 1856, Chatham, Canada West, reprinted from the *Syracuse Chronicle.*

Gavrilovich, Peter, and Bill McGraw, eds. *The Detroit Almanac: 300 Years of Life in the Motor City.* Detroit: Detroit Free Press, 2000, p. 190.

Green, John M., ed. and publisher. *Negroes in Michigan History.* Detroit: 1985. Originally published in 1915 as the *Michigan Manual of Freedmen's Progress,* compiled by Francis H. Warren.

Hamilton, Kendra Y., ed. *The Essence of a People II: African Americans Who Made Their World Anew in Loudoun County, Virginia, and Beyond.* Leesburg, Va.: Black History Committee, Friends of the Thomas Balch Library, 2002.

Hayden, Robert C. *Eight Black American Inventors.* Reading Mass.: Addison-Wesley Publishing Company, Inc, 1972, pp. 92–103.

Head, James W. *History and Comprehensive Description of Loudoun County, Virginia.* 1908, pp. 71–76.

Hill, Daniel G. *The Freedom-Seekers: Blacks in Early Canada.* Toronto: Stoddart Publishing Company Ltd., 1992.

Hine, Darlene Clark, Elsa Barkley Brown, and Rosalyn Terborg-Penn, eds. *Black Women in America: An Historical Encyclopedia,* Vol. II, *M–Z.* Bloomington: Indiana University Press, 1993, pp. 766–67.

"Historic Slave Sanctuary Doomed by Wrecking Crew," *Syracuse Herald,* March 30, 1936.

Hopkins, Leroy T. "Black Eldorado on the Susquehanna: The Emergence of Black Columbia, 1726–1861." *Journal of the Lancaster County Historical Society,* Vol. 89, No. 4 (1985).

Kanoyton, Darcelle. "Lovejoy Marker Dedication Held," *Michigan Chronicle,* May 17, 1975.

Kavanaugh, Kelli B. *Detroit's Michigan Central Station,* Images of America Series. Charleston, S.C.: Arcadia Publishing, 2001.

Kay, Marvin L. Michael, and Lorin Lee Cary. *Slavery in North Carolina, 1748–1775.* Chapel Hill, S.C.: University of North Carolina Press, 1995, pp. 185–86.

LaBrew, Arthur L. *The Detroit History That Nobody Knew (or Bothered to Remember) 1800–1900, Part 1.* Privately printed, 2001, pp. 381, 220.

"Letter from William Whipple," *Frederick Douglass's Paper,* May 13, 1852.

Livingston County, Kentucky: history and families, 1798–1989, Vol. I. Smithland, Ky.: Livingston County Historical and Genealogical Society, 1989.

Loudoun County Chancery Cases, Archive Room at the Loudoun County Courthouse, Leesburg, Virginia.

Loudoun County Land Deed, Archive Room at the Loudoun County Courthouse, Leesburg, Virginia.

Loudoun County Will Book, Archive Room at the Loudoun County Courthouse, Leesburg, Virginia.

Malone, Thomas, ed. *Dictionary of American Biography,* Vol. XI. American Council of Learned Societies, 1933. New York: C. Scribner's Sons p. 617.

Marshall, Albert P. *"The Real McCoy" of Ypsilanti.* Ypsilanti, Mich.: Marlan Publishers, Inc., 1989.

May, Jeanne. "Railroad station provided one-way tickets to freedom," *Detroit Free Press,* Dec. 21, 1987.

McCutcheon, Marc. *Everyday Life in the 1800s.* Cincinnati: Writer's Digest Books, 1993.

Michael, Peter H. *An American Family of the Underground Railroad.* Bloomington, Ind.: Peter H. Michael, 2005. This tells the story of the Michael family's involvement in the Underground Railroad and maintains that all signs indicate the family farm in Cooling Springs, Md., harbored the Wanzer party during their flight to freedom.

Moffett, Ella B. "Forty-Eight Years Ago To-Day 'Jerry' Was Rescued—The Story," *Sunday Herald (Syracuse, N.Y.),* Oct. 1, 1899.

Nelson, Allen Uzikee. Interview at his home in Washington, D.C., Tuesday, May 13, 2008.
———. Telephone interview, Feb. 26, 2008.

Nelson, Winona. Telephone interview, Feb. 19, 2008. She is a descendant of one of Wanzer's daughters, Harriet Anne. She had visited Frank Wanzer's gravesite in Toronto in Aug. 2007.

New York: A Guide to the Empire State. Compiled by workers of the Writers' Program of the

Work Projects Administration in the State of New York, American Guide Series. New York: Oxford University Press, 1940. See pp. 333–34.

Pearson, Henry Greenleaf. *James S. Wadsworth of Geneseo, Brevet Major-General of United States Volunteers.* New York: Charles Scribner's Sons, 1913.

Peebles, Robin S. "Fifty Years of Progress, Michigan and the 1915 Freedmen's Exhibit," *Michigan History,* Vol. 68, No. 1 (January/February 1984): pp. 13, 14.

Prince, Bryan. *I Came As a Stranger: The Underground Railroad.* Toronto: Tundra Books, 2004, pp. 101, 142.

Presgraves, Jim, ed. *Loudoun County Families and History.* Wytheville, Va.: Wordsprint, 1999.

Prospect Cemetery in Toronto. Telephone interview with officials of the cemetery, where Frank Wanzer is buried in Section 15, grave 1683. According to cemetery data, Wanzer died on Aug. 13, 1911, at the age of 82.

Psychiatry's Betrayal. Citizens Commission on Human Rights, Louisiana, 1995.

Quarles, Benjamin. *Black Abolitionists.* New York: Oxford University Press, 1969, pp. 82, 146, 206, 208, 209, 242.

"The Real McCoy," *Observer and Eccentric,* Sep. 2, 1999.

The Rev. J. W. Loguen, As a Slave and as a Freeman: A Narrative of Real Life. Electronic edition. Syracuse: J.G.K. Truair & Co., 1859.

Robinson, Gwendolyn, and John W. Robinson. *Seek the Truth: A Story of Chatham's Black Community.* Printed and bound in Canada, 1989.

Robinson, Wilhelmena S. *International Library of Negro Life and History: Historical Negro Biographies.* New York: Publishers Company, Inc., under the auspices of the Association for the Study of Negro Life and History, 1967. See Rev. Jermain Loguen on p. 97 and William Whipper on p. 142.

Rothstein, Edward. "Early America's Imported Hero," *New York Times,* Nov. 16, 2007, p. B 29.

Saffer, Wynne. *Loudoun County, Virginia 1860 Land Tax Maps.* Leesburg, Va.: Thomas Balch Library, 2002.

Schedule 1, Free inhabitants in Salem in the county of Livingston of Kentucky, the federal 1860 census for Livingston County, Ky.

Scheel, Eugene M. "Important Events in the History of African Americans in Loudoun County." Presented as a public service by the Thomas Balch Library, Leesburg, Va., 1999, last revised 2007. See p. 8 for quotations about slavery from Catherine Broun's diary.

———. *Loudoun Discovered, Communities, Corners & Crossroads,* Vol. 3. Leesburg, Va., Friends of the Thomas Balch Library, 2002, p. 10.

Schwarz, Philip J. *Migrants Against Slavery: Virginians and the Nation.* Charlottesville, Va.: University Press of Virginia, 2001, p. 33.

Sernett, Milton C. *North Star Country: Upstate New York and the Crusade for African American Freedom.* Syracuse: Syracuse University Press, 2002, pp. 136–41.

Shadd, Adrienne, Afua Cooper, and Karolyn Smardz Frost. *The Underground Railroad: Next Stop Toronto.* Toronto: Natural Heritage Books, 2002.

Share with Us Waterford Virginia's African-American Heritage: An Interpretive Guide to Your National Historic Landmark Village. Waterford, Va.: Waterford Foundation, Inc., 2002.

Simon, Kevin, ed. *The WPA Guide to Kentucky.* Lexington: University of Kentucky, 1939.

"Slaveholders in Loudoun County, 1860 Census." Black History Committee, Friends of the Thomas Balch Library, Leesburg, Va.

Statistical gazetteer of the state of Maryland and the District of Columbia. Baltimore: J. S. Waters, and Washington: William M. Morrison & Co., 1856.

Stevenson, Brenda E. *Life in Black and White: Family and Community in the Slave South.* New York: Oxford University Press, 1996, p. 253.

Still, William. *The Underground Railroad.* Philadelphia: Porter & Coates, 1872, pp. 116–22.

Switala, William J. *Underground Railroad in Pennsylvania.* Mechanicsburg, Pa.: Stackpole Books, 2001, pp. 12, 13, 70.

Tilman, Lori. The Christmas Eve Escape. Paper submitted in fulfillment of the History 199 Independent Study class for the Historic Preservation Certificate Program at Northern Virginia Community College.

Wallace, Marie Albertina (Stark). Handwritten manuscript of her parents' adventures as settlers on Saltspring Island. Archives of Victoria Provincial Museum, Victoria, British Columbia, no date. Xerox of 30-page typescript.

Washington, Booker T. *Up from Slavery: An Autobiography.* Grand Rapids, Mich.: Candace Press, 1996, pp. 83–84.

CHAPTER 8

Cohen, Irwin. *Echoes of Detroit: A 300-Year History,* Haslett, Mich.: City Vision Publishing, 2000.

Cole, Celeste. "Black Bards of Song," *Michigan Challenge,* Lansing, Mich.: Michigan State Chamber of Commerce, June 1968, p. 30.

Connor, R.D.W., W. W. Pierson, and C. P. Higby, eds. *The James Sprunt Historical Publications,* published under the direction of the Department of History and Government, Vol. 18, Nos. 1–2. Chapel Hill: University of North Carolina Press, 1926. See "Slaveholding in North Carolina: An Economic View," by Rosser Howard Taylor, p. 93, for discussion of shoes purchased by North Carolina slaveholders.

Detroit Free Press, May 24, 2000, p. 7B. Obituary, Leontine Smith, social worker, genealogist.

"Detroit Loses Her Wealthiest Negro, Lomax B. Cook, well-known citizen dies at the age of 70," *Detroit News,* Jan. 2, 1906, p. 7.

"Family Has Long History," *Michigan Chronicle,* February 16, 1963.

Fox, Jean M. *Tracking the Underground Railroad.* Monograph #3, The Farmington Hills Historical Commission, Farmington Hills, Michigan, 1993, pp. 27–28. See p. 29 for the story of runaway slaves Ellen and Aaron Wilson.

Glazer, Sidney, ed. *Negroes in Michigan During the Civil War.* Lansing, Mich.: Michigan Civil War Centennial Observance Commission, 1966. The names of many Michigan UGRR agents appear on p. 12.

Green, John M. *Negroes in Michigan History.* Detroit: John M. Green, 1985. A reprint of *Michigan Manual of Freedmen's Progress,* compiled by Francis H. Warren, secretary of Freedmen's Progress Commission, Detroit, 1915.

Hagedorn, Ann. *Beyond the River: The Untold Story of the Heroes of the Underground Railroad.*

New York: Simon & Schuster, 2002, pp. 18–20. This book talks about antislavery sentiments in eastern Tennessee.

Hargrove, Hondon. Remarks at the Fred Hart Williams Genealogical Society's Memorial Service Honoring the 102nd U.S. Colored Troops, Nov. 11, 1985. Burton Historical Collection, Detroit Public Library, 5201 Woodward, Detroit, Mich., 48202.

Haskins, James, and Kathleen Benson. *Conjure Times: Black Magicians in America.* New York: Walker Publishing Co., July 2001.

Hayden, Robert C., and Karen E, Hayden. *African-Americans on Martha's Vineyard & Nantucket: A History of People, Places and Events.* Boston: Select Publications, 1999. See pp. 63 and 64 for the Charles Shearer story.

Hine, Darlene Clark. Black Women in the Middle West: The Michigan Experience. A lecture delivered at the annual meeting of the Historical Society of Michigan in Kalamazoo, Mich., Oct. 14, 1988.

Hine, Darlene Clark, Elsa Barkley Brown, and Rosalyn Terborg-Penn, eds. *Black Women in America: An Historical Encyclopedia,* Vol. I, *A–L.* Bloomington, Ind.: Indiana University Press, 1993. Elleanor Eldridge information is on pp. 389–90.

———, eds. *Black Women in America: An Historical Encyclopedia,* Vol. II, *M–Z,* Bloomington, Ind.: Indiana University Press, 1993, pp. 766–67.

"James H. Cole Very Near Death, Richest Negro in Detroit is Critically Ill of Pneumonia," Scrapbook, Burton Historical Collection, Detroit Public Library, *Detroit News,* May 16, 1907, p. 126.

Katzman, David M. "Early Settlers in Michigan," *Michigan Challenge,* Lansing, Mich., Michigan State Chamber of Commerce, June 1968, p. 11.

LaBrew, Arthur L. *The Detroit History That Nobody Knew (or Bothered to Remember) 1800–1900,* Part 1. Privately printed, 2001, pp. 381, 220.

Leach, Nathaniel. *Second Baptist Church of Detroit, Abbreviated History.*

Leontine Cole Craig Smith manuscript collection, Burton Historical Collection, the Detroit Public Library. Binder #17, "The story of James H. Cole, Great-Grandfather of Leontine (Cole) Smith. "Is This the way It was?" Binder #27, Mme. Florence Cole Talbert McCleave. Binder #11, 1 of 2, information about the Civil War, Binder #11, 2 of 2, information about the Civil War, and Binder #41, "A Brief History of 75 Years of Negro Progress," Charles H. Wesley and John C. Dancy.

Lewis, Ferris E. *Michigan Yesterday and Today,* 8th ed. Hillsdale, Mich.: Hillsdale Educational Publishers Inc., 1975, pp. 225–48.

Livingston County, Kentucky: History and Families, 1798–1989, Vol. I. Smithland, Ky.: Livingston County Historical and Genealogical Society, 1989.

McGraw, Bill, compiler. *Great Pages of Michigan History from the Detroit Free Press.* Detroit: Detroit Free Press, Wayne State University Press, 1987.

McRae, Norman. *Negroes in Michigan During the Civil War.* Lansing, Mich.: Michigan Civil War Centennial Observation Commission, 1966.

Miller, Francis Trevelyan, ed. in chief. *The Photographic History of the Civil War in Ten Volumes,* Vol. 8. Articles cited include "Boys Who Made Good Soldiers," by Charles King, pp. 189–94; "The Secret Service of the Federal Armies," by George H. Casamajor," p. 261 and "The Secret Service of the Confederacy," by John W. Headley, p. 285. Information about boys who fought in the war comes from the article by Charles King, brigadier general, United States Volunteers. Frank Robinson, a drummer in Musician

Company E of Michigan's 102nd U.S. Colored Infantry, was only 10 years old when the Civil War finally staggered and bled to a close.

Our Untold Stories: A Collection of Family History Narratives, compiled and written by members of the Fred Hart Williams Genealogical Society, Burton Historical Collection, Detroit Public Library, 2001. See pp. 124–26 for an account of James H. Cole's life written by his great-granddaughter, Leontine Cole-Smith.

Pawlak, Debra Ann. *Farmington and Farmington Hills.* Charleston, S.C.: Arcadia Publishing, 2003, pp. 22–30.

Peebles, Robin S. "Fifty Years of Progress, Michigan and the 1915 Freedmen's Exhibit," *Michigan History,* Vol. 68, No. 1 (Jan./Feb. 1984): pp. 13, 14.

Rice, Dorothy J. Bibb. "Orphan Train Riders," *Southern Indiana Genealogical Society Quarterly,* Vol. XXVIII, No. 3 (July 2007): p. 109.

Schedule 1, Free inhabitants in Salem in the county of Livingston of Kentucky, the federal 1860 census for Livingston County, Ky.

Simon, Kevin, ed. *The WPA Guide to Kentucky.* Lexington: University of Kentucky, 1939.

"Son of slave mother, slaveholder father got rich in Detroit," *Detroit Free Press,* Feb. 2, 1986.

Turner, Arthur, and Earl R. Moses, eds. and compilers. *A Brief History of Detroit's Colored Population and a Directory of Their Businesses, Organizations, Professions and Trades.* Detroit: 1924.

Uys, Errol Lincoln. *Riding the Rails: Teenagers on the Move During the Great Depression.* New York: TV Books, L.L.C., 1999.

Walker, Juliet E. K. "Racism, Slavery and Free Enterprise in the United States Before the Civil War," *Business History Review,* Vol. 60, No. 3 (Autumn 1986): pp. 343–82.

Washington, Booker T. *Up from Slavery: An Autobiography.* Grand Rapids, Mich.: Candace Press, 1996, p. 15.

Wilson, Sunnie, with John Cohassey. *Toast of the Town: The Life and Times of Sunnie Wilson.* Detroit: Wayne State University Press, 1998.

Woodford, Arthur M., principal author. *Detroit: American Urban Renaissance.* Tulsa: Continental Heritage, Inc., 1979.

CHAPTER 9

African Americans: Voices of Triumph. Alexandria, Va.: Time-Life Books, 1993.

"Court Records from 1800s Testify to Slaves Courage," *Los Angeles Times,* March 18, 2003.

"Freedom Suits Document a Stark History of Slavery," *Los Angeles Times,* Feb. 28, 2003.

Horton, James Oliver and Lois E. *Slavery and the Making of America.* New York: Oxford University Press, 2005, p. 157.

Missouri: A Guide to the Show Me State. Compiled by Workers of the Writers' Program of the Work Projects Administration in the State of Missouri. Sponsored by the Missouri State Highway Department. New York: Duell, Sloan and Pearce, 1941.

CHAPTER 10

Batty, Peter, and Peter J. Parish. *The Divided Union: A Concise History of the Civil War.* Charleston, S.C.: Tempus Publishing, Inc., 1999.

Claxton, Melvin, and Mark Puls. *Uncommon Valor: A Story of Race, Patriotism and Glory in the Final Battles of the Civil War,* Hoboken, N.J.: John Wiley & Sons, 2006.

Guelzo, Allen C. *Lincoln's Emancipation Proclamation: The End of Slavery in America.* New York: Simon and Schuster, 2003.

Hesseltine, William B. *Lincoln and the War Governors.* New York: Alfred A. Knopf, 1955.

Leech, Margaret. *Reveille in Washington.* New York: Carroll & Graf Publishers, Inc., 1969, orig. pub. 1941.

Moore, Stacy Gibbons. "Established and Well Cultivated, Afro-American Foodways in Early Virginia," *Virginia Cavalcade,* No. 39, Autumn 1989.

Paige, Howard. *African-American Cookery.* Southfield, Mich.: Aspects Publishing Co., 1995. Paige describes George Washington's breakfasts when he had guests and relates the story of Alethia Tanner's successful garden on p. 94.

Pearson, Henry Greenleaf. *James S. Wadsworth of Geneseo, Brevet-Major-General of United States Volunteers.* New York: Charles Scribner's Sons, 1913.

Recipes gathered in interviews with Barbara Wynder, who grew up in Cheriton, Virginia; the late Fred L. Williams of Detroit; Janice Berry of Detroit and Shervonne Taylor, an Ohioan.

Russell, Hilary. *Final Research Report: The Operation of the Underground Railroad in Washington, D.C., c. 1800–1860.* Washington, D.C.: Historical Society of Washington and the National Park Service, 2001.

"Slavery's Place in the Capitol," editorial, *New York Times,* Dec. 21, 2007, p. A30.

Stoddard, William O., Jr., ed. *Lincoln's Third Secretary: The Memoirs of William O. Stoddard.* New York: Exposition Press, 1955.

The War of the Rebellion: A Compilation of the Official Records of the Union and Confederate Armies. May–November 1864; Series 1, Vol. 39, Chapter 51, part 1, U.S. War Department, Serial Set, 1817–1980, Vol. No. 2993, Session Vol. No. 35, 1892, 52nd Congress, 1st Session, H. Misc.Doc 233 pt. 1, 1046 p.

Ward, Geoffrey C. "Death's Army," *New York Times Book Review,* Jan. 27, 2008, p. 8.

Wilson, Joseph T. *The Black Phalanx.* Hartford, Conn.: American Publishing Company, 1890. Reprinted Salem, N.H.: Ayers Company Publishers, Inc., 1992.

CHAPTER 11

African Americans, Voices of Triumph: Leadership. Alexandria, Va.: Time-Life Books, 1994, pp. 83–84.

African Americans, Voices of Triumph: Perseverance. Alexandria, Va.: Time-Life Books, 1993, pp. 62–65.

Aptheker, Herbert, ed. *A Documentary History of the Negro People in the United States.* New York: The Citadel Press, 1951, p. 481.

Bacon, Margaret Hope. *Valiant Friend: The Life of Lucretia Mott.* New York: Walker and Company, 1980, p. 62.

Bates, Beth Tompkins. *Pullman Porters and the Rise of Protest Politics in Black America, 1925–1945.* Chapel Hill, N.C., and London: University of North Carolina Press, 2001.

Batty, Peter, and Peter J. Parish. *The Divided Union: A Concise History of The Civil War.* Charleston, S.C.: Tempus Publishing, Inc., 1999.

Bernikow, Louise. *The American Women's Almanac.* New York: Berkley Books, 1997.

Blanton, Wyndham B. *Medicine in Virginia in the Nineteenth Century.* Richmond: Garrett & Massie, Inc., 1933, pp. 241, 264, 297.

Christian Recorder, Nov. 25, 1880. Obituary for Lucretia Mott.

Claxton, Melvin, and Mark Puls. *Uncommon Valor: A Story of Race, Patriotism and Glory in the Final Battles of the Civil War.* Hoboken, N.J.: John Wiley & Sons, 2006.

Daniel, Walter C. *Black Journals of the United States.* Westport, Conn.: Greenwood Press, 1982, p. 8.

DeRamus, Betty. "Slaves met tricksters, spies on freedom's trail," *Detroit News,* Feb. 8, 2000.

Fauquier County, Virginia 1759–1959. Warrenton, Va.: Fauquier County Bicentennial Committee, 1959.

Franklin, John Hope, and Loren Schweninger. *Runaway Slaves: Rebels on the Plantation.* New York: Oxford University Press, 1999, pp. 56, 64.

"The Fugitive Slave Case in Philadelphia," *National Era,* April 14, 1859.

"Fugitive Slave Excitement at Harrisburg," *National Era,* April 7, 1859.

Hamilton, Kendra, ed. *The Essence of a People II: African Americans Who Made Their World Anew in Loudoun County, Virginia and Beyond.* Leesburg, Va.: Black History Committee, Friends of the Thomas Balch Library, Leesburg, Va., 2002.

Harris, Jessica B. "Juneteenth," *American Legacy,* Summer 2005, pp. 15–16.

Hine, Darlene Clark, Elsa Barkley Brown, and Rosalyn Terborg-Penn, eds. *Black Women in America: An Historical Encyclopedia,* Vol. I, *A–I.* Bloomington, Ind.: University of Indiana Press, 1994, pp. 505–6.

Kelly, Donovan, "S Is for Slaves, Escaped," *Elan* magazine, Feb. 2007.

Lee, Deborah A. "Daniel Dangerfield, 1831–Unknown," in *The Essence of a People II: African Americans Who Made Their World Anew in Loudoun County, Virginia and Beyond,* Leesburg, Va.: Black History Committee, Friends of the Thomas Balch Library, 2002, pp. 32–37.

Loudoun County, Virginia Clerk's Office, deed book, 5S, p. 366.

Scheel, Eugene. *Important Events in the History of African Americans in Loudoun County, Virginia: A Chronology.* Orig. ed., 1999, Leesburg, Va.: Thomas Balch Library.

"Slavery's Place in the Capitol," editorial, *New York Times,* Dec. 21, 2007, p. A30.

Stevenson, Brenda E. *Life in Black & White: Family and Community in the Slave South.* New York: Oxford University Press, 1996.

Stevenson, Brenda, ed. *The Journals of Charlotte Forten Grimke.* New York: Oxford University Press, 1988, pp. 357–58.

White, Slave and Free Negro Population in Loudoun County, Virginia 1800–1850, Appendix C. from federal U.S. Census Schedules, Thomas Balch Library, Leesburg, Va.

Wigham, Eliza. *The Anti-Slavery Cause in America and Its Martyrs.* London: A.W. Bennett, 1863.

Yanak, Ted, and Pam Cornelison. *The Great American History Fact-Finder.* New York: Houghton-Mifflin Co., 1993.

CHAPTER 12

"Archaeologists find location of Ramptown," WMU News, June 17, 2002, Western Michigan University, Kalamazoo, Michigan, www.wmich.edu/wmu/news/2002/0206/01 02-421.html. Accessed on Oct. 10, 2002.

Campbell, Amanda J., and Michael S. Nassaney. *The Ramptown Project: Archaeological and Historical Investigations of Underground Railroad Activities in Southwest Michigan.* Kalamazoo, Mich.: Department of Anthropology, Western Michigan University, 2005.

Carroll, Kenneth. *Joseph Nichols and the Nicholites.* Easton, Md.: Easton Publishing Co., 1962.

Chardavoyne, David G. "The Kentucky Raids on Calhoun and Cass Counties," *Court Legacy,* Special Annual Meeting Issue, Vol. XII, No. 3 (2004).

The Court Legacy, Special Annual Meeting Issue, Vol. XII, No. 3 (Sep. 2004).

DeRamus, Betty. "Adrian house opened a window to freedom," *Detroit News,* Feb. 1, 2000.

———. "Kentucky Raid epitomizes races pulling together," *Detroit News,* Aug. 15, 2005.

———. "Slaves met tricksters, spies on freedom's trail," *Detroit News,* Feb. 8, 2000.

Dorson, Richard M. *Negro Folktales in Michigan.* Cambridge: Harvard University Press, 1956.

Durham, Michael S. "I Am Going to Be Thomas Day," *American Legacy,* Winter 1998, pp. 49–53. This talks about the backgrounds of some of the North Carolinians who moved to Cass County, Michigan, after the Nat Turner uprising.

"Ethiopians' Eden. One of the Old Stations to the Underground Railway," *Daily Inter Ocean,* Jan. 3, 1880, issue 235.

Farrell, Patrick, and Kassie Bracken. "A Tiny Fruit That Tricks the Tongue." *New York Times,* May 28, 2008, pp. D1, D3. This talks about a West African berry that changes an eater's sense of taste, making everything eaten following the berry taste sweet.

Fox, George R. "Place Names of Berrien County," *Michigan History,* Vol. III, No. 1 (Jan. 1924).

Giltner v. Gorham et al., Case No. 5,453, Circuit Court, D. Michigan, 10 F, Cas. 424; 1848 U.S. App. LEXIS 355; 6 W.L.J. 49; 4 Mc Lean 402. June, 1848, Term. Platt & Norvell for plaintiff. Mr. Emmons, for defendants. Opinion By: McLean. This was an action brought to recover the value of six slaves claimed by the plaintiff, a resident of Carroll County, Kentucky. The slaves were arrested by agents of the plaintiff in Marshall, Michigan, and then rescued by the defendants.

Graff, George P. *The People of Michigan Bicentennial Publication.* Lansing, Mich.: Michigan Department of Education State Library Services, 1974.

Grimm, Joe, ed. *Michigan Voices: Our State's History in the Words of the People Who Lived It.* Detroit: Detroit Free Press and Wayne State University Press, 1987, pp. 51–52. Letter from Reverend Parsons.

"Kidnappers in Michigan and Indiana," *New York Herald,* Oct. 8, 1847, issue 27.

Lansing Republican, Lansing, Michigan, June 9, 1857.

"Letter from St. Louis," *Daily Evening Bulletin,* Oct. 9, 1860, issue 2.

Long, John H., ed. *Kentucky Atlas of Historical County Boundaries,* a project of the Dr. William M. Scholl Center for Family and Community History. New York: Charles Scribner's Sons, 1995.

Lucas, Marion B. *A History of Blacks in Kentucky,* Vol. 1, *From Slavery to Segregation, 1760–1891.* Frankfort, Ky.: Kentucky Historical Society, 1992.

Lutz, Tom, and Susanna Ashton. *These "Colored" United States: African American Essays from the 1920s.* New Brunswick, N.J.: Rutgers University Press, 1996, pp. 129–34.

Marty, Debian. "The Banality of Goodness: A Collective Biography of an Abolitionist Community." A speech delivered at the Indiana Association of Historians meeting, Feb. 2008, Purdue University, Indianapolis, Ind. Marty is associate professor and chair, department of philosophy, prelaw and peace studies, Division of Humanities and Communication, California State University, Monterey Bay. This lecture examines the moral choices of southwestern Michigan's antislavery Quakers and the forces that shaped their decisions.

———. Email of Jan. 19, 2007. Marty notes that the number of people reported captured by the Kentuckians in 1847 has "varied over time, with the most reliable estimate between nine and ten, but I've seen the figure as high as sixteen."

———. Email of Aug. 12, 2005, about the significance of the Kentucky raid, which "shows us not only what is possible, but what is required in response to injustice. It's possible for people with different racial identities to work together to better our lives, mindful of our different roles and responsibilities in a particular situation. It's also simply necessary that we do act together, for peaceful co-existence cannot be accomplished alone."

Mathews, Alfred. *History of Cass County, Michigan. With Illustrations and Biographical Sketches of Some of Its Prominent Men and Pioneers.* Chicago: Waterman, Watkins & Co., 1882.

Mebane, Mary E. *Mary, Wayfarer: An Autobiography.* New York: Viking Press, 1983. Mebane talks about the psychological as well as physical differences between growing corn and growing tobacco.

Michigan: A Guide to the Wolverine State. Compiled by Workers of the Writers' Program of the Work Projects Administration in the State of Michigan. New York: Oxford University Press and the Michigan State Administrative Board, 1941, pp. 192–97 and 410.

Michigan Pioneers: The First One Hundred Years of Statehood. Detroit: J. L. Hudson Co., Sep. 1937.

Mort Crim Communications, Inc. Email about the dedication of the plaque commemorating the Kentucky raid, July 26, 2005.

Mose-Ursery, Sondra. Interview, Vandalia, Michigan, 2003.

Mose-Ursery Private Collection, 1949 funeral record of Melissa Brown and 1929 obituary of Andrew Jones.

Mumford, Lou. "Black wants 'white history month,' " *South Bend Tribune,* May 7, 1999.

"Negro Votes in Cass County," *National Democrat,* April 12, 1856, Cassopolis, Michigan.

"Out of Bondage: How Perry Sanford Escaped from Slavery: Thrilling Experience on His Way to Michigan," reprinted in *Heritage Battle Creek* 9 (Winter 1999), p. 78.

Portrait and Biographical Record of Berrien and Cass Counties, Michigan, Containing Biographical Sketches of Prominent and Representative Citizens and of the Presidents of the United States. Chicago: Biographical Publishing Co., 1893.

Portrait and Biographical Album of Calhoun County, Michigan. Containing Full Page Portraits and Biographical Sketches of Prominent and Representative Citizens of the County Together with Portraits and Biographies of all the Presidents of the United States and Governors of the State. Chicago: Chapman Bros., 1891.

Prince, Bryan. *I Came as a Stranger: The Underground Railroad.* Toronto: Tundra Books, 2004.

Pritchard, James. "WMU team verifies fugitive slave site," Associated Press, Oct. 6, 2005.

"Quaint Old Characters," *Niles Daily Star (Mich.),* Feb. 16, 1901, p. 1.

Rogers, Howard S. *History of Cass County, from 1825 to 1875.* Cassopolis, Mich.: W. H. Mansfield, Vigilant Book and Job Print., 1875.

Rombauer, Irma S., and Marion Rombauer Becker. *Joy of Cooking,* Indianapolis: Bobbs-Merrill Co., Inc., 1964.

Romig, Walter, L. H. D. *Michigan Place Names: The History of the Founding and the Naming of More Than Five Thousand Past and Present Michigan Communities.* Grosse Pointe, Mich.: Walter Romig, 1978.

Sawyer, Marcia Renee. Surviving freedom: African-American farm households in Cass County, Michigan, 1832–1880. Ph.D. dissertation, Ypsilanti, Mich.: Michigan State University, 1991.

Schoetzow, Mae R., compiler. *A Brief History of Cass County.* Marcellus, Mich.: Cass County Federation of Women's Clubs, 1935.

"Searching for site of escaped slave settlement," WMU News, Dec. 12, 2001, Western Michigan University, Kalamazoo, Michigan. www.wmich.edu/wmu/news/20001/0112/0102-185.html. Accessed on Oct. 10, 2002.

Shadd, Adrienne, Afua Cooper, and Karolyn Smardz Frost. *The Underground Railroad: Next Stop Toronto.* Toronto: Natural Heritage Books, 2002. See p. 6 for a discussion of nineteenth-century washing machines.

Shugart, Zachariah. Account Book, Day Book and Diary. Niles Community Library, Niles, Michigan.

"In Slave Days, History of the Underground Railroad," *Ann Arbor Courier,* May 13, 1885. This is an interview with Erastus Hussey, Underground Railroad conductor in Battle Creek, Michigan, reprinted from the *Battle Creek Call,* publication date unknown.

Stecker, Naseem. "A Stop on the Long Road to Freedom," www.michbar.org/journal/article.cfm?articleID=881&volumeID=67. Accessed on July 12, 2005. This article explains why a plaque was erected to commemorate the Kentucky raid and why the Michigan Bar Association considers the 1847 incident a legal milestone.

Steffens, Marcia. "MSU professor talks about Ramptown, Chain Lake Baptist," *Dowagiac Daily News,* June 20, 2007.

Stewart, Roma Jones. "The Migration of a Free People," *Michigan History,* Vol. 71, No. 1 (Jan./Feb. 1987): pp. 34–38.

"Troutman Again," *Michigan Liberty Press,* April 7, 1849.

Troy, Rev. William. *Hair Breadth Escapes from Slavery to Freedom.* Manchester: Bremner, 1861, pp. 10–11. This is runaway slave Joseph Sandford's description of the Kentucky raid.

Wilson, Benjamin C. "Black History of Cass County, Michigan," *Chronicle,* Vol. 16, issue 3 (Fall 1980).

———. "Kentucky Kidnappers, Fugitives, and Abolitionists in Antebellum Cass County, Michigan," *Michigan History,* Vol. 60 (Winter 1976).

CHAPTER 13

Chadwick, Bruce. *Traveling the Underground Railroad.* Secaucus, N.J.: Carol Publishing Group, 1999.

Diggs, Mamie Sweeting, great-granddaughter of Daniel Hughes. Interview, Williamsport, Pa., 2003.

Frock, Karen. *Follow the North Star to Freedom.* Documentary film, Williamsport, Pa, 1997.

Hunsinger, Louis, Jr. "Daniel Hughes: Giant of Freedom Road," *Susquehanna Parent Magazine (Williamsport, Pa.),* Feb. 2002

Switala, William, Jr. *Underground Railroad in Pennsylvania.* Mechanicsburg, Pa.: Stackpole Books, 2001.

U.S. Federal Census Mortality Schedule, 1850–1880, for Daniel Hughes, Ancestry.com. He is described as male, black, married and 63 years old and the cause of death as "Gravel & Para."

Van Auken, Robin, and Louis E. Hunsinger, Jr. *Williamsport: Boomtown on the Susquehanna.* Charleston, S.C.: Arcadia Publishing, 2003, pp. 53, 54.

CHAPTER 14

African Americans, Voices of Triumph: Leadership. Alexandria, Va.: Time-Life Books, 1994, pp. 83–84.

African Americans, Voices of Triumph: Perseverance. Alexandria, Va.: Time-Life Books, 1993, pp. 62–65.

Aptheker, Herbert, ed. *A Documentary History of The Negro People in the United States.* New York: The Citadel Press, 1951, p. 481.

Batty, Peter, and Peter J. Parish. *The Divided Union: A Concise History of the Civil War.* Charleston, S.C.: Tempus Publishing, Inc., 1999.

Bernikow, Louise. *The American Women's Almanac.* New York: Berkley Books, 1997. Mary Elizabeth Bowser's spying is mentioned on p. 15.

Blanton, Wyndham B. *Medicine in Virginia in the Nineteenth Century.* Richmond: Garrett & Massie, Inc., 1933, pp. 241, 264, 297.

Claxton, Melvin, and Mark Puls. *Uncommon Valor: A Story of Race, Patriotism and Glory in the Final Battles of the Civil War.* Hoboken, N.J.: John Wiley & Sons, 2006.

Daniel, Walter C. *Black Journals of the United States.* Westport, Conn.: Greenwood Press, 1982, p. 3.

DeRamus, Betty. "Slaves met tricksters, spies on freedom's trail," *Detroit News,* Feb. 8, 2000.

Dyer, Frederick H. *A Compendium of the War of the Rebellion,* 3 vols. New York and London: Thomas Yoseloff, special contents of this edition, Sagamore Press, Inc., 1959.

Emery, Theo. "Watch Night Services Link Past and Future for Blacks," *New York Times,* Dec. 31, 2006.

Farmer's Almanac for the Year of Our Lord 1864. New York: M. T. Cozans, 122 Nassau Street.

Fauquier County, Virginia 1759–1959. Warrenton, Va.: Fauquier County Bicentennial Committee, 1959.

Foote, Shelby. *The Civil War: A Narrative, Red River to Appomattox.* New York: Vintage Books, 1974.

Franklin, John Hope, and Loren Schweninger. *Runaway Slaves: Rebels on the Plantation.* New York: Oxford University Press, 1999, pp. 56, 64.

Funkhouser, Darlene. *Civil War Cookin', Stories, 'n Such: One Hundred Twenty-Nine Recipes Used by the Troops in the Field.* Weaver, Iowa: Quixote Press, 2000.

Hagedorn, Ann. *Beyond the River: The Untold Story of the Heroes of the Underground Railroad.* New York: Simon & Schuster, 2002.

Moore, Frank. *Women of the War; Their Heroism and Self-Sacrifice.* Hartford, Conn.: S. S. Scranton & Co., 1866. On pp. 309–10, Moore describes the massacre of black troops at Fort Pillow, Tennessee, in April 1864 by Confederate forces led by General Nathan Bedford Forrest: "Of the negro troops hardly one escaped. They were shot down like hogs. They were stabbed and beaten when wounded. The sabres were often plunged into the hole made by the pistol ball. Some were pinned to the ground and burned. Some were buried alive."

Morris, Charles. *Famous Men and Great Events of the Nineteenth Century.* Washington, D.C.: W. E. Schull, 1899.

Nalty, Bernard C. *Strength for the Fight: A History of Black Americans in the Military.* New York: The Free Press, 1986. Bowser, Truth and Harriet Tubman are mentioned on p. 44.

Poland, Charles P. Jr. *From Frontier to Suburbia.* Marceline, Mo.: Walsworth Publishing Co., 1976, pp. 129–41.

Powell, Lew. *On This Day in North Carolina.* Winston-Salem, N.C.: John F. Blair, 1996. See p. 96 for story of Blind Tom.

Pybus, Cassandra. *Epic Journeys of Freedom: Runaway Slaves of the American Revolution and Their Global Quest for Liberty.* Boston: Beacon Press, 2006.

Rawick, George P., ed. *The American Slave: A Composite Biography,* Vol. 7, *Oklahoma and Mississippi Narratives.* Orig. pub. 1941, reprinted, Westport Conn.: Greenwood Press, 1972 p. 146, narrative of Isaac Stier, Natchez, Mississippi.

Sharp, Saundra. *Black Women for Beginners.* New York: Writers and Readers Publishing, Inc., 1993.

Tutelian, Louise. "A Bit of Paradise on Island No. 999," *New York Times,* Aug. 24, 2007, p. D1.

The War of the Rebellion: A Compilation of the Official Records of the Union and Confederate Armies. May–November 1864; Series 1, Vol. 39, Chapter 51, part 1, U.S. War Department, Serial Set, 1817–1980, Vol. No. 2993, Session Vol. No. 35, 1892, 52nd Congress, 1st Session, H. Misc. Doc 233 pt. 1, 1046 p.

Ward, Geoffrey C. "Death's Army," *New York Times Book Review,* Jan. 27, 2008, p. 8.

White, Slave and Free Negro Population in Loudoun County, Virginia 1800–1850, Appendix C from federal U.S. Census Schedules, Thomas Balch Library, Leesburg, Va.

Wigham, Eliza. *The Anti-Slavery Cause in America and Its Martyrs.* London: A. W. Bennett, 1863.

Williams, James. *Life & Adventures of James Williams, A Fugitive Slave, with a full description of the Underground Railroad,* 3rd ed. San Francisco: Women's Union Print, 1874.

Williams Genealogical Society, Detroit Public Library, 2001, p. 17. This tells the story of Kitt, a runaway slave who used several aliases while in the Army.

CHAPTER 15

"Abolitionist Movement," Microsoft Encarta Online Encyclopedia, 2007, http://encarta .msn.com.

Adams, James Truslow, editor-in-chief. *Album of American History,* Vol. II *1783–1853.* New York: Charles Scribner's Sons, 1945.

African Americans, Voices of Triumph: Perseverance. Time-Life Books, 1993.

Athearn, Robert G. *American Heritage Illustrated History of the United States,* Vol. II, *The Gilded Age.* New York: Choice Publishing, Inc. Created in Association with the editors of American Heritage and for the updated edition, Media Projects Inc., 1988, pp. 908–10.

Bacon, Margaret Hope. *Valiant Friend: The Life of Lucretia Mott.* New York: Walker and Company, 1980.

Banwejw, Neela. "A Midnight Service Helps African Immigrants Combat Demons," *New York Times,* Dec. 18, 2007, p. A20.

Bathwaite, Edward. *The Development of Creole Society in Jamaica, 1770–1820.* Oxford: Clarendon Press, 1971, p. 162. The author talks about a good obeah being able to use "blood, feathers, parrot beaks, dog teeth, alligators teeth, broken Bottle, Grave Dirt, Rum, Eggshells or any other materials relative to the practice of Obeah or Witchcraft."

Beasley, Delilah L. *The Negro Trail Blazers of California.* Los Angeles: Times Mirror Publishing and Binding House, 1919. See p. 54 for the story of Gordon, a black man who came to California from Baltimore with his wife and several of her sisters. He opened a barbershop in the basement of the Niantic Hotel, which was owned by Mr. Fink. One of his wife's sisters ran a millinery store at the same location. The hotel was located in San Francisco at Bush and Samsone streets. On October 1861, Gordon was shot and killed at his barbershop by a white man named Robert Schell. Schell pistol-whipped Gordon as he lay dying on Samsone Street. Schell had been accused of stealing by his wife's sister. Robert Cowles, a light-skinned black man, was a witness. Cowles was not allowed to testify because of his race, but the testimony of a white witness led to a murder conviction.

Bell, Madison Smartt. "The Fugitive: A novelist's biography of Harriet Tubman," *New York Times,* June 24, 2007, p. 8.

Bennett, Lerone, Jr. "The Mystery of Mary Ellen Pleasant, Parts 1 and 2," *Ebony,* April, May, 1979.

Bibbs, Susheel. *Heritage of Power.* MEP Publications, 1998.

Biographical entry for Zachariah Morgan. *The Traverse Region,* Chicago: H. H. Page & Co., 1884.

Brown, Dee. *The Westerners.* New York: Holt, Rinehart and Winston, Inc., 1947, pp. 121–28. Describes the Gold Rush.

Brown, Patricia Leigh. "Fall Foliage in California—Ritual with an Itch," *New York Times,* Sep. 27, 2007, p. A18.

Bruce, Marian. "Former Slave's Story," *Vancouver Sun,* May 6, 1974.

Calhoun, Ada. "Ladies of the Evening: How two sisters in Chicago created the early 20th century's most glamorous brothel," *New York Times Book Review,* August 12, 2007, p. 9.

Carey, Benedict. "Do You Believe in Magic?" *New York Times,* Jan. 23, 2007, pp. D1, D6.

Casey, Maura J. "Of Witches and the Wait for Justice," *New York Times,* Editorial Notebook, April 13, 2008.

Curtis, Nancy C. *Black Heritage Sites: The South.* New York: New Press, 1996.

Daily Evening Bulletin (San Francisco). Aug. 4, 1884, p. 2, issue 101, col. F. Marriage Notice for Mrs. Lucy Breckinridge, daughter of William Sharon.

Daily Evening Bulletin (San Francisco). Nov. 14, 1885, p. 3, issue 33, col. H. Death Notice for William Sharon.

Daily Evening Bulletin (San Francisco). Sep. 9, 1886, p. 2, issue 132, col. D. This is a notice about Bell and Mary Pleasant providing a bond for J. E. Browne and Mrs. Weile after their original insurer withdrew from their case.

Daniels, Douglas H. *Afro-Americans, the San Francisco Bay Area and the Golden Gate National Recreation Area.* San Francisco: National Park Service, 1980.

Davis, Kenneth C. *Don't Know Much About History.* New York: Crown Publishers, Inc., 1990.

De Graaf, Lawrence B. "Race, Sex and Region: Black Women in the American West, 1850–1920," *Pacific Historical Review,* Vol. 49, No. 2 (May 1980): pp. 285–313.

DeRamus, Betty. The Real Mother of the Civil Rights Movement. An address delivered at LeMoyne-Owen College, Memphis, Tenn., Nov. 2005.

DuBois, W. E. B. *The Souls of Black Folk.* Atlanta: Atlanta University Press, 1903. He writes on p. 216, "Association with the masters, missionary effort and motives of expediency gave these rites an early veneer of Christianity, and after the lapse of many generations the Negro church became Christian."

Ellis, Pat, ed. *Women of the Caribbean.* London and U.S.A.: Zed Books Ltd., 1986. This book mentions that a nanny instills confidence and pride in her group. On p. 27, she writes: "All legends and documents refer to Nanny of the First Maroon War as the most outstanding woman of this time, leading her people with courage and inspiring them to maintain their spirit of freedom, that life of independence which was their rightful inheritance."

Federal Census for city of San Francisco, 1880, Series T9 Roll: 79 p. 126. According to the census of June 1880, Mary E. Pleasant was then aged 65, black and born in Pennsylvania. She was described as servant and housekeeper in the Thomas Bell household.

Federal Census for city of San Francisco, 1870, Series M593 Roll: 80 p. 486. In the 1870 census, Mary Pleasant is described as 50 years old, black, owner of a boarding house and from Pennsylvania. John Pleasant is described as a ship cook.

Flucke, A. F. "Early Days on Saltspring Island," *British Columbia Historical Quarterly,* Vol. 15, July–Oct. 1951.

"Former slave's son enters 90th year," *Daily Colonist (Victoria, B.C.),* March 16, 1956. This article tells the story of Ernest Harrison, a descendant of one of Saltspring's original black settlers.

Gibbs, Mifflin W. *Shadow and Light: An Autobiography.* New York: Arno Press and the New York Times, 1968.

Hamilton, Kenneth Marvin. *Black Towns and Profit: Promotion and Development in the Trans-Appalachian West, 1877–1915.* Urbana, Ill.: University of Illinois Press, 1991.

Goode, Kenneth G. *California's Black Pioneers: A Brief Historical Survey.* Santa Barbara, Calif.: McNally and Loften, 1973.

Griffin, Mary Crosley. *Hangtown: Tales of Old Placerville.* Universal City, Calif.: Crosley Books, 1994.

Grimes, William. "Murder by Mail in Gilded Age New York," *New York Times,* Oct. 24, 2007, p. C1.

"Hair of a Witness Examined," *San Francisco Bulletin,* March 20, 1862, p. 2.

Hayden, Robert C. *Eight Black American Inventors.* Reading, Mass.: Addison-Wesley Publishing Company, Inc., 1972, pp. 34–35.

Hayden, Robert C., and Karen E. Hayden. *African Americans on Martha's Vineyard and Nantucket: A History of People, Places and Events.* Boston: Select Publications, 1999. See p. 247 for quotation about Mary Ellen Pleasant.

Hine, Darlene, et al., eds. *Black Women in America: An Historical Encyclopedia,* Vol. II, *M–Z.* Indiana University Press, 1994.

Holdredge, Helen H. *Mammy Pleasant's Partner.* New York: G. P. Putnam's Sons, 1954.

Hudson, Lynn M. *The Making of "Mammy Pleasant": A Black Entrepreneur in Nineteenth Century San Francisco.* Urbana and Chicago: University of Illinois Press, 2003.

Hudson, Lynn M. "Strong Animal Passions in the Gilded Age: Race, Sex, and a Senator on Trial," *Journal of the History of Sexuality,* Vol. 9, No. 1/2 (Jan.–April 2000): pp. 62–84.

Hudson, Lynn M. When "Mammy" Becomes a Millionaire: Mary Ellen Pleasant, An African American Entrepreneur. Submitted to the faculty of the University Graduate School in partial fulfillment of the requirement for the degree Doctor of Philosophy in the Department of History, Indiana University, July 1996.

Irby, Charles C. "The Black Settlers on Saltspring Island, Canada," reprinted from the *Yearbook of the Pacific Coast Geographers,* Vol. 36, 1974. This piece provides a decade-by-decade count of the blacks who moved to the island off the coast of British Columbia, talks about intermarriage on Saltspring and explains why blacks on the island developed no social cohesion.

Kahn, Charles. *Salt Spring: The Story of an Island.* Madeira Park, B. C.: Harbour Publishing, 1998.

Kaspar, Sydney H. "You Can Still Strike It Rich in the Gold Country," *Early American Life,* Vol. XIII, No. 1, Feb. 1982, Harrisburg, Pa.: The Early American Society, 1982, p. 82.

Katz, William Loren. *Black People Who Made the Old West.* New York: Thomas Y. Crowell, 1977.

Katz, William Loren. *The Black West.* Seattle: Open Hand Publishing, 1987. This talks about Sylvia Stark firing through the roof to run off Indians and, on p. 152, about California's passage of its own fugitive slave law.

Kennedy, Patricia. *San Francisco, California,* Images of America Series. Charleston, S.C.: Arcadia Publishing, 2001.

Lapp, Rudolph M. *Blacks in Gold Rush California.* New Haven: Yale University Press, 1977.

Larson, Kate Clifford. *Bound for the Promised Land.* New York: One World Books, 2004. See p. 48 for reference to female preacher Zilpha Elaw, who may have influenced Mary Ellen Pleasant in Nantucket.

Louisiana, A Guide to the State. Compiled by the Workers of the Writers' Program of the Work Projects Administration in the State of Louisiana. New York: Hastings House, 1941.

Magical Arts. Time-Life Books. Alexandria, Va.: Time-Life Books, 1990, pp. 8, 9, 80–83.

"Marie Laveaux, the Queen of the New Orleans Voudou Negroes," *St. Louis Globe-Democrat,* Feb. 20, 1886, p. 16, issue 273.

McKinley, James C., Jr. "Travelers in Search of Mexico's Magic Find Town of Witches and Warlocks," *New York Times,* March 27, 2008, p. A6.

Miller, Robert H. *Reflections of a Black Cowboy.* Englewood, N.J.: Silver Burdett Press, Inc., 1991.

Nelson, Truman, ed. *Documents of Upheaval: Selections from William Lloyd Garrison's The Liberator, 1831–1865.* Clinton, Mass.: The Colonial Press, Inc. 1966.

Paige, Howard. *African American Family Cookery.* Southfield, Mich.: Aspects Publishing Co., 1995.

Parker, Elizabeth L., and James Abijian. *A Walking Tour of the Black Presence in San Francisco,* p. 2.

Parkman, Francis. *The Oregon Trail.* New York: Dodd, Mead & Co., 1945; New York: Pageant Books, 1960.

Peterson, Audrey. "France's Freedom Fighters," *American Legacy,* Summer 2005, p. 62.

Pleasant, Mary Ellen. "Memoirs and Autobiography," *The Pandex of the Press* 1, Jan. 1902.

Pratson, Frederick. *Guide to Western Canada,* 2nd ed. Chester, Conn.: Pequot Press, 1990.

"A Quiet Wedding, Judge Terry and Sarah Althea Married to-Day at Stockton." *Daily Evening Bulletin (San Francisco),* Jan. 7, 1886, p. 3, issue 77, col. E.

Riegert, Ray. *Hidden San Francisco and Northern California,* 4th ed. Berkeley, Calif.: Ulysses Press, 1990.

Riley, Glenda. *A Place to Grow: Women in the American West.* Arlington Heights, Ill.: Harlan Davidson, 1992.

Romero, Simon. "A Language Not Quite Spanish, with African Echoes," *New York Times,* Oct. 18, 2007, p. A4.

———. "Venezuela Dances to Devilish Beat to Promote Tourism," *New York Times,* June 12, 2007.

Rucker, Walter. "Conjure, Magic and Power: The Influence of Afro-Atlantic Religious Practices on Slave Resistance and Rebellion," *Journal of Black Studies,* Vol. 32, No. 1 (Sep. 2001): pp. 84–103.

Sacramento Union, June 2, 1858, p. 2. Story about Archy Lee.

Savage, W. Sherman. "Blacks in the West." An Essay in *Contributions in Afro-American and African Studies,* No. 23, Westport, Conn.: Greenwood Press, 1976.

"The Sharon Divorce Case. Plaintiff Invokes the Aid of a Colored Sorceress. Persistent Efforts to Win Back the Love of the Defendant. A Weird Story as Told on the Witness Stand," *Daily Evening Bulletin (San Francisco),* April 16, 1884, issue 8, p. 2. This relates the story of Laura Scott's testimony about charmed socks during the Sharon trial.

Sharon v. Hill, Circuit Court, D. California, 26 F. 337; 1885 U.S. App. LEXIS 2397; 11 Sawy. 290, Dec. 26, 1885.

Sherman, William Tecumseh. *Memoirs of General W. T. Sherman.* New York: Penguin Books, 2000, pp. 67, 75.

Slave Narratives. New York: The Library of America, 2000.

Smith, James R. *San Francisco's Lost Landmarks.* Sanger, Calif.: Word Dancer Press, 2005.

Snyder, David L. *Negro Civil Rights in California: 1850.* Sacramento: California State Archives, Sacramento Book Collectors Club, 1969. This includes the story of Sarah Carroll, a free black Sacramento property owner, who was unable to sue a white man for allegedly stealing her property.

Stauffer, John. *The Black Hearts of Men: Radical Abolitionists and the Transformation of Race.* Amherst, Mass.: Harvard University Press, 2004. Traces the intertwined lives of John Brown, Gerrit Smith, Frederick Douglass and William McCune Smith.

Stevenson, James. "Balloons over Broadway," *New York Times,* Op-Ed, Nov. 17, 2007, p. A31.

Still, William. *The Underground Railroad,* copyright 1871, William Still, reprinted, Johnson Publishing Co., Inc., 1970, pp. 773–75.

Stodghill, Ron. "Driving Back into History," *New York Times,* May 25, 2008, Travel Section, pp. 1, 8, 9.

Strausbaugh, John. "When Barnum Took Manhattan," *New York Times,* November 9, 2007, p. B29.

"Terry Shot Dead, He Slapped the Face of U.S. Justice Field. A Deputy Marshall Thereupon Kills Him. A Sensational and Tragic Scene in the Dining Car of a California Hotel, Mrs. Sarah Althea Hill Terry Witnesses the Affair," *Milwaukee Sentinel,* Aug. 15, 1889, col. B.

Thurman, Sue Bailey. *Pioneers of Negro Origin in California.* San Francisco: Acme Publishing Co., 1952, p. 8.

Transcript of Argument of William M. Stewart, *Sharon* v. *Hill* (Ninth District, 1885), Bancroft Library.

Twain, Mark. *Roughing It.* New York: Harper & Brothers Publishers, 1913.

Wadler, Joyce. "Southern Gothic: Ghosts Welcome," *New York Times,* May 31, 2007. This piece talks about painter Hunt Slonem's various plantation houses, including an 1832 pink plantation house in Batchelor, Louisiana. The article also discusses Slonem's psychics and his belief in ghosts.

Washington, Guy. National Park Service, 174-page database on blacks in California.

"Wealthy Negroes, Colored Citizens Worth from Half a Million Down," *Observer and Gazette (Fayetteville, N.C.),* Jan. 6, 1887, issue 12, col. F.

The Wild West. The editors of Time-Life Books. New York: Warner Books, 1993.

Williams, James. *Life & Adventures of James Williams, A Fugitive Slave, with a full description of the Underground Railroad,* 3rd ed. San Francisco: Women's Union Print, 1874.

Yanak, Ted, and Pam Cornelison. *The Great American History Fact-Finder.* New York: Houghton Mifflin Company, 1993, p. 180.

PERMISSIONS

INDEX